TWO FLOORS ABOVE GRIEF

A Memoir of Two Families in the
Unique Place We Called Home

KEVIN M. O'CONNOR

Two Floors Above Grief: A Memoir of Two Families in the Unique Place We Called Home
Published by 18th Floor Publishing
Ft. Lauderdale, FL

ISBN: 979-8-9870213-0-9
Personal Memoir

Cover and interior design by Victoria Wolf, wolfdesignandmarketing.com, copyright owned by Kevin M. O'Connor. Front cover image by Laura Marie Sanchez.

The stories and conversations in Two Floors Above Grief all come from the author's recollections. The stories do not represent word-for-word transcripts. Rather, the author has retold the stories in a way that evokes the feeling and meaning of what was said, and in all instances, the essence of the dialogue is accurate.

18TH FLOOR
PUBLISHING

To Leon, for his loving care and support

CONTENTS

INTRODUCTION

We lived in an environment considered funereal. I convert the word into an adverb, "funereally." Amidst the wakes and funerals being conducted in the first-floor funeral home, we did have moments, days, and years of joy and fun in the apartments where we lived on the second and third floors. Really.

In 1930, Uncle Lawrence and Aunt Mildred founded O'Connor Funeral Home in Elgin, Illinois. Dad and Mom joined them ten years later. Ninety-three children, grandchildren, great grandchildren, and great-great grandchildren descend from their marriages. We identify as the "Offspring of 364 Division Street," the address of our house on the corner of College Street.

We offspring sustained our relationships through stories, phone calls, music, and times together from the late 1920s to 1984 when my parents sold the business. Many of the stories come from 700 pages of letters saved by my parents and me. I organized 270 tabbed, dated entries in clear plastic sleeves ordered sequentially in four, three-ring notebooks. The gathered texts were either handwritten or typed on materials, including stationary from the family business, letterhead from Mom's places of work, tablets of paper, backsides of theater programs, typing paper, half sheets of notes sent by others, aerograms, postcards, and greeting cards. Aunt Mildred used the notepads from the Royal Garment Company, the provider of a selection of dresses for deceased females to wear at their "showings." I maintain mental snapshots of these letter writers sitting at desks and kitchen or dining room tables to reveal their penmanship or press the keys of manual, and later, electric typewriters.

I revel in the authenticity to our family history conveyed by the thoughts embedded in their written words. The excerpts of letters included in this book were written in the times before email, text, Zoom, and the immediacy with which communications are now created, delivered, received, and responded. Due to the cost of long-distance phone calls, my family used the phone sparingly to make contact. Hence, written communications were the primary means of maintaining connections with one another.

Our families looked forward to the delivery of mail mid-morning each day. We skimmed through the envelopes of bills and promotions, hoping to find a personal card or letter. If there wasn't one there, we had no choice but to wait for the next delivery twenty-four hours later—or forty-eight hours on a Saturday. There was no delivery on Sundays. Today, when I send out an email or text, I find myself checking within thirty minutes, an hour, and throughout the day to look for a reply.

These letters are part of the glue holding our families together. Mom foreshadowed this book in a letter she wrote on September 28, 1970:

"Grazie for keeping us so well informed with your letters. Will be fun when you come home to go over them with you. We are going to try to keep them in order for you. Should almost be like a diary for you, and that wouldn't be a bad idea . . ."

Some narratives, such as memoirs, biographies, and autobiographies are revealed in a sequenced fashion. I have *not* written this book in strict chronological order, but rather in the style of a non-linear memoir. Although I organized my letter artifacts in sequence, I realize the patterns and connections in life—and one's family history—are not ordered by the dates on a calendar. This book is intended as a love letter to the offspring of 364 Division Street and to all who revel and cherish the history of their families.

PROLOGUE

We smiled at each other. *Or did we?*

We cried. *Or did we?*

These moments are at times blurry.

My brother, Kerry, and I looked at each other across the feet of the woman who lay in the bed at the hospice wing of Aventura Hospital in Miami.

We both sighed, knowing what next must be done. As the sons and nephews of undertakers, we had been called upon to assist in the work of our family funeral home many times before. The difference this time was the deceased was neither a stranger nor funeral home client. She was our mother.

Ninety-three years of life.

It was half past midnight on October 1, 2010.

We were doing what Dad and our Uncle Lawrence did—providing exquisite care for the deceased. They treated death in a way similar to a midwife or an obstetrician assisting at the entrance of life. Respectfully. Gently. Carefully.

The hospice nurse, Millicent, opened the door to the room. "I will call the funeral director," she whispered. "He will be here within the hour. Since it is late, you can go home."

Offering our thanks, we let her know we preferred to wait for the undertaker to arrive. On numerous occasions, we had been tasked with being assistants in a "death call," the time when the body of the deceased makes their journey from place of death to a funeral home where their body is either embalmed or prepared for cremation. The location of death could be a home, a hospital room, a morgue, or an accident scene. There are few, if any, ways to predict the location of death. When the time comes, undertakers are there to help the deceased start their journey.

Now we moved a bit around the dark, single-bedded room. Amy, Mom's caregiver of two years, came to join us. She was there during most of the three days of Mom's hospital stay. We welcomed her presence for Mom's transition.

We made a call to our brother, Barrett, in Scottsdale, Arizona. He had visited Mom the week before. He and I took turns pushing her in a wheelchair to eat sandwiches at an Atlantic Ocean café on Hallandale Beach across the street from her condominium. We took our usual mother-son pictures, not knowing those would be the last of us together.

Kerry and I made other calls to family members to provide the update about Mom's passing. Sitting still in the room, I recalled what Mom wrote to me on November 9, 1970, three days after *her* mother died:

"[I] am sure I will always think of what might have been done or that just a little more patience on my part would have made her last days more pleasant. I do have to get a hold of myself and pray that she is now with Dad and not lonely anymore. The priest gave a great sermon. He did not dwell on what a wonderful person or great worker she was or anything like that, but that she was a mother and got to see her children raised and lived a full life with her husband. He mentioned sacrifices and what she did when we were growing up and Dad was out of work. We always got something new before she got anything for herself. He talked of hard work and of the many times she probably had her hands in water. I can remember crying myself to sleep when I was little, thinking of Mother dying, and now the time is here, but I can't wish her back because she was so miserable in the rest home . . . I wanted so bad for her to talk again to us, but she didn't. I did pray God would take her, but it was such a shock when the news came."

How prescient of how we now felt. Even though we knew Mom was failing in health, her death, as she wrote forty years previously about her own mom's passing, "was such a shock."

The undertaker arrived. We introduced ourselves. He indicated families did not usually stay in the room for this part of the process. We explained our familiarity and our desire to be part of Mom's journey. We positioned ourselves so the gurney was taut against the side of the bed. There was a sheet beneath Mom's body. Kerry and I pulled one side of the sheet to guide Mom's body toward the inside of the open body bag on the gurney. Once her body was positioned, we rolled her on to her side and pulled the sheet out from underneath. The sheet was placed back on the bed. The undertaker stepped back.

It had been more than thirty years since I last helped in this process.

My brother and I brushed our fingers across Mom's face to gently finish the closing of her eyes. Then together we gripped the tag of the open zipper at the bottom of the body bag and guided the zipper up past her reposed face and to the top of her head. Zip. Done. We secured the body bag by pulling two straps from under the gurney. We tightened one strap near the knees and the other across the chest.

Amy observed as Kerry, the undertaker, and I rearranged the position of the bed to move the gurney out of the room. Kerry and I extended a hug to Nurse Millicent. We walked along each side of the cart as the undertaker pushed it through the halls to the elevator door. We rode the elevator to the first floor. The undertaker guided us to the exit where he had parked the hearse. He opened the wide single back door. Together we lifted and rolled the gurney into the vehicle. As a child, I was fascinated by the mechanics of these carts, with wheels attached to legs that rolled up as the gurney was pushed inside. Rolling the bag containing mom's body into the hearse fascinated me in a similar way.

We thanked the undertaker. He drove off to the funeral home where we knew he was to embalm and prepare her for the next steps in her journey. Kerry and I walked with Amy to my car and drove her to our mother's condominium. We escorted her upstairs, as we did not want her to enter alone at the early morning hour. Kerry and I walked through each room to say a bit of goodbye to where Mom had made her home for the past three months. Eventually, we each gave Amy a tearful hug. We drove to the funeral home, finding the empty hearse at the rear door. We knew the embalmer had likely started his work. We drove to my nearby home, and I readily fell asleep.

Mom's departure was the final death in a parental quartet who raised me, my brothers, and our cousins Maureen, Kathleen, and Sharon in adjoining apartments on two floors above a funeral home. Our unique stories were lived two floors above grief.

MY FAMILY TREE: FATHER'S SIDE

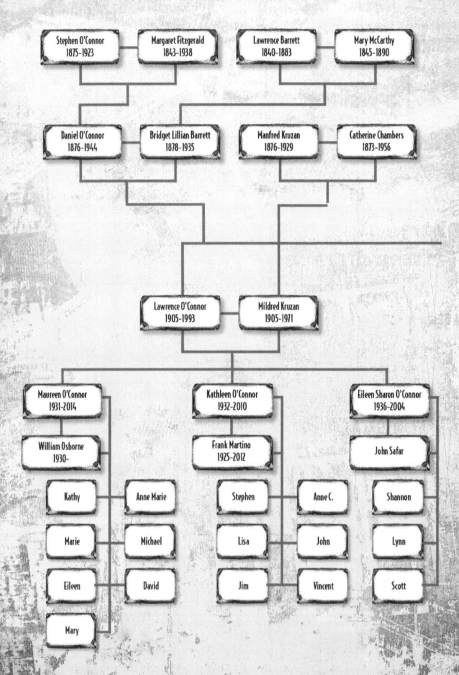

Stephen O'Connor 1875-1923 — Margaret Fitzgerald 1843-1938

Lawrence Barrett 1840-1883 — Mary McCarthy 1845-1890

Daniel O'Connor 1876-1944 — Bridget Lillian Barrett 1878-1935

Manfred Kruzan 1876-1929 — Catherine Chambers 1873-1956

Lawrence O'Connor 1905-1993 — Mildred Kruzan 1905-1971

Maureen O'Connor 1931-2014

William Osborne 1930-

Kathy — Anne Marie

Marie — Michael

Eileen — David

Mary

Kathleen O'Connor 1932-2010

Frank Martino 1925-2012

Stephen — Anne C.

Lisa — John

Jim — Vincent

Eileen Sharon O'Connor 1936-2004

John Safar

Shannon

Lynn

Scott

MY FAMILY TREE: MOTHER'S SIDE

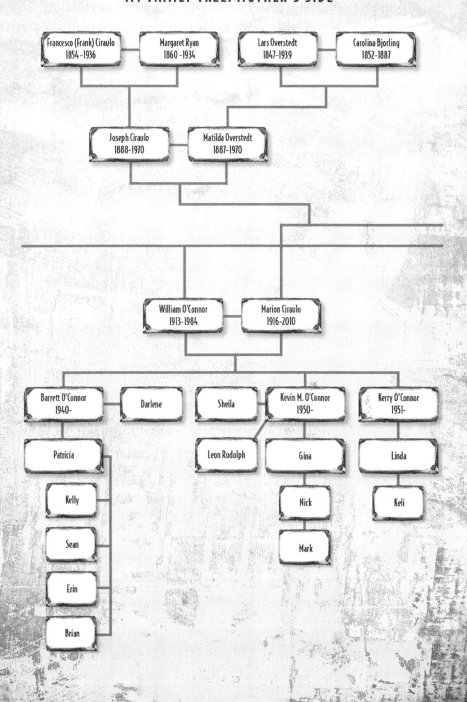

MY FAMILY TREE: FATHER'S SIDE

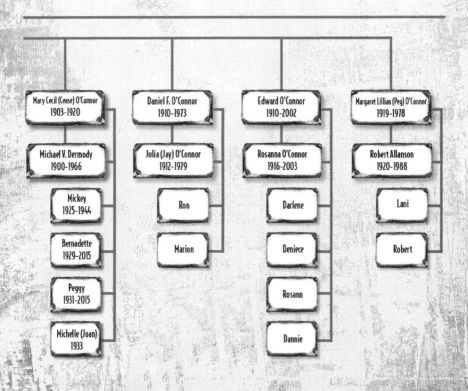

Mary Cecil (Cease) O'Connor 1903-1920	Daniel F. O'Connor 1910-1973	Edward O'Connor 1910-2002	Margaret Lillian (Peg) O'Connor 1919-1978
Michael V. Dermody 1900-1966	Julia (Jay) O'Connor 1912-1979	Rosanna O'Connor 1916-2003	Robert Allanson 1920-1988
Mickey 1925-1944	Ron	Darlene	Lani
Bernadette 1929-2015	Marion	Deniece	Robert
Peggy 1931-2015		Rosann	
Michelle (Joan) 1933		Dannie	

MY FAMILY TREE: MOTHER'S SIDE

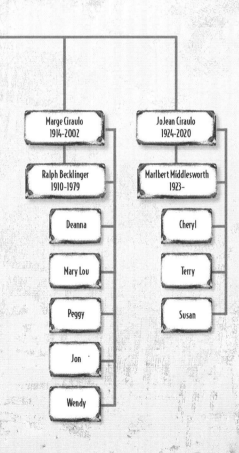

Marge Ciraulo
1914-2002

JoJean Ciraulo
1924-2020

Ralph Becklinger
1910-1979

Marlbert Middlesworth
1923-

Deanna

Cheryl

Mary Lou

Terry

Peggy

Susan

Jon

Wendy

PART I

CONCEPTIONS AND BEGINNINGS

How did I live in an apartment above a funeral home? Simply, I did not know any differently. I imagine my brothers and cousins have responded in like fashion. Becoming funeral home children happened at the moment of our births. Without evidence or detail from our parents, my cousins, brothers, and I were presumably conceived in the very buildings where our deceased clients reposed in the coffins chosen by their families. Hang on to that thought of conception. Now let it go. The chapters in this part of the book are about other beginnings; they are about Uncle Lawrence, Aunt Mildred, and their families making the decision to start a funeral home business.

In the mid-to-late '20s, Lawrence began formulating plans for his future. He worked at Burns Funeral Home in Hammond, Indiana. His family was acquainted with the Burns family. Lawrence told me about his initial interest in becoming an undertaker when the funeral home profession was in the midst of changes. Most funerals at the time were held in the homes of the families of the deceased. In rural areas, the funerals and burial of bodies occurred shortly after death. In several locations, the undertakers were also furniture makers. Building caskets was an extension of their business. Sometimes the dying person was in their house in their last hours, listening as a craftsman from the family or neighbors constructed their casket. You know the comment of "putting the last nail in the coffin?" Think of listening to the pounding of the nails, knowing of your placement in the coffin being assembled.

Away from rural areas, establishments in towns provided embalming services to preserve bodies. Embalming slows down decomposition of the body. It became a more common practice during the Civil War to preserve deceased soldiers' bodies for burials near their homes. By the turn of the twentieth century, embalming was customary in bigger towns and urban areas. Embalming gave families more time to plan funerals. In the Hammond-Chicago urban area, funeral homes began to replace the traditional practices of holding services in the home. Mr. Burns established a business in Hammond to provide funeral preparations and planning for families away from their homes.

Lawrence and Mildred based their decision to start their own funeral business on elements connected to their circumstances. As they proceeded in their venture, they found a first location for the business and a second location on Division Street nine years later. Ultimately, they included my parents in the business.

CHAPTER 1

Courting and Marrying

The establishment of funeral homes like the one owned by Mr. Burns was becoming more common. Through his work experiences, Lawrence was interested in getting more involved in the profession. He was also interested in Mildred Kruzan.

Mildred and Lawrence's dating years occurred in what is historically referred to as the "Roaring Twenties," a time of Calvin Coolidge and Herbert Hoover's presidencies, the prohibition of alcoholic beverages, and shared national interests in music and fashion generated by radio programs and newspaper advertising.

They were born a month apart in 1905, two years after the Wright Brothers flew at Kitty Hawk. They met in 1927. Mildred was from the neighboring town of East Chicago. She was taken by Lawrence's brown eyes, wide smile, thick dark hair, and slender six-foot frame. He carried himself with authority and confidence. He had graduated from Worsham College of Mortuary Science in Chicago and established himself as a businessman who cared about the families in his care.

He was living at home with his parents, Daniel and Bridget O'Connor, three younger brothers Dan, Bill (my father as a teen), Ed, and younger sister, Peg [Margaret Lillian]. His older sister, Cease, her husband, Mike, son, Mickey (born in 1926), and daughter, Bernadette (born in 1929), also lived in the house. With the combined salaries of Mike, Lawrence, and Dan, the family was crowded but secure in their intergenerational home. Then, the stock market crashed, and the Great Depression ensued.

The family's plans went into a tailspin. Mr. Burns continued to provide funeral services but at charges lower than before. He decreased Lawrence's pay. Lawrence looked for other work. He thought he found opportunities to start a funeral home in the Gary area. Those plans did not work out.

Mr. Burns put Lawrence in contact with a friend of his in Elgin, Illinois, who knew of an older house on a main street that could be converted into a funeral home on the first floor with an apartment upstairs. After the passing of two funeral directors in Elgin, there was a need for a Catholic-oriented undertaker to open a funeral home. There were two Catholic churches within four blocks of the house. Lawrence drove to Elgin, met with Mr. Burns's friend, and toured the house and neighborhood.

He was delighted to share his excitement about the opportunity to start his own business. Mildred did not immediately share in his excitement, as is conveyed in this imaginary conversation I created between the two of them:

"Lawrence, what do you know about Elgin? Have you been to Elgin? Have you seen the house?"

"Yes, I have. I was there two days ago. I did tell you I was going to Chicago. I didn't tell you I was also going to Elgin. I wanted to go there before I talked to you."

"I don't like when you keep secrets. What did you find out?"

"The house has possibilities. I talked to Cease, and she and Mike think our moving might help with the money we have in the family and how crowded it is getting in the house on Walter Street."

"You've already talked to Cease about this? She didn't say a word to me."

"I asked her not to until I talked to you first. Cease and I thought you and I could take Ma and Pa with us. They can help us get the funeral home started."

"Hold on. Hold on. I love your parents. I love your family. But you want them *to live with us*? This is getting to be too much. How does that help if your dad and mom are in Elgin with us and your brothers and sister are going to school here in Hammond?"

"Well, there is more. Ma wants to have Bill and Peg with her and Pa. She wants them to move to Elgin, too."

"Now you say it is not just your dad and mom. Bill and Peg, too? Are you crazy? Lawrence, we are planning our wedding, and now you are letting me know I will start my life with you *and* your parents! *Plus,* your brother and sister?"

"It's too difficult for Ma and Pa, Cease and her family, the four other kids, and you and I to all live together in one house in Hammond. Since we're the ones getting married, it seems logical for us to move out. If we take Bill and Peg with us, Mike and Cease can stay in the house with Mickey and Bernadette. Dan started work, and he will stay with them and help with the rent. Cease says the principal at Catholic High will provide an athletic scholarship for Ed's tuition. Cease and Mike can take care of him. You and I, Ma and Pa, will take care of the other two."

"But why?"

"Because we can start our own business in Elgin. Mike's job with the fire department will hold them here in Hammond. But the money is still tight in the family. We thought with two households, we all might be able to live more comfortably."

"We will be lucky to put food on the table. These are big decisions. I want to be included. What about my family? I'll be leaving my mother, brothers, and sister. My father died a month ago. There is so much to consider."

Would Lawrence have pursued his idea if Mildred said no? I presume he never asked her the question about the move being a choice. They proceeded with wedding plans. When they went to obtain their wedding license, he wrote "Elgin" as the town of his residence. Lawrence was convincing. He had a way about him—full of surprises. Starting married life with in-laws and young children to raise wasn't what Mildred had in mind. Actually, a part of her may have been relieved Lawrence's parents were going along. She was ready to be a wife. Not a parent.

Mildred and Lawrence married on June 4, 1930. The wedding was held on a Wednesday at noon at her family's Catholic Church. The reception was held at her mother's home with an offering of cake and punch. At the reception, the radio was tuned to a station playing "Happy Days Are Here Again," "Georgia on My Mind," and other songs popular at the time. During the month of their wedding, Lou Gehrig and Babe Ruth were making headlines about the home runs they were hitting. A gangster involved in illegal alcohol sales was shot and killed by Al Capone's gang within days of their wedding.

Wedding of Mildred Kruzan and Lawrence O'Connor,
Hammond, Indiana, June 4, 1930.

Mildred left her job as a secretary and stepped into an intergenerational in-law position. In a term I never heard her use, this move was certainly a BFD, a big fucking deal. I admire her determination and sense of adventure, leaving her home area and pursuing a new life. She welcomed it as an opportunity with an attitude of "make the most of it." I assume her perception of the role of wife was in line with the social norms of the times. She recognized Lawrence as the head of the household. She was dependent on him and his business potential to provide financial support. She didn't drive a car. She moved to Elgin knowing only those with whom she traveled.

Mildred and Lawrence were pioneers, taking risks and making monumental decisions to pursue their venture into a life of helping people to manage the grief of death. Lawrence's determination propelled them. Mildred was unable to consider how she would find joy in what lay ahead. Not realized by her at the time, their first years together in marriage provided the ignition to ensuing brighter family stories.

CHAPTER 2

Early Years of Marriage

Many of you have moved away from the town where you spent your childhood. You took chances. You have these experiences in common with Lawrence and Mildred. They made the decision to veer away from accustomed traditions. They moved to Elgin, a town and region as foreign to them as Hammond was to the areas of Cork, Ireland, and Glamorganshire, Wales, where their ancestors lived prior to coming to this country.

Lawrence and Mildred drove away from Hammond with family in tow. They experienced excitement combined with anxiety about the unknown as they made their journey. They traveled fifty miles along highways and streets through south Chicago and the southwest/west suburbs to Elgin. Did they have two cars or a car big enough for all six of them to make the trip? Did they drive a hearse they purchased with optimistic hope it would be used in their first cortege as funeral business owners? Perhaps friends and family helped with driving in a caravan. This is all a mystery. There are no pictures.

I do have a picture in my mind of the Clampett family as they moved from the Dakotas to Hollywood, California, in the 1960s TV show *The Beverly Hillbillies*. Look up this show and watch an episode or two. The characters are different than Lawrence and Mildred, but the Clampetts and O'Connors share stories of generations of family creating new lives. On the bright side, the Clampett vehicle was more dilapidated than anything Lawrence drove.

The route led to the two-story rental house at 18 Villa Street that Lawrence had inspected the month before. At the time, the house was on the direct route of US Highway 20 through Elgin from Chicago to Rockford and beyond. Before the construction of Interstate 90 and the bypass around downtown Elgin in the late '50s, Villa Street was busy with car, truck, and delivery traffic. This location put the business at a convenient place for visibility. In the funeral business, being located in a high traffic area is beneficial.

"Pa" Dan and "Ma" Bridget helped Lawrence and Mildred start what was to be their first funeral home location. They painted, wallpapered, and did what many young couples do when moving into a house or apartment. They worked together to create residence areas on a back section of the first floor and second floor. The front section of the first floor was remodeled for wakes and funerals to be presented in an appealing way for grieving families and those who came to pay respects. They designed space in the basement to include an embalming preparation room and casket storage and display.

A funeral home business does not have a product to display in a shop window. A mortuary is not like a plumbing or electric business you contact and schedule a time to do your requested work. A funeral home has routine, but no schedule. Such is the way of death. Building trust through relationships is essential to a funeral home business. Lawrence knew his business needed to be marketed through the appearance and quality of service provided, advertising, and the word-of-mouth of customers.

The family joined St. Mary Parish two blocks from their home and became involved in church, business, and community organizations, which helped them market the business. On August 20, 1930, Lawrence conducted his first funeral as a certified undertaker with the state and the Illinois Funeral Directors Association. The name of the deceased, according to the Elgin Death Index, was Edward Keating. He was 63. Additional business followed.

Maureen came into Lawrence and Mildred's family on May 8, 1931. Kathleen was born November 30, 1932, and Eileen Sharon on July 27, 1936. I have always been intrigued with the "een" pattern in their names. Lawrence and Mildred must have discussed names for their expected children. Unlike many of their prior generations, they did not give names to their children that had been used before in the family. All the girls' names were in line with Irish heritage. What if Eileen had been a boy? What name ended with "-een"? Eugene?

All of us in the family referred to the oldest two by their first names. In our immediate family, Maureen was never Mo. Kathleen was never Kathy or Kate. We didn't say Eileen by name in our interactions. She was called Sharon by family and friends alike. Using middle names is not unusual in the family. Many referred to my dad alternately as "Bill" or as "Virg," the shortened version of his middle name, Virgil. We referenced Cecil when we spoke of Mary Cecil. This was sometimes shortened to "Cease." Dad's younger sister, Margaret Lillian, was never called Margaret. Many of us called her Lillian or Peg. She spent most of her life using the names interchangeably with her family and friends.

Dan and Bridget's other responsibilities focused on Dad and Peg. Dad started his junior year at Elgin High in 1930. Peg attended elementary school at St. Mary's. Dad graduated in 1932. Peg went to high school at Mount St. Mary Academy in St. Charles. She was a resident student in their dorm and came home on weekends to Elgin. She graduated in 1937, two years after

Bridget died suddenly of pneumonia at St. Joseph Hospital in Elgin. She was fifty-six. In all the letters I have or in the stories I have been told, there is little mention of Grandmother O'Connor. Many years after her death, in a closing to a letter to me from Mildred dated January 25, 1971, she typed:

"With that, I'll sign off as of right now. 'I'm not in the NUDE'—as your Grandmother O'Connor used to say—to write more. So until next time, lots of love. —Auntie M."

This tidbit from Mildred reveals to me something about her humor and Grandmother O'Connor's. They knew each other rather well. After all, Mildred agreed this grandmother, her mother-in-law, could join Lawrence and her in the days after they married to start the business in Elgin. Within the confines of the first Elgin apartment, Mildred knew her well in her every mood (or 'NUDE'?).

Lawrence and Mildred started their married life and family with the challenges of a business in a new town. Mildred had responsibilities more extensive than other young brides. I imagine Lawrence developed the plan for the move and new business. The culture of the times influenced them. He saw Mildred less as a business partner and more as a wife who was expected to go along with what he, the provider, proposed. Lawrence valued Mildred's support in their new adventure. His engaging personality helped him to readily meet people and generate business for the new funeral home.

The intergenerational work of Lawrence, his parents, and Mildred provided the support needed by my teenage dad and aunt. The business thrived in those first seven to nine years. They did their initial marketing to Catholic families in Elgin. I have a sample of the marketing they did in the first years of the funeral business using a poster displayed at church and community functions. The poster has a color representation of a painting done by artist Carl W. Rawson in 1931. The scene is of four horses. A military commander is atop one of the horses. Behind the horses are four football players known as "The Four Horseman of the Apocalypse" of Notre Dame executing a play on an imaginary field. Behind them in the clouds is the face of Coach Knute Rockne. The title of the painting is *The Spirit of Leadership*. In the area below the framed representation of the painting, bold blue letters spell out:

O'CONNOR FUNERAL HOME
1400
118 VILLA ST. << >> ELGIN, IL

1400 represents its phone number at the time.

Rendition of painting by Carl Rawson used in poster for funeral home marketing, early to mid-1930s.

Why did Lawrence use this image of Rockne for his marketing in the first years of the business? He explained his motivation for the poster to me during a driving trip we took to South Bend in September 1983 to celebrate my cousin, Michelle Dermody's twenty-fifth anniversary as a nun. Lawrence was reminiscing about his youth.

Rockne was the coach from 1918 to 1931 when Lawrence was in his teens and twenties and enamored with Notre Dame football. While Rockne was building the program, there was a cloud of discrimination fostered by the Klu Klux Klan. Its members were instrumental in influencing Indiana state policies and politics. They discriminated against Blacks, Jews, Catholics, and the Irish. In 1924, the Klan held a rally in South Bend attended by their supporters. Students came from the school to challenge them. Fights broke out. Rockne spoke at the rally to help quell the combat between the students and the Klan. The fighting abated. Due, in part to this event, the team became known as the "Fighting Irish."

The team won their first national title in 1925. Rockne led the team to more than one hundred wins and three national championships. Catholic-Irish families strongly supported the team and the university. The following he fostered in northern Indiana extended to national audiences. The success of the team contributed to the acceptance of Irish culture after years of discrimination.

Rockne converted to Catholicism. He used his platform and stature to give his political support to Al Smith, governor of New York and the most prominent Irish American leader of his generation. Rockne's support helped Smith to become the Democratic nominee for president in 1928. He was defeated by Herbert Hoover, the last Republican to win a national election until 1952.

Rockne died at the age of forty-three in an airline flight headed to Los Angeles. He was going to participate in the production of a movie, *The Spirit of Notre Dame*. I surmise Lawrence was tying the roots and struggles felt by Irish Americans against discrimination with the allegiance to Notre Dame shared by many in the Chicago area. The portrayal in the painting brought together the broadly known story of Rockne and his death, the growing support for Irish Americans, and the appeal Lawrence wanted to make to Catholics in Elgin to consider his young business.

Lawrence was a funeral director *and* a marketeer. In addition to the poster, he created advertisements for area publications, under the heading "A Service for Elgin within the Means of All." He combined sketches of the outside of the "quiet and dignified" funeral home with a hearse and a rendition of an interior funeral parlor. Lawrence's marketing, combined with Mildred's support, the assistance of his father and mother, and the teenage work support of my dad and his sister, continued through the 1930s. By the end of the decade, the business and family outgrew the location on Villa Street.

Newspaper advertisement for Villa Street
location of the funeral home, 1930s.

CHAPTER 3

Division Street House: A Main Character

Much of our family history comes from the setting of the house Lawrence discovered at 364 Division Street. Most of the specifics about the Villa Street location are lost. The Division Street house is a key character in the stories of our family.

By 1938, Lawrence and Mildred, their three girls under the age of five, Dad, Peg, and our grandfather resided in the apartment above the funeral home on Villa Street. The living areas became crowded with elementary children and toddlers running from room to room, floor to floor. Amidst helping his father and family to conduct the funeral for his grandmother, Margaret Ellen Fitzgerald O'Connor in Hammond in April, Lawrence proceeded with negotiations to purchase the house on the corner of College and Division Streets, five blocks northeast of the original house on Villa Street.

This location had potential for the business on the first floor, areas on the second floor for bedrooms, a bathroom, and a kitchen, plus a third-floor ballroom for conversion to an apartment for either Dad or his brother Ed. Both Dad and Ed completed their education, apprenticeships, and certifications at Worsham College by 1936. They worked in the funeral business with Lawrence and their father and were ready to start their own careers. The Division Street house provided for those opportunities. There was enough business to provide an income for two, possibly three families.

The house has been referred to in articles in local newspapers, historical journals, and publications. Additionally, the house has been a part of Elgin Historical House Tours. The programs from these tours have details about the history of the house. It is referred to as a mansion in some Elgin history books. The house was originally built by families instrumental in developing the dairy industry in Elgin. The Elgin economy of the mid-1800s was girded by milk production facilities. Cattle grazed on land outside of Elgin and within city limits, including our property.

The house was constructed in 1886-87 for William Hubbard, a merchant in town. The house was referred to in an article in the December 24, 1886, edition of the *Elgin Daily Courier-News*: "The finest new house which this year has produced…is an elegant stone structure of pressed brick and brown stone and built in the latest and most approved style of architecture. It is heated throughout with steam and fitted with all modern improvements. The building presents a very fine appearance, and the interior finish is a marvel of beauty and elegance. The cost of the building is $12,000 and will cost half as much more to complete."[1]

The house was described in the program brochure for The Gifford Park Association's 28th Annual Historic Elgin House Tour held on September 12, 2009: "The exterior design of this massive home is predominately Romanesque

Revival, a style ... commonly employed for large public buildings such as courthouses, train stations, office buildings and the like. Romanesque-influenced homes began appearing in the 1880s. The structures were always masonry, large and often became local landmarks. Typical to the style, the building sits on a rough-faced or ashlar stone base. Not typical, however, is the extensive use of smooth brick and the red stone, used in narrow horizontal bands, providing a contrast in texture and color to the brick. These are elements of the Chateauesque style.... Other Romanesque features are the prominent tower, large rectangular window openings with single panes of glass and occasionally used arched windows and openings." [2]

Wraparound porches, two on the first floor and one on the second floor, accented the house's exterior. The porches included fancy woodwork railings with spindles of matching design. Gable slanted rooflines created a triangle vertical wall section where dormer windows appeared. During my time of living there, the bedrooms of my brothers and parents and our kitchen all had these dormer windows. Four chimneys rose from the deeply pitched rooflines, connected to three fireplaces on the first floor and another fireplace in one of the bedrooms on the second floor. The side entrance of the house was what we might refer to as a carport in today's terminology. Architecturally, it is referred to as a porte cochere. The roof of this port was (and still is) supported by large wooden columns joined by decorative spindle work friezes and a rock base similar to the basement foundation.

Alfred B. Church purchased the house from Hubbard in 1873. Church was the stepson of Gail Borden and son of his wife, Emeline Church Borden. The Borden name was renowned for its dairy businesses, wherein Borden developed the process of condensing milk. The Borden and Church families lived in the house next door at what is now 378 Division Street. Church was a banker and real estate developer. Church and businessmen at the time recruited businesses to come to town. These included The D.C. Cook Publishing Company and Brethren Publishing Company.

Church owned the property until 1902 when he moved to New York. The property was sold in 1903 to Thomas Loucks for $28,000. In 1911, Mr. Loucks's son, John Loucks, died. His funeral was conducted in the house. I find it serendipitous that there was a funeral in the house almost thirty years prior to the first funeral conducted by O'Connor Funeral Home. Adding to the serendipity is the deceased's middle name, which was Connor.

Loucks resided in the home until 1922 when he sold it to Emil Johnson, owner of the Seybold Piano and Organ Company. (Adding to serendipities, when my brother Kerry, his wife, Linda, her daughter, Keli, and her family were looking for a used spinet piano in 2005, they found a vintage Seybold in excellent condition.) Johnson and his wife experienced financial difficulties during the Great Depression. Henry Muntz bought the property for $5,700 while Mr. and Mrs. Johnson resided in the house. In 1937, Mr. Johnson died. His funeral was also held in the house, another precursor to the upcoming purchase of the house as a funeral home. Mrs. Johnson, now a widow, moved out. The house fell into disrepair. There were few prospective buyers.

Enter Lawrence.

My Uncle Lawrence started the proceedings to buy the property. He petitioned the Elgin City Zoning Board in December 1937 to let them know he wanted to buy and convert the building into a funeral home. According to Elgin historian and teacher, E.C. Alft, in an article titled "Days Gone By: The Division Street Mansion" published in *Northwest Herald* on March 24, 2007,[3] the zoning in the 1930s did not allow for a funeral home. Lawrence's petition started a discussion in the town and neighborhood. The neighbors feared increases of traffic and parking. Lawrence noted the presence of the Holy Trinity Lutheran Church across the street. Traffic and parking were already present on Sundays and days of church services. The congregation had no parking lot. Neighbors also expressed concerns about their property values and whether a funeral home was too commercial for a residential area.

Lawrence persisted, and Muntz eventually sold the property to him in 1938. Lawrence still did not have the approval of the zoning board. He was taking a risk but confident in his position. In May 1939, he received permission to convert the property from residential to commercial.

Those on the board, as well as some of the neighbors at the time, realized the property was no longer practical for a single family. If the property sat empty, the city received no taxes. Lawrence's proposal offered the potential of a business for taxes as well as a solution to provide purpose to a vacant and dark structure with what I presume may have presented itself as gothic and haunted.

The zoning board required no exterior alterations, except for a possible elevator shaft on the north side, and a stipulation the building needed to be used as a residence and a business. This worked perfectly into Lawrence's intention to create residences on the second and third floors of the house. An additional stipulation was for funerals to leave the premises on the northeast corner of College Street. The protocol has been maintained by the business, even as owners changed.

Lawrence's vision and tenacity, supported by Mildred, his father, and brothers helped pave the way for the creation of our lives together on Division Street. Soon, Dad and Mom would join them in the business and family adventure.

CHAPTER 4

Dad and Mom: Their First Business

During the time Lawrence was searching for a new location for the funeral home, Dad and Mom made their plans. They had met at Elgin High School and might have seen recently released movies such as *Calling Dr. Kildare*, *The Hardys Ride High*, and *The Wizard of Oz*. The main song of *The Wizard of Oz* was "Over the Rainbow," recognized now as one of the most recorded songs of the past one hundred years. During those same years, singers Frank Sinatra, Ella Fitzgerald, and Ethel Merman and orchestra leaders Benny Goodman and others performed songs, including "I've Got You under My Skin," "Pennies from Heaven," "Moonglow," and "The Way You Look Tonight." To get a music sense of Dad and Mom, locate those songs on your music apps and listen. You will become more acquainted with them when listening to the melodies.

Mom was familiar with the funeral home. Her grandmother, Maggie Ryan Ciraulo, died a few days prior to her graduation in 1934. Her grandfather, Frank Ciraulo, died in 1936. Both funerals were held at the funeral home. Her father, Joseph Ciraulo, and Uncle Lawrence signed Frank's death certificate. These two funerals gave opportunities for Mom's family to meet Dad. Mom's father's family had been established in Elgin and surrounding areas since the mid-to-late 1800s. Her mother was raised in Rockford with three sisters and a brother, all born in villages west of Stockholm, Sweden, prior to immigrating. She was the first child born in the family outside of Sweden. Three years after her birth, her mother died in giving birth to a younger brother. He, too, died. She became the baby in a family without a mother. She was named Otelia at birth. She changed her name to Matilda earlier in her life. Her name was further adapted to Tillie, or Till, by her friends and siblings. My cousins and I called her "Mamie," not Grandma. We called our grandpa, "Joey." His two younger sisters and two brothers also lived in Elgin.

Dad and Mom married on Wednesday June 28, 1939, at noon. Mom's maternal grandfather, Lars Overstedt, died ten days before the wedding. The family was involved in his funeral and the preparations for the wedding at the same time. The wedding was attended by many in her family, Dad's five siblings, and many of his forty-two first cousins, plus aunts and uncles from the Hammond and Chicago areas. Through their high school and dating years, they created a cacophony of friends with varied interests and occupations. At the start of their marriage and throughout their lives, they socialized with friends two to three times a week as individuals and as a couple. According to a newspaper account, more than one hundred guests attended the wedding and reception. Some of their wedding day pictures were taken on the front lawn area of the Division Street house. Lawrence had finalized his purchase the prior month. He was beginning to make modifications to the house while the business continued operating from the Villa Street location.

Wedding of Marion Ciraulo and Bill O'Connor,
Elgin, Illinois, June 28, 1939.

At the time of their marriage, in addition to work he did at the funeral home, Dad was employed at a produce store in Elgin. When Dad and Mom came out of the front doors of St. Mary's attired in his tuxedo and her white wedding gown and hat, his store colleagues greeted them in a decorated produce truck with two chairs on the flatbed. The wedding party lifted them onto the bed of the truck. The driver proceeded to drive them through town with cars following behind.

They arrived at the home of Mom's family for the afternoon reception of cake, punch, coffee, and alcoholic libations served by Mom's dad, a bartender in area restaurants and bars. Mom told us the story of moving about the reception and noticing a family friend sipping from a chipped cup. Knowing her mother's embarrassment, Mom went over to the person and offered to take their cup to the kitchen. She hid it. She did not tell her mother.

From the reception, Dad and Mom drove to their honeymoon in Milwaukee. Mom wrote a letter on stationery from the Shorecrest Hotel and mailed it with thirteen cents of special delivery postage postmarked on the day after the wedding:

"Dearest Mother and Family, We got away so quick that I didn't get a chance to give you all half as big a kiss as I wanted to. I miss you already and am just a little blue at this moment. We have a beautiful room right on the lake. I can hear the water and the fog horns as I am writing this. I just took a shower and feel a lot better. My whole body ached when we got up here. My dress is up to Lu Adams's house. She might bring it over, otherwise we will go over and get it when we get back. My hat won't stay on unless I put the band under the chin which I don't like very well, but maybe I can fix it if I can get some thread someplace. Give Dee Sue and Marilu [Mom's nieces] a big kiss for me. I am going to bed now to rest my weary bones. Thanks again, Mother and Dad, for a grand wedding and reception and all my love to you all, Marion."

P.S. Me, too. Thanks a million for everything, mostly for your daughter and sister. We're both very happy about everything. Remember me—I'm the new guy in the family. Bill"

This letter helps me to visualize Mom with a youthful newlywed vulnerability I had not experienced as her son. She was homesick after one night away from her family. She was grateful for all her parents did for her and Dad. She was starting a new part of her life. I do not sense apprehension in her writing. Rather, I sense a woman experiencing the emotions of a first separation from her family. I see Mom as a young bride with words conveying she was ready to start her life with Dad. His note at the end was a special bonus.

Think of the emails and texts and phone messages you leave with those you love in the hours after a shared major occasion. When I send a text, I more than occasionally catch myself wondering why my addressee hasn't responded within one to two minutes after I sent it. I do the same with email. I look for a return in the first five minutes or an hour. When a day goes by, I catch myself asking, "Why didn't they respond?"

Letter writing prior to the times of email and text was different. Mom's letter, unlike our modern-day ways of communication, was received two to three days after it was written. Her words expressed the feelings she was having. So authentic. Her letter, like so many I have read from members of the family, was one of the lifelines with which Mom and family members communicated with each other. Mom's letter tells you who she was. I have the original letter. How many texts and emails have I kept in printed fashion to provide a history to my written conversations? Very few.

Dad and Mom set out to open their own funeral home in Aurora, twenty miles south of Elgin. They made a plan almost identical to what Lawrence and Mildred accomplished ten years earlier and found a house to rent in Aurora similar to the house on Villa Street. They borrowed money from family members to pay the rent and purchase the initial necessary equipment. Mom continued to work at Collingbourne Mills in Elgin as a bookkeeper and model of their linens, shawls, and lace clothing pieces.

She commuted to work on the Chicago, Aurora, and Elgin train line each day to and from Aurora. The train was referred to as "The Third Rail." The

Third Rail ceased operating for passengers in 1957. Freight was stopped in 1959, and all operations ceased in 1961. The tracks have been removed and replaced by the Prairie Path Bike Trail.

While Mom was at work, Dad involved himself in community and religious organizations to get acquainted and be present in the Aurora community. They kept a ledger in the first years of marriage, endeavoring to live within their limited means. It contains itemized details of their income and where their money was being spent. They made payments of six dollars a month to pay off their refrigerator. I notice Lawrence made the payment for them in August 1940. Throughout the ledger, it is noted that Dad paid himself a salary of ten dollars per week. The ledger is mostly in Dad's handwriting. There are notations from Mom as well. The ledger does not indicate the wages she was earning from her job. The itemizations provide a glimpse of Dad and Mom at the time:

Cigarettes: 10 cents
Bread: 10 cents
Jelly: 10 cents
Pen and holder: 5 cents
Golf ball: 10 cents (they played golf regularly through their married years together)
Tomato: 4 cents

They paid dues, donations, and fees to their church, clubs, and to the "Irish Fellowship." There is also a notation indicating 'Book rental . . . 51 cents' for *The Patriot*, a novel published in 1939 and written by Pearl S. Buck, a popular author of the time. It is the story of a young man from Shanghai who fights with Chiang Kai-Shek. I wonder whether it was Mom or Dad who read the book. Maybe both. I wonder, too, what drew them to a story about China. The ledger also indicates the names of people they entertained in their home. These include family members and friends from their high school years. Many of those friendships continued throughout their lives. The last date in the ledger was July 17, 1941. I don't know if they kept additional ledgers.

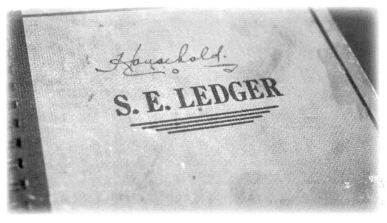

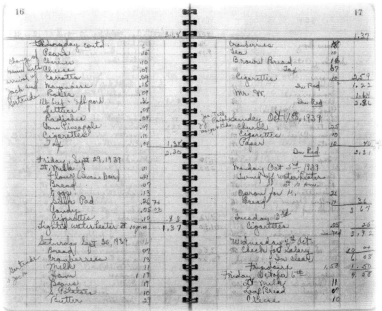

Marion and Bill's budget ledger from first year of marriage, 1939–40.

By June 1940, the O'Connor Funeral Home in Aurora had conducted one funeral. Mom and Dad had depleted their financial resources. Mom was in the early months of pregnancy with Barrett. They gave up their dream of having their own business. At about the same time, Dad's younger brother, Ed, and his wife, Rosanna, started to join with Uncle Lawrence to establish the business at the location on Division Street, but they decided to take a position with a funeral home in Chicago. Their departure created an opportunity for Lawrence to extend an offer to Dad to join him in the business.

As they came together to form the business, Lawrence and Dad now shared their schooling experiences from Worsham College and the first ten years of the business on Villa Street. Dad's schooling combined with experience in Aurora and expanding knowledge of the mortuary business contributed to the potential of the funeral home. When I was in elementary school, I thought Dad was a partner in the business. It wasn't until my late teens I discerned he was never a co-owner with Lawrence. Dad was Lawrence's employee. I think this arrangement might have been due to Dad and Mom's lack of financial resources in the first year of their marriage. Also, Lawrence may have thought it better to not share in ownership. Rather, as the older brother, he wanted to provide Bill with the opportunity he needed as a new husband and father-to-be. The decision was possibly influenced by Lawrence's and Dad's interpretation of their father's letter to his six children written two years prior. Their father wanted them to work together as a team and be concerned for each other. Part of Dad's agreement with Lawrence provided Dad and Mom with the about-to-be designed living space on the third floor. I am not sure if this arrangement was legally confirmed or implicitly understood by them, Mildred, and Mom. They did not discuss these arrangements in my presence. I never asked. I am interested now. I wish I'd inquired more during my time with those from earlier generations.

Dad and Mom moved to 364 Division Street in summer 1940. Barrett was born in December, 1940. His first name is the maiden name of Dad's mother. His middle name, Joseph, is Mom's father's name. Mom's familiarity with people in Elgin through her upbringing, schooling, and employment helped encourage business in providing impetus for families to consider O'Connor Funeral Home. Her influence continued in the years to come.

The turn of the decade marked endings as well as beginnings. Dad and Mom courted, married, became pregnant, started a business, dissolved it, and adapted to new family alliances in the funeral home business with Mildred and Lawrence. Together, they developed a relationship and collective family culture, raising my cousins, brothers, and me.

Their joined families were just beginning.

CHAPTER 5

Transforming Victorian Parlors to Chambers for the Dead and Living

The design of the house—from its origins, followed by the adaptations Lawrence and Dad created—brought our two families together as one. The relationships, connections, and coexistence came as a result of the house itself. The house spoke to us not only through its architecture, but also in the way it would intertwine itself in our individual and family lives. Our families developed our distinctive cultures *because* we lived in the house at 364 Division Street.

Dad and Lawrence's initial task was converting the neglected house from a single-family home to their business and apartments. There were nonfunctional radiators, torn and faded window treatments, and evidence of water leakage. The house had not been built to be a funeral home and multi-family residence. There was limited plumbing for kitchen and bathroom use for two families of five adults and four children. Additionally, they needed to maintain the business on Villa Street while they prepared the Division Street location. Although they worked with contractors, the two brothers—with support and ideas from Mildred and Mom—tackled much of the work themselves.

Lawrence and Dad began to design and refurbish the first floor and basement for the business, and the second and third floors as apartments. While Dad had a designer's eye, Lawrence managed the finances. Lawrence saw the potential for a funeral home business when he first visited the house. From the street and curved driveway, he was intrigued by the welcoming ten-foot-wide stairway leading to a roofed porch at the top of the stairs. The entry to the first floor featured two side-by-side, ten-foot, carved wooden doors. Above them was a frosted glass transom window etched with the numerals 204, the address given to the house when it was originally built. Through changes made on the street design in Elgin between the 1890s and 1920s, the address shifted to 364.

These front doors led into an eight-by-eight vestibule. The entrance continued through two crystal glass doors leading into the foyer with inlaid wood flooring bordered by patterned dark and lighter tone triangles. The foyer was accented with three focal points: a three-window angled bay area with stained glass at the top of the center window, a tile-surrounded fireplace with a slate wood mantel, and a winding staircase leading down to the basement and up to the second floor. The fireplace was surrounded by intricate etched glass door cabinets with stretched lace curtains, creating a mystery of what was behind. The sides and floor area of the fireplace were accented by beige and red tone tiles. The ceilings of the first floor were twelve feet high.

Dad and Lawrence added couches and chairs to the foyer to provide sitting areas for families. They placed the organ from Villa Street into the bay window area. Two adjoining parlors separated by pocket doors of dark stained wood beckoned across the room from the fireplace. The front parlor featured a fireplace designed like the one in the foyer and positioned on the eastern side of the room. To the left of the fireplace, a ten-foot exterior exit door led to a porch used as an outdoor area for the prior residents. A large rectangular window on the south side with a stained-glass accent section above as wide as the window provided a view to the front lawn.

The second parlor was designed as a dining room for the original residence. When Lawrence first viewed this room, he noticed a round disc about the size of a silver dollar protruding from the floor. This was placed at a position at the head of a dining table in the original house. The host of dinner sat at the head of the table. When service was needed at the table, the host pressed his foot on the button on the floor, which sent a signal to ten brass arrows in a wooden box with a glass door located on the wall of the servants' area. Each of the arrows indicated a different part of the house. When the button on the floor was pressed, the arrow next to the words "dining room" pointed in an upward direction. This indicated service was needed from the kitchen staff. Kerry and Linda have this servants' box hanging in the back entrance of their house, a memento to family history.

Steam heat radiators projected from the walls of the foyer and parlors. Walking straight from the front door through the foyer, past the parlor entrances on the right and staircase on the left, led to a door with access to the outside for the staff. This room contained the sinks and faucets to wash dishes. Lawrence and Dad replaced this doorway with a wall and removed the kitchen sinks. Using the available plumbing, they converted the space into a toilet area for use by those attending wakes and funerals. This was a necessity as there was no toilet on the first floor.

To the left of this entrance to the sink area was a room designated as the butler's pantry. Such a pantry was common in Victorian homes. There was an entrance to this room from the outside. A spacious porch with two stairway access points extended from this entrance to the driveway and carport area. Lawrence and Dad converted the original pantry into the office for the business. There was a fireplace in the office and desk area to the right of it. Behind the desk on either side of a large window were more built-in, glass door cabinets and drawers. These were used in the original house to store dishes, silver, linens, and other items needed to serve meals for the family and their guests. For the funeral home, these storage areas held the materials and forms for the business.

On the opposite side of the desk from where Lawrence or Dad sat, they placed side chairs and a small couch for the family to sit while they "made arrangements" (aka planned) for the wake and funeral service. "Making arrangements" is a common term in the funeral home industry with which I was readily familiar as a child. The undertaker leads a dialogue with the family to learn information for legal documents, the customs of the family for funerals, the type of service they like, their preferences for music selections, and where they plan to bury or cremate the deceased. When Dad was preparing for a funeral in the office, he made phone calls from the desk, completed forms, wrote the obituary for the newspaper, and contacted the businesses involved.

The wall next to the desk divided the office from a third parlor area or back room of the funeral home. Originally designed as a working kitchen area attached to the butler's pantry, this connected room provided an entrance to another flight of stairs leading up to the second floor and two doors leading outside to the porches and steps to the driveway. This back room became known as the back parlor, large enough to be a third area for wakes but usually closed off to the public and used to hold deliveries, stacks of folding chairs, and other equipment.

To the left side of the doorway from the office was another staircase entrance to the basement. Lawrence and Dad adapted the basement to the needs of a funeral home. The basement could also be accessed from the front foyer and through a porch at the back of the house. I often wonder how a builder in the 1880s excavated and created a basement with a seven-foot-high foundation for this mansion. Lawrence and Dad and their hired contractors built interior walls, creating designated areas for the boiler/furnace room, a preparation room to embalm bodies, and a casket display room.

The furnace was heated from coal delivered in trucks that pulled up to the side of the house. The truck driver shoveled coal into a chute that opened through the basement wall into bins near the furnace. Barrett remembers Dad shoveling coal into the furnace, though shortly after my birth, the furnace was converted from coal to oil. Two large cylindrical metal drums supported by iron legs secured to the floor were placed next to a basement wall. A pipe similar to a gas line on a car was connected from the drums and through the basement wall to an outside opening. In later years, the furnace was converted from oil to natural gas with pipelines provided underground by the utility company.

Dad and Lawrence designed and created an ambience in the business spaces with their clients in mind. They provided seating places that fostered the closeness of conversations. At times of grief, there are feelings of uncertainty and vulnerability. The atmosphere of the funeral home was intended to counteract and soothe those emotions.

Concurrent to establishing the design of the funeral home areas, they also converted the second floor to a living space for Lawrence and Mildred's family. In the original design of the house, the second floor was entered from the top stair into an expansive loft-type area. A wooden railing provided a barrier over the open staircase leading down to the entrance to the basement. Beyond the railing, three sixteen-foot-high windows looked over the driveway and neighborhood.

By 1948, the Elgin area's Jewish congregation had constructed a synagogue across the street, adding to the view from the house. The design of the synagogue's exterior wall included a fifteen-foot representation of the Ten Commandments tablets. This view from our windows was a reminder of the universality of the religions in our neighborhood. As I shoveled sidewalks, mowed the grass, walked, or drove from the driveway, I might pause to view the oversized tablets.

In the original construction of the house, the five rooms on the second floor joined themselves through openings, allowing a resident to walk through all rooms in a circuitous route. Contractors closed off the connections between rooms to create a living room, three bedrooms, a kitchen, and a dining room on the landing. The front room was entered with a right turn at the top of the stairs. A bay window in this room was directly above the bay window in the front foyer of the funeral home. A fireplace in the room provided heat in addition to the steam heat from the radiators. In the far-left corner, an opening led to a built-in vanity and sink area purposed as a washing station for both the front room and another room with a fireplace, closet, and expansive front window. The sink area was similar to the "Jack and Jill" bathroom concept where two bedrooms have access to one bathroom. A contractor built a bookshelf wall in place of the opening between the sink area and front room. With this wall in place, the front room became the living room for the second floor.

The former adjoined room became Mildred and Lawrence's bedroom with access to the sink area and a small closet with built-in drawers and hanging area. The fireplace was sealed. This master bedroom was connected to another area accessed using sliding pocket doors. By closing the pocket doors, the room became the girls' bedroom. This room also had a mantle, sealed-off fireplace, steam heat radiators, and a walk-in closet. The hallway between the living room and the entrances to the bedrooms contained three additional walk-in closets with more built-in drawers and hanging areas. These closets and the ones in each of the bedrooms provided space they did not have on Villa Street.

An entrance on one wall of the girls' bedroom led to a bathroom with a tub and a pedestal sink. This bathroom was also accessed from the back hallway. Originally, there was no toilet in this bathroom; instead, it was located in a narrow closet next to the bathroom hallway. This toilet was designated in the original design as a 'water closet' or WC. The toilet was attached to an overhead tank holding a reserve of water. When the chain from this tank was pulled, water flowed into the toilet. This was the only toilet in the original house. Dad and Lawrence employed plumbers to move pipes to the bathroom to create a toilet area next to the bathtub. The WC area became a closet for storage.

Next to this closet was a room later referred to as the back bedroom, with a walk-in closet that went through to a room converted to the second-floor kitchen. A shelf and drawer cabinet were built on the wall, closing off the back bedroom. This space became a dinette area lit by a large window and a half-moon window toward the top of the ceiling. This newly created kitchen was designed with a U-shaped counter and cabinet area for food preparation with a centered sink under a window looking west toward Division Street and downtown. Opposite the U space, on the left-hand side of the kitchen exit, was an entrance to a single-doored pantry.

The exit from the kitchen went to the back hallway and the stairway to the third floor.

Moving to the top of the stairs, Dad and Mom worked from an empty canvas of the third-floor ballroom to create their apartment. Prior to Barrett's birth, they began to reconfigure the area. For those of you who watch HGTV, I envision Mom and Dad as lead characters in a home design series called *Unstaging a Ballroom.*

The ballroom included two performance stages. The finished wood floors gleaned with a patterned border setting of linear laid wood. The walls and ceiling corresponded to the roof line. Paneled wainscot rose from the floor to the sloping plastered ceiling.

I wish I knew more about how Mom and Dad transformed the ballroom into two bedrooms, a living room, a kitchen, a family room area we called the 'back room,' a bathroom, and laundry room. How much did they do themselves? Did the contractors who worked on the first and second floors also work on the third? How did they do the design and construction while awaiting Barrett's birth and during his first years?

The bedroom at the top of the stairs was designed for Barrett. With my birth in 1950 and Kerry's in 1951, Barrett shared his space with cribs and later, two additional twin beds. Our bedroom's ceiling was like the rest of the third floor, sloping according to the rooflines. At the highest points, the ceiling was ten feet in height, giving our room and entire apartment the appearance of an expansive, high-ceilinged attic. Above the stage, two west-facing rectangular windows, each measuring about three by four feet, brought in outside light. We didn't need window coverings for privacy on the third floor. We saw the sky from the windows.

In the mid-1950s, Dad and Mom made the decision to remove the stage and expand the useable floor space. They placed our three beds along the long wall under the windows. This created space in parts of the room for shelves and desks. Unfortunately, the walls under the windows and the attic above our room were not insulated. Our room was particularly colder than the rest of the apartment. In winter, the temperature could be cold enough for the formation of ice crystals on the wood paneling. To help us keep warm, we wore extra layers of clothing as we sat at our desks to do homework or on the floor to listen to music and the radio. The windows became so frosty, it was often difficult to view the sky. We received electric blankets one Christmas to provide further warmth.

The room featured a walk-in closet about twenty-five feet in depth and five to six feet wide. While we talked in our beds prior to falling asleep, Kerry and I terrorized each other with imaginative stories of the creatures in this foreboding space. One single lightbulb hanging from a black electrical cord provided light to the closet. The light was turned on by a toggle switch next to the frame of the closet door. There was a sharp click sound each time the toggle was turned. Kerry and I had a tendency to leave the light on in the closet. Sometimes, we'd hear Lawrence calling from the bottom of the stairs, "Kevin! Kerry! I hear a light bulb crying. It wants to be turned off. It says we need to save on electricity." We'd dutifully turn off the light. But how did he know we left the light on? Did he sneak upstairs and peek into the room and then go back downstairs? If so, why didn't he turn off the light himself? Another mystery. I developed a respect of turning off lights to conserve electricity.

Moving on to the living room. Coming out of our bedroom, Dad constructed a closed gate on the left at the top of the stairs. This was intended to prevent a downward fall. Looking opposite the gate, my eye was drawn to the living room. This room was accented on one cornered end by the bay area with a window overlooking the front yard. The bay was usually set up with a bench, chairs, or two-person couch. I used this area to lay out the Sunday *Chicago Tribune*, the *Elgin Courier-News*, or *Time* magazine on the floor and position myself on my knees to read. The remainder of the living room was large enough to accommodate two to three sitting areas with couches and chairs, an area for a small dining table, and a place to keep a cabinet console record/radio system.

When they first moved into the third-floor area, Dad built a bookshelf unit of five sections. It included a center corner piece and sections of shelves extending from either side. He designed the shelves specifically to accent the wainscot woodwork and color already in the house. Over time, Dad alternated the position of the shelving unit in different locations in the living and dining room areas. In the final years of their residence, Dad placed the shelves in the back room of the apartment. I wish I took those shelves on the day he and Mom moved out of our residence in 1984. The shelves represented Dad's creativity and carpentry and could have served any of our family offspring.

The entrance to Dad and Mom's bedroom was near the end of the east wall of the living room. The roofline was a bit lower in that part of the house. The furniture was purchased when they married. Mom's dresser was lower in height, typical of bedroom furniture of those times. Dad's dresser was "high boy" design. Dad and Mom's walk-in closet was incredibly small by today's standards, with a built-in wall drawer unit on both sides and an area above to hang clothes. The small closet may be one of the reasons Dad and Mom had minimal attire.

Back to the top of the stairway entrance to the third floor, a four-to-six step turn to the left led to a transomed window door entrance to the kitchen.

Dad and Mom enhanced the room with cabinetry, spaces for appliances, and an area for a five-foot diameter round table in planked picnic table design built by Dad. The table was tucked beneath one of the two square windows under the sloping ceiling. Curved benches and two captain's chairs provided seating around the table.

Opposite the table, there was a smaller area with matching window. This area provided bench seating, a place for the family telephone, and an interior window with a view into our bathroom—another sign our house was not typical of other homes. This interior window was a source of practicality during its time. Dad and Mom put Kerry and me in the bathtub, walked out of the bathroom, through the hallway/dining room area at the top of the stairs, and into the kitchen. From there, they watched over us while we played in the bathtub, and they attended to kitchen work. All right, some of you might be thinking I made this up. But no, it's the truth. This window added to our architectural and family uniqueness.

Aside from mealtime, the kitchen table was a gathering space for those from the second floor and visitors. Mildred was often positioned at the table with coffee in hand and conversation at the ready. When Maureen, Kathleen, and Sharon came upstairs, they headed directly to the kitchen table. The table was accessorized by a round lazy Susan (also constructed by Dad), a rotating tray popular in the homes of our friends and in restaurants. Mom and Dad would place bowls of prepared food on it, and each of us conveniently served ourselves. As we finished putting food on our plates, the Susan was turned to the next person. This was repeated until we all put what we wanted on our plates. We said a prayer and started eating.

Kerry and I explored an interest in the physics of propulsion and thrust using the lazy Susan. We'd place an object on the Susan, then discover how continual turning accelerated its speed. The spinning object eventually took flight. One episode occurred with a white Corningware sugar bowl, which flew through the kitchen and directly out into the hallway, landing on its side, miraculously intact. However, thousands of sugar granules found their way into every fiber of carpet and the crevices on the baseboard and stair railing at the borders of the floor.

Mom was not a milk drinker. Dad routinely provided glasses of milk for us three boys and himself. He insisted on not having milk poured from a dairy jug or bottle placed on the table. Instead, the milk was poured from the dairy container into a ceramic brown pitcher in the shape of a cow's head. The mouth of the cow was the spout of the pitcher. The pitcher had a place on the counter next to the table. Dad poured the milk into each glass and responded to our requests for more. At one dinner in the mid-1950s, each of us three boys knocked over our glasses of milk. Dad paused his dinner the first two times to wipe up the mess, leaving the spilled glasses empty. At the third occurrence, he rose from his seat without speaking a word and retrieved the cow pitcher. And then he stepped to the table and poured the remaining milk over the head of the third perpetrator. He calmly returned the pitcher to the counter, sat down, and in his inimitable voice of patience, said, "All glasses are now empty. Let's finish dinner. I will clean up later." To this day, Barrett, Kerry, and I can verify this occurrence. But none of us can remember *who* received Dad's final pour.

After dinner concluded, Dad and Mom each lit a cigarette. This was our signal to leave the table. We went to the back room to watch TV, to the living room to read the newspaper and listen to music, or to our bedroom to do homework. Dad and Mom washed dishes together unless Dad went downstairs for a wake or work-related task that needed attention.

Dad and Mom's bar was located on the right when entering the kitchen. The space was created when they remodeled in the early 1960s, with a section of counter and cabinetry matching the rest of the kitchen. Glassware was housed above the bar counter. The liquor was stored below the counter. Mom and Dad engaged in drinks when guests visited. There was a blender on the countertop. Dad used it nightly to prepare a chocolate shake at 10 p.m., which he carried to the back room to watch Jack Paar and later, Johnny Carson, deliver the opening monologue on *The Tonight Show*. This was one of Dad's rituals.

Going beyond the kitchen, to the right past the kitchen door was an open area along the railing for the stairwell. This area was set as a dining room with table and chairs. It was the route to the bathroom, laundry area, and back room, with its own stage in the same four-by-eight-foot proportions as the stage in our bedroom. My brothers, cousins, friends, and I played on and under the stages. These stages added to my interest in music and theater already present in the family. The interest in theater stemmed from Dad's father, a musical revue performer in church productions in Hammond, as well as Lawrence and Dad who performed in community productions in Hammond and Elgin. I have been drawn through our heritage to enjoy performing and involvement with theater productions.

The backroom stage was positioned under two large windows in the upper pitched ceiling. The windows sat right under this triangle point of the ceiling, allowing ample light, with a view of the sky and the branches of the large trees that reached to the third story. As air conditioning units became available, one window area was designed to accommodate an AC unit. During hot, humid weather, we closed the wooden entrance door from the back room to the rest of the apartment. This room was our refuge from heat.

In the redesign of the early '60s, the stage was removed, allowing space for two couches and three to four chairs suitable for TV watching, reading, and napping. Another section of the room was large enough to design a double sliding door closet constructed by Dad. Under the floor of the closet, he built in long storage drawers, similar in size to those in hospital morgues. Who else but Dad would combine his refurbishing skills with his many morgue experiences? During some play times, we removed the stored items, laid in the drawers, then had our playmates push them closed. I felt confined in that dark environment The area outside the side door of the closet became Barrett's bedroom during his later high school and college years.

There was substantial woodwork on the third floor. Whether he was working on the wainscot lower half portion of the walls, the doorway moldings, or the transom windows above three of the four doorways in the apartment, Dad took particular care with wood refinishing and staining. Sometimes Mom joined him in the projects. I became aware of the term "stripping the woodwork" when I watched them put on the chemicals to remove the stain and varnish. Fumes permeated the air for a few days, lessened only when the windows opened.

Dad taught himself to be a competent carpenter and home remodeler, using his skills in building furniture and refinishing woodwork in the funeral home and both apartments. He was known for frequently rearranging furniture. Mom remarked at times, "Every time we get a new ashtray, Dad insists on rearranging the furniture."

Dad and Mom's skills, coupled with tenacity and vision, created the evolving atmosphere of our third-floor home. Each project was an adventure that represented them as individuals and a couple. The structural designs gave us the physical aspects of how we lived. The cultures of two autonomous families living together were imparted to our later generations. We lived in the midst of the funeral home business Dad and Lawrence created and maintained on the first floor. The professional and personal lives of the families intertwined on a daily basis.

PART II

TWO FAMILIES, TWO APARTMENTS, TWO CULTURES

We lived integrated, yet unobtrusive, lives. Each couple and their family maintained their own individual identities. This is true of most families—the families from which you came and the families you create and continue to engender for children and grandchildren. These identities are important factors for descendants to understand in creating heritage in the lives of brothers, sisters, cousins, parents, aunts, and uncles.

Our cohesion was founded on the autonomy each family developed in their own living spaces. The strength of our collective cultures contributed to our security. There was no sense of competition between the two families. This might have to do with the age differences between us cousins. Lawrence and Mildred's daughters grew up in the 1930s through early 1950s. Our family of boys grew up in the late 1940s through the early 1970s. The differences of years, characters, and time, coupled with the experiences of each of the four parents, were infused into the architecture and the character of the house.

CHAPTER 6

Second-Floor Family Culture: Intersecting our Pathways

Lawrence and Mildred created an atmosphere and culture in their second-floor environment with their three daughters. Their way of life was influenced by the physical structure of the house and our connection to the uniqueness of the funeral home business.

The kitchen and back hallway area became a hub, a pivot point for family, delivery people, friends, and guests whose paths crossed there. Mildred was often at the landing to say hello to whoever was coming up or down the stairs. Lawrence was there occasionally. They each made a point to take time to get acquainted with our friends and engaged them in conversation. Mildred's welcoming greeting, smile, and hugs made the environment on the second floor consistently accepting and inclusive. In addition to our connected families, her aging mother, Grandma Kruzan, came to live in the house in the late 1940s. She remained there until her death in 1956. Her residency continued the previous intergenerational living experiences of the O'Connors and my mother's family.

As a toddler and preschooler, I had more awareness of my immediate family interactions than those of the second-floor family. I don't recall when Maureen lived in the house but do have memories with Kathleen and Sharon. Lawrence and Mildred included us three brothers more in their lives as their daughters finished their schooling, became employed, married, and moved to locations away from Elgin. Mildred used her yellow kitchen wall phone to converse daily with one or all three daughters, taking her position on the step stool next to the phone. When long coiled telephone lines became available, she spoke on the phone as she walked about the kitchen or took the kitchen stool and herself into the pantry. There she gained a sense of privacy for her conversation. The phone was her connection to a world beyond the apartment and the funeral home. She chatted with friends and family or phoned in orders for groceries and household goods to Goggin Drugs or Zenk Brothers, one of the many small food stores scattered throughout the neighborhoods. Mildred did not own a car or drive. She ordered over the phone, and items were delivered to the house. She was the forerunner of Instacart, an online grocery shopping service now used by many. She and the vendors were years ahead of their time.

Mildred also connected to the world outside of her kitchen through a radio in a wooden console box placed on one of the counters. The volume depended upon what she was doing, whether she was on the phone or involved in conversation with me or others in the kitchen. The radio was usually tuned to WRMN, Elgin's AM radio station. She listened to the morning news at 7 a.m. I heard the broadcast when I woke up in my bedroom at the top of the stairs. She kept the radio on during the day. The noon news included a reading of the obituaries with names of the deceased and the services planned. Mildred verified the arrangements made for our clients and the services at the other funeral homes in Elgin. As she listened to these obits, Mildred provided a resource for the funeral home as she dutifully maintained a written running record of funerals conducted by our competitors.

Part of the second-floor culture was Lawrence's personal hygiene standards. He rarely had dirty hands. He had a concern regarding the funeral home and bodies of the deceased. He thought there may be germs emulating from the deceased where the prep work was done or in the funeral home itself when a body was laid out in the casket. He wanted to be sure the germs remained in the downstairs areas and not on our hands. It was customary for him to request me and my brothers to wash our hands with soap and water after we worked in or walked through the funeral home areas. He insisted we rub isopropyl (rubbing) alcohol on our hands to further ensure protection, and he kept a bottle of rubbing alcohol under each sink on all floors. To this day when I smell alcohol in a doctor's office, in the health room of the schools where I worked, or on the cotton swab I now use on a needle to take blood sugar readings, Lawrence's face and voice come into my memory.

Lawrence maintained his health. He ate the meals Mildred provided. He did not take part in preparing meals. He exhibited a belted girth around his midsection, making him appear the heaviest of his brothers. His body was similar to William Frawley's character, Fred Mertz, on *I Love Lucy*. Coincidentally, Mildred bore a body, face, and clothing resembling Vivian Vance who played Ethel Mertz on the same series. Lawrence did not routinely exercise at home. He announced regularly that he was going to the YMCA to swim laps in the pool. He made routine visits to his chiropractor, perhaps stopping along the way at a favorite tavern where he lunched on a sandwich, enjoyed a brew, and conversed with the bartender. Although I was not knowledgeable at the time about the work of a chiropractor, Lawrence's visits influenced me to first seek out treatments when I was in my forties.

I go regularly now, wishing for the opportunity to talk to Lawrence about what led him to go.

Lawrence showed his positive spirit and care when he met and worked with people who entrusted him with the care of their deceased loved ones. This was part of his personality that also came through with our family and friends. He treated me and my brothers as sons. This is evidenced in a letter he wrote to me on November 29, 1970:

"I have several times been on the verge of writing to you, but each time I attempted to do so, I became engulfed by a feeling of futility. 'What can I say?' sort of thing. Knowing that you get all the news from all the other family sources left me in somewhat of a quandary, but still, I want to write to divulge some of my precious collection of 'Gems of Thawts.' [He shared information from Maureen, Kathleen, and Sharon's families]. Thanks for your check. [It was in the amount of five dollars, sent to him from Rome where I was attending school.] I am returning it to you as you better use it for school. I did not know anything about the phone calls [long-distance charges I incurred on the business phone the summer before], but I do appreciate your remembering and sending the check. It shows that you have honorable traits.

Now that Kerry is in residence again here at 364, the back stairs are once again put to good use, and it is refreshing to have the fellows coming and going. Brings back a lot of fond memories of when you and everyone else were creating pleasurable activities around the premises. Take good care of yourself. Looking forward to when you will be back in this area. Affectionately, Lawrence."

His care and humor also came through when he wrote to me at school in Rome five months later on April 8, 1971. I was almost overdrawn in my checking account and wrote to Kerry to help me out, so Dad and Mom would not know I put myself in a precarious position. Unbeknownst to me when I sent the request, Kerry was on his way to Rome for a surprise visit. Lawrence's note stated:

> "Dear Kevin, The card you addressed to Kerry was read by me. You wrote it before you knew Kerry was coming your way. I heeded your poignant plea about being overdrawn and deposited $200.00 to your account to cover. Nobody looks good in stripes, Lawrence."

Opening each other's mail was not customary. There was a high regard for the privacy of each family. Our families worked together to navigate the challenges of privacy presented by our shared living environment. By location on the third floor, there was more sense of privacy than the second floor. When Dad and Mom were having a discussion in their living room, and they heard someone coming up the stairway, they paused the discussion if they thought it necessary. Out of respect, Lawrence, Mildred, and the girls stood at the bottom of the stairs and announced "Marion? Bill? Are you up there?" before they came up the stairs. The absence of complete privacy was part of our environment. We knew no different.

When Lawrence and Mildred wanted to talk privately to each other or their daughters, they closed the doors to rooms or spoke in quieter tones. At any given time, one of us from the third floor may have been walking through their living areas or sitting in the second-floor living room reading, listening to music, or watching TV.

One evening in December 1965, I was laying on my stomach and reading by the living room's bay window when Mildred received a call on the kitchen phone. She was grieving with tears, gasps, and sobs. Her sister had died in East

Chicago. I overheard Lawrence muster the words to help Mildred. They were having a private moment but not upset with me for being where I was at the time. Nor did they close their kitchen door to avert sound from traveling at their time of sorrow. Our families respected each other's privacy. Yet, aloneness was not a part of our families' cultures.

Mildred was especially gracious during the summer of 1970. Five or six of my friends came to Elgin from Loyola in Chicago to share a meal, play some games, watch TV—and maybe indulge in some of the alcohol we might find on the premises—and stay overnight. After the friends stopped with me at the second floor back hallway and introduced themselves, we engaged in conversation. Mildred excused herself and asked me to join her in the living room. My friends walked upstairs to the third floor.

"Kevin, I met two of your friends before. Nice boys. Tell me about your friend with the poncho."

I stammered for a bit.

"How far along is she? Where is her family?"

"She has been a good friend in our group through most of this school year," I replied. "She is probably about six months."

Mildred knew I was aware and had observed the 20 pregnancies of her daughters and my sister-in-law. I was not a stranger to the physical signs of pregnancy. I instinctively knew Mildred was concerned about my friend, while at the same time, I worried that she wondered why I brought her to our house.

"She must be so hot in that poncho," Mildred said.

"I think she thinks people won't notice as much if she wears the poncho. She does not have support from her family. We are helping her in any way we can."

"It's ninety-five degrees outside; I think tonight, I will have her sleep in the girls' room. I bet she wants some time to herself in the bathroom. Maybe take a shower. What do your Dad and Mom think?"

"I don't know," I admitted. "I imagine they are talking to her now."

"I'll make sure she has what she needs. You bring her back here to me when you are deciding where your friends will sleep."

I wish I knew what happened to Melinda and her baby. By September, I was in Rome and into a world far apart from hers.

Mildred's generosity was not a one-time thing. Mildred and Lawrence offered their apartment to others in the family needing accommodations. Dad and Lawrence welcomed their cousin, Tom, in the house when he was going through a divorce process from his second wife.

As obliging as Mildred was, she did let me know her view of challenging aspects of being married into the O'Connor family. She took it in stride and humor. Her letter to me dated January 9, 1971, allowed her to vent a bit about the living situation with Tom:

"The more I get to know him, the more of a crackpot I think he is, and my sympathies sometimes go to his about-to-be-former wife. That is probably heresy among the blood relatives, but he surely is a Mr. Do-Gooder! I guess I feel this way because one day last week he tried to tell me what I should do and say, and at that time, I had had it. I will still invite him to come here whenever he wants, as I guess he has a terrible apartment, and I can sympathize with him, as I know he's never been used to that kind of living, but I will scream if I hear once again 'may I offer you a suggestion?' I don't need TWO [referring to Lawrence] like that. Do you have space for one more in your room? I may just fly over to be a housemother, chaperone. Something!"

A few weeks later on January 25, 1971, she wrote:

"Cuz is still in trouble. The court date keeps being postponed, so I think the lawyers are keeping their rent paid. Sometimes I feel sorry for him. This past weekend I learned how to make Jell-O a la Chef

Cousin. Really, I laughed right out loud when he saw me making some Jell-O and told me HOW IT SHOULD BE DONE! He is almighty right in all things, so he thinks, but I mean it that I invited him to come here any time he wanted, as we do have the room, and I know he sure isn't used to living as he is now, and for that he does have my sympathy. He looks terrible and has lost fifteen pounds. Wish I could lose fifteen pounds, or at least ten. I have written this between a couple of phone calls—and in between a lecture from LS. [Lawrence] I think MOST of the original O'Connors are NUTS. Love from your Auntie."

Lawrence and Dad's father was the brother to Tom's father. Their mother was the sister to Tom's mother. Hence, Dad, Lawrence, and Tom called themselves double cousins. They looked similar enough to be mistaken for brothers. Tom took an interest and conversed with my brothers and me plus the children of his other cousins. He was a conduit who helped to keep our family extended. To this day, I have followed his lead. I reach out to the children of my first cousins like he did to us.

Tom paid his gratitude forward to me for the accommodations he received from Lawrence and Mildred. In September 1979, I was newly separated, working as a second-grade teacher in McHenry and commuting from Elgin each day. I was waiting to occupy a condominium in Woodstock. Tom lived in a house in McHenry. I accepted his offer to stay in a room at his house. I saved commute time. For six weeks, I either drove my car or rode my bike to and from Tom's and work. He fed me breakfast in the morning, gave me the supplies to pack my lunch, and prepared dinner each evening. He made Jell-O. Evidently, he had learned the right way to make it from his observations of Mildred's culinary skills. I was grateful to have the place he provided in his home.

I have heard from some of our offspring about being unaware of Mildred's humor and smiles. She kept me up to date on what was happening in Elgin. In

September 1969, she wrote:

"The olde town is getting a new face. The city hall is now leveled, and I'm sure that leaves you with a nostalgic feeling. I read in the *Courier-News* where someone stole the hands from the tower clock. Would you now say that the person has time on her hands?"

Referencing my trip to Oktoberfest in Munich, she wrote to me in October 1970:

A long time ago, Anita, beauty shop operator and from Germany, gave me an insight of these days of revelry in Germany. Some of the things she told me 'just weren't very nice,' so I am hoping you retained your INNOCENCE! Did your papa tell you of the birds and bees??? Let me say, they sing and dance."

Mildred experienced health difficulties causing hair loss. She adapted to wearing wigs. She kept her humor in a letter written on November 6, 1970:

"Have to BATHE! Going to sorority tonight, so I better start getting ready. It takes me quite a while to adjust my wig, and pretty soon, I'll be adjusting my TEETH. And my wooden leg. Lots of love to you and your roommates. Auntie Mildred."

She wrote comically about other health issues on November 23, 1970:

"I was supposed to work at the bazaar, but I got a pain in the middle so stayed home. Tomorrow I am to go to the lab for GI X-rays ... you know ... when you swallow the cement. I remember several years ago I had those tests at St. Joe Hospital, and I guess someone slipped up and didn't give me the usual laxative when it was all over, so I got into deep trouble until a nurse came to the rescue. Ever since then, she has called me Gravel Gertie!"

In her New Year's 1971 letter to me, less than three months before she died, she wrote:

"Saturday night we are invited out, and then I guess the tree will come down. All decorations will be put away and so into the year 1971. We have all had our share of happiness and some tears, but for the most part, I think we have all been lucky and have much to be thankful for. Love, Mildred."

I consider myself incredibly fortunate to have been so readily included in the culture provided by my second-floor family. As blessed as I was to have my parents, the second-floor culture enhanced my development and the enriched perspective I maintain for extended family.

CHAPTER 7

Third-Floor Culture: Dancing through Life

Similar to Lawrence and Mildred, Dad and Mom brought their own individual characters to their relationship, our immediate family, and the interplay of the two families. Dad and Mom created an atmosphere with a foundation for my brothers and me to develop and proceed with our own interests in high school, college, and beyond. Mom and Dad's love story can be summarized in the song "After the Lovin'," first recorded in 1976 by Engelbert Humperdink. They mentioned this song as one of "their" songs when they danced together. They loved dancing with one another to the music of orchestras and combos playing in the Elgin or Chicago areas. Dancing is a metaphor for the way Dad and Mom lived their lives. As Dad led, Mom flowed with him. When I watched them dance, I wasn't aware Dad was leading. They danced as one. As a couple. As a team. I saw them in this flow during my life. I did not sense Dad was in charge or made decisions and Mom followed. Mom and Dad choreographed their way through life, setting out on plans while making adjustments to whatever real or imaginary music was playing in their heads and the adjustments they needed to make on life's dance floor.

Some people say the roles in marriage are clearly defined. In 1950–60s family TV shows *Father Knows Best*, *Leave It to Beaver*, and *The Dick Van Dyke Show*, the father was portrayed as income producer dressed in suit and tie and leaving for work in the morning. The mom was generally attired in an apron, getting the children ready for school and serving breakfast. Little mention, if any, was given to the mom leaving the house during the day or having her own employment.

Dad and Mom did not model this type of parenting; they shared parenting responsibilities without regard to perceived gender roles. When a diaper needed changing or a baby needed to be fed or rocked, Dad was as engaged as Mom. When it came to mealtime and preparations, Dad and Mom were equally involved.

Mom did not work outside the home through much of the '40s and '50s, although she worked part time during the holidays at a department store or office. In 1958, she went to work full time as a secretary and bookkeeper at the Elgin National Watch Company's factory, directly across the street from one of her childhood residences. She and her family lived in the apartment above the restaurant operated by her parents. Ciraulo's Restaurant served breakfast and lunch to the employees of the factory. My grandfather operated the counter, a chef worked at the grill, and my grandmother baked desserts. Mom knew what it was like to live in a building where parents operated a business.

When Mom entered the full-time workforce, it was to provide the money needed for Barrett's college education. This was my first experience of not having Mom at home when we left for school or when we arrived home. After

Mom left for work in the morning, Dad provided breakfast, helped to get our lunch bags organized, and checked with us to make sure we had what we needed for school. When we came home, he was in the apartment or working downstairs. Mildred would greet us when we reached the second-floor landing, asking about our day and letting us know if Dad was upstairs or downstairs. Dad would start the preparation for dinner during the day while Mom was at work. When she arrived home from work around 5 p.m., she'd finish the dinner preparations.

Dad was the primary housekeeper. He kept our apartment in pristine, comfortable condition. Mom was no stranger to housework, but for the most part, it was Dad's domain. It wasn't unusual to find Dad vacuuming, dusting, or doing other chores in his briefs in our apartment. I laugh now when I picture him mid-task. He took special pride in the linoleum and vinyl floors in our kitchen and family room, mopping them weekly and waxing three to four times a year, usually after we went to bed, as he wanted the floor to dry before breakfast. After Mom went to work and we went to school, Dad recuperated by sleeping during the day, unless the phone rang, and business beckoned. Dad provided a role model for me of a man who considered it respectable to have a dust rag in his hand, push a vacuum, change or make a bed, and prepare breakfast, lunch, or dinner.

My parents pursued eclectic interests. In addition to dancing, both enjoyed playing bridge with other couples and friends. Our bedroom was next to the living room where the games and conversations occurred. I often left the door open, so I could hear the adults' conversation and fall asleep to words such as "pass," "trump," or the names of the card suits. Dad enjoyed poker and played frequently at the local Elks Club in late afternoons. When it came time for dinner and we knew Dad wasn't working on the first floor, or we could not find him in the house, Mom made a call to the bar at the Elks Club to remind him to come home. He managed to break away from his game, ideally with some quarters and dollar bills in his pocket from his winnings. Mom enjoyed playing a variety of card games with her friends. One group was called "Club" and was composed of friends from high school who came together weekly for more than fifty years.

Mom and Dad were well-known for the way in which they planned events that brought people together. They relished in opportunities to continue longtime friendships in settings that included class reunions. They graduated only two years apart at Elgin High School, so their friendships intertwined. Starting with Dad's twenty-fifth reunion in 1957 and Mom's in 1959, they served on the planning committees for their reunions every five years. They helped to keep up with address changes and ways to contact people. They organized reunions without the benefit of Google, the Internet, Facebook, or People Finder. Dad's fiftieth reunion was in 1982. Mom attended her fiftieth reunion two months before Dad died in 1984. She continued helping with her class reunions at five-year intervals through the next twenty-five years. My brothers and I have followed their lead and coordinate reunions for our elementary, high school, and college classes. Mom and Dad inspired me to keep on nurturing the friendships of my youth.

At social events like reunions and the occasions they planned for their ever-expanding social circles, Dad's musical talents with piano and organ playing were recognized by friends and family. As soon as Dad's fingers touched a keyboard, people gathered and joined in song. I knew of few times when Dad could walk past a piano without sitting down to play. In the mid '70s, Kerry gifted Dad with an upright piano to place in the living room, giving Dad welcome opportunities to play. Buying the piano was special. The challenge came in finding piano movers willing to hoist the piano up the steps to the ground level porch area and up the two flights of stairs to the third floor. Dad and Mom enhanced their music appreciation in the apartment with the piano readily available. Dad would listen to a tune on the stereo system or radio, put his fingers to the keyboard, and then transfer the tune to his own rendition. He'd commit the tune to his musical memory, adding it to his repertoire for piano locations he found in town or while traveling. He was a truly gifted play-by-ear musician who read very little sheet music.

His piano prowess brought strangers together. For example, in the fall of 1977, after dining in the restaurant at the Silverado Country Club in Napa, California, I recall walking through the crowded bar area where a piano sat alone. Dad instinctively put his hands to the keyboard and began to play. People broke into song and then requested more songs for him to play. If he knew the song, he played it. If he wasn't sure, he said something like, "Sing me the beginning." When they sang for him, he joined in the tune with his magic hands. These memorable scenes with my father repeated during his lifetime.

Mom and Dad also influenced us through activities in which they were involved as a couple and individually. Dad was one of the first people I knew who took an interest in yoga. Classes were held at the YMCA two blocks from our house. On April 10, 1971, he wrote me:

"I think you would love yoga. I signed up for the next session. I hope I can keep it up. Four lessons. Four weeks. I've tried to keep it up on my own. It takes a lot of nerve at my age to be in the class with only two young guys and about fifteen girls and women. While I'm doing it, I enjoy it and try to do some at home every day or evening. I may not last due to the conditions and circumstances, but at present, I really enjoy it and practice at home. I don't know a soul in my class and hope they don't know me. If I can keep going long enough to learn enough to get into the advanced class, they have one called "Professional Men." But you have to have a good form and be in condition to catch up with them. I think I'd like that, but we'll see."

I joined him once for a class when I was home from college. He also introduced me to massage sessions. To this day, I am involved in yoga and massage. Dad's sense of new experiences was ever-present. We jumped at the chance to take a mud bath when we were in Calistoga, California, in the mid '70s. Mom declined to join us. I enjoyed sitting in a tub next to Dad's tub, soaking in the steaming mud poured over us by the attendants. Had Dad not offered his encouragement, I may have missed the experience.

Both Mom and Dad enjoyed watching and commenting about movies. Dad sometimes went to movies on his own. When the first beepers evolved in the '60s, we sometimes located Dad at a theater via the device when business responsibilities occurred. When Dad and/or Mom went to a movie, he often included a written review to me, as evidenced in a letter dated January 6, 1971:

"… I wanted so badly to see *Love Story*. So, Mother and I were standing in line by 8:50 p.m. at the Crocker Theater, finally got in, and sat up in the balcony for the 9 p.m. show. They have features running from 12:45 p.m., and the last show starts at 11 p.m.! It opened Christmas Eve, and I guess the lines are like that for every show—if you can imagine that at our Crocker. It is great. I like Ali McGraw, but I can see why they looked and looked for the right guy. He is fabulous. It's like the book almost to a T, for which I am glad. They let her swear throughout as in the book. Don't miss and hope you enjoy it, too. The book here is now on top for 43rd week. The book and movie move, but there's so many angles to continually analyze in relationships, etc. to decide."

A later personal experience related to the book *Love Story* occurred in April 1973, when I wrote to Dad and Mom about volunteer work I was doing at the Bank of America in San Francisco where I was employed. I was part of an employee group involved in providing English as a Second Language (ESL) lessons to employees seeking more proficiency in their reading and writing of English. My student was Mae Chu. Mae was from Burma and lived not too far from me in the Golden Gate Park neighborhood of the Richmond District in the city. I wrote in a letter to Mom and Dad:

"Tutoring is going fine. Mae is reading *Love Story* out loud, and we pick it apart—grammatically, structurally, vocabulary, and story line. I'd forgotten about all the language in the book. I'd like to skip over some of the words, but I want her to know all the new vocabulary. Seems silly to go over a word without knowing what it means. But how do I explain 'beating off' to a thirty-three-year-old Burmese woman or 'tight ass' or 'up yours.' Should be a broadening experience for both of us, especially for shy, reserved Mae who cringes when someone says 'shit.' She seems to like the story itself though."

I found myself in Dad and Mom's company when they discussed their social plans, purchases they wanted to make, and how they wanted to design and decorate their living spaces. Dad often took it upon himself to rearrange furniture and start with a decorating idea prior to conversing with her. She trusted the way he sought out design and color schemes. She appreciated and acknowledged him for his artistic qualities.

Dad was seldom without a project involving his handiwork with furniture and woodwork. He wrote in a letter dated November 1, 1971:

"Guess I have too many projects going. I am rebuilding and refinishing the corner bench that I built many years ago, sanding and repainting the metal capping on the chapel roof (nice days only), regular housework around here, puttering with your room design, embalming, and keeping up with funeral work. (No complaints there! We need it as it's been slow.)"

He took pride in his work. He acknowledged his successes and took setbacks in stride. One complication occurred when he was redesigning our bedroom in the mid-1950s. He was putting wood paneling on the walls. I was watching from what he determined to be a safe distance. The paneling was supported by two sawhorses. Dad was cutting piece after piece with a handheld electric saw. Suddenly the saw stopped. He didn't know why. He looked under the paneling he was cutting. He had cut the electric cord with the blade of the saw as it went through the paneling on one of the edges. What a mistake. He was lucky he was not hurt. He unplugged the cord. Then, he wrapped the strands of exposed wire together with black electrical tape. The saw worked again, and he continued, not dwelling on the error. When we teased him about this accident, he laughed right along with us. In the 1970s, when I was trimming the bushes outside of my house, I sawed right through the electric cord, leaving myself in a momentary state of bewilderment when the trimmer stopped. I laughed to myself, put down the trimmer and made a call to Dad to share in the story. We laughed together.

In addition to Dad's interests and the activities in which they were involved together, Mom was an athlete. During her youth, she participated in basketball and softball teams. She played tennis in city-sponsored leagues and tournaments. Starting just after high school and into her nineties, she played golf in leagues and with friends. Mom set aside spring, summer, and fall afternoons for her golf outings. She was a founding member of Elgin Golferettes. On Tuesdays, she left home in the morning with her golf clothing and equipment in the car. After work, she went directly to the golf course. She changed clothes and was ready at the first tee by no later than 5 p.m. After the game, she came home and ate her portion of the dinner that Dad had prepared. She referenced her golf games in her letters, such as the following from June 23, 1971:

"Last night I had a 50 playing golf, which is my best score so far this year. Couldn't do anything wrong."

In her letter written on June 3, 1975:

"... by the way, I had a 47 last Tuesday night in our league. Finally put my game together after having a miserable start."

I imagine her secret ambition was seeing herself as a professional athlete, like female golfers Babe Zaharias, Patty Berg, Mickey Wright, or Kathy Whitworth.

Through their shared interests in design, card playing, entertaining, and providing for individual interests such as piano playing and golf, Mom and Dad modelled two people who universally danced through life. Their relationship was mirrored in the spins, twirls, jitterbugs and two-step maneuvers that came to them so effortlessly. The smiles on their faces and the manner in which they flowed across a dance floor provided the release to whatever struggles they may have been experiencing.

Mom and Dad lived their lives not as shoulds or woulds or coulds. They experienced each day according to the rhythm of their everyday choreography. My memories of their dancing provide a backdrop to their stories and inspiration to me to prance, cavort, and waltz through my own life.

This caricature was created for Bill and Marion in celebration of their 40th Wedding Anniversary, June 28, 1979. Frank Martino was the artist. He was the husband of Kathleen O'Connor. Frank was a professor of art education and taught K-12 and college level courses in New York City and Long Island. His drawings conveniently represent the stories presented in this chapter about their marriage.

CHAPTER 8

Support and Encouragement in Our Family Life

M om and Dad's dance through life influenced the support they provided to my brothers and me and in turn, the buttress we have provided to each other through our lives. Like siblings in any family, Barrett, Kerry, and I have our own personalities. Dad and Mom acknowledged us for our individual talents and strengths without statements such as, "Why don't you do this like your brother?" or "Your brother never did that." Mom did refer to me as "you big lug" when she felt I was unfair or mistreating Kerry. She and Dad occasionally referred to us in one word, "KevinandKerry." We were close in age, known as "Irish Twins," in some Celtic circles. They peppered their letters with elements of humor as conveyed in this October 15, 1972, letter from Mom:

"Kerry was asked when he was going to get married. He said 1978. I wished he wasn't so impulsive!"

Dad and Mom embedded the concept of brotherhood among us. Dad remarked that since Barrett was an only child from his birth in 1940 to my arrival in 1950, they prepared him intentionally for my presentation to the family. He had established routines and habits as an only child. Being no longer alone and a big brother to me and Kerry fifteen months later must have challenged his position in our family. He went from autonomy and preferential treatment to having to share space with us in our apartment. After having slept alone in a large bedroom, he was now in the company of cribs where his brotherly occupants challenged the quiet to which he was accustomed. The doting he received from Lawrence and Mildred, Maureen, Kathleen, and Sharon, was now shared with Kerry and me. Even with these scenarios, Barrett has always been caring and supportive of his little brothers. Whether he was helping us in sports or modeling his fathering skills for us to employ in our own parenting, Barrett has always been the consummate older brother and mentor.

Barrett once rescued Kerry and me while swimming in a lake in Northern Wisconsin. I was five years old. Barrett was on the shore with our family friend, Jeff. Kerry and I ventured out enough to the drop-off from the beach area. I recall the sensation of bobbing up and down in the water as Kerry and I held hands. Each time my vision came above the water, I saw Barrett sitting on the beach. I am not sure how many times we came above the water. I imagine I bobbed up thousands of times. Realistically, it was once or twice. The fear is still grounded in me. Barrett ran into the water and grabbed both Kerry and me and brought us to shore. By this time, Dad and Mom dashed out from the nearby cottage. As I was coughing up water, I felt the softness of a cotton towel on my shoulders. I don't recall if Barrett got in trouble for not paying attention to us or if he was recognized for his rescue. Probably the latter.

By the time Kerry and I were in mid-elementary years, we became interested in team sports and athletic activity. Barrett was there to guide and help us, as he was active in sports in his elementary and early high school years. During his college years of 1958–62, Kerry and I did not have much interaction with Barrett. When he was home for the summer, he worked during the day and spent most evenings with his friends. Nonetheless, he came to our baseball games and provided coaching.

At the start of my seventh-grade year, Barrett was newly married, living in Elgin and visiting our house frequently. He still attended our basketball games. He helped us with shooting and dribbling on the funeral home's parking lot turned basketball court with a backboard and hoop that had been mounted on the trunk of an oak tree when Barrett was in grade school. The blacktop surface sloped down a bit toward the tree and backboard. We marked a line for free throw shooting and a space adapted for our own version of a basketball court. It was a gathering area for games with friends. I particularly enjoyed shooting baskets with Kerry and Barrett at the backyard hoop. I felt more comfortable with them in this activity than with friends who came to join us. When Kerry had friends over, I sometimes played, albeit nervously, or excused myself and did not go outside to join the game. My self-consciousness and lack of confidence got the best of me. I watched from the kitchen window, looking down to the court three floors below. Kerry didn't disparage me for my self-perceived lack of skills in sports. Some of my better memories are shooting baskets and playing H-O-R-S-E or other games alone with Kerry in the backyard. Just us.

After watching Kerry play basketball on the fifth-sixth grade team at St. Mary's, I tried out for the seventh-eighth-grade team. Truthfully, I do not remember a tryout. Anyone who wanted to play on the team was given the opportunity. I joined the team because I realized it was a way to enhance the acquaintances with other boys in my class. I knew little about what to do with a basketball. Being on the school team helped me become part of a circle of friends. Kerry was a confident player and was recognized for his skills. With Barrett's support of Kerry and me, he helped each of us to develop our skills. I was challenged with the practices of my teams and started to be more comfortable with who I was through Barrett and Kerry's help. Conversely, I was so nervous and anxious about my skills that I sometimes became nauseated. Prior to practice on each Monday and Wednesday evening at 7 p.m., I spent some time in the bathroom at home with spells of diarrhea. I allowed myself just enough time to eat dinner, have my bathroom visit, and either walk or get a ride to practice from Mom or Dad.

During practices, I was self-conscious of my perceived lack of ability compared to my teammates. I spent most games hoping to stay on the bench. In reality, the bench was a line of folding chairs set in a row. I do recall the feeling of cold metal on my bare legs and thinking the coldness was preferable to playing in the game. When I got into the game, I mustered everything Barrett, Kerry, and the coaches taught me. But I was not able to dribble a basketball. When the ball did come to my hands, I passed it quickly to someone else. If I was near the basket, I shot the ball. I made a point or two.

The best part of the eighth-grade season was that Kerry and I were on the same team. He was a first-string guard. I played a bit more as an eighth grader. By the end of the school year, the pre-practice and pre-game diarrhea ended. My enhanced play turned into an award as "Most Improved Player."

While gaining more confidence with basketball, I was fostering an increasing interest in musical artists and performances beyond the pop and rock interests of my peers. Before my teen years, I became a fan of Judy Garland, Barbra Streisand, Broadway scores, and the albums in the Division Street listening repertoire. I sang along with every Streisand recording and knew the order of the songs on the *Judy at Carnegie Hall* 1961 concert album I received as a gift from Mom and Dad for Christmas. I know that none of my friends received *this* gift under their trees.

I enjoyed a pretend world, performing along with singers and recorded musical productions. After leaving the dinner table, I frequently retreated to the living room to listen to a record or cassette and sing and dance along with the tunes. The two stages that had been in the apartment were sacrificed to create more useable living space. Consequently, when I wanted to do my personal performance on a bigger area, I carried the cassette tape recorder and available tapes to the expanse of the viewing areas of the funeral home. In those environments, absent of any wakes or funerals, I leaped, tapped, or cross-stepped through the length of my pretend performance venue. I do not know if anyone ever saw me. I was not concerned. I didn't close a door and lower the volume. My space. My venue.

When I graduated from eighth grade in June 1964, Dad and Mom gifted me with the cast album of Streisand's *Funny Girl*. To be sure, I was the only graduate of my class to be gifted with this recording. I dared not tell my friends who only listened to the Top 40 tunes about these aspects of my musical tastes, as I feared it would jeopardize my relatability. Nonetheless, Dad and Mom consistently supported my musical tastes.

I also enjoyed playing with dolls. This started with a doll Dad and Mom gave me when I was three or four. I referred to this uniformly plush, stitched doll as "Snooper," indistinguishable as a boy or girl. The interest in this doll led to enjoyment in playing with Barbie-type dolls alongside my cousin, Wendy, or neighbor, Ruth, who sometimes loaned me their dolls. Admittedly, I was teased about my doll play from others in the neighborhood or classmates, but I don't recall any direct challenge or judgment from my brothers or parents. Doll play was simply part of who I was at the time.

So, there I was at age fourteen . . . with a foundation in doll play, a most improved basketball player who danced and sang in the funeral home parlors while listening to show tunes on the cassette player. I was on my way. To where? I did not know.

In the midst of my passages into these parts unknown, Dad and Mom augmented their support for us with unexpected joy and humor in the surprises they planned for us. One occurred when I was seventeen and Kerry was almost sixteen. Dad summoned us.

"I want you both to come with me and Mom in the car," he said. "We have a surprise for you."

It seemed imperative for us to go. We drove fifteen to twenty minutes to arrive at a house in Barrington. A Volkswagen convertible was in the driveway.

"Whose house is this, Dad?" Kerry asked.

"I'll tell you later. Look at the Volkswagen. The car is yours. To share," Dad announced to our surprise and delight.

"This is for us?"

"With this car, you can drive back and forth to school and go out with your friends."

The owner of the car came into the driveway. Dad and Mom introduced everyone. As they conversed, I realized the purchase of the used car was the result of an advertisement Mom saw in the newspaper. They had called the owner and made arrangements. Dad extended an envelope to the owner with the agreed-upon amount of cash.

"How we going to get this home?" I asked.

"You two are going to drive it."

"Alone?" Kerry said.

"Kevin will drive because he has his license. Kerry, you will be the passenger. You will be able to drive it once you get your license."

"I am not sure how to drive a stick shift car," I said.

"Why do you think we arranged to have Barrett teach you to drive his Mustang a few weeks ago? We wanted you to be ready. You DO know how to drive a stick."

Kerry and I slid into the car. The owner gave Dad the key, who then handed it over to me. I put it into the ignition, and the car turned on immediately. I put my right hand on the round knobbed gear shift. I felt my feet trying to do what I practiced with Barrett. With a chug and another chug of my first-time experience, I slowly led the car in a stop and start forward motion. The driveway was lengthy. I drove a bit in first gear and then second gear. I came to a stop. I needed to turn right onto the street while holding the steering wheel and grasping the knob of the gear shift while creating the proper sequence and juxtaposition of my feet on the clutch and gas pedal. More chugs. More stops and starting. More resultant jerking of our heads and bodies. We came to the first stop sign. Dad got out of his car while Mom stayed in the passenger seat.

Dad came over to the driver's side window. He said to follow him and Mom in their car. We followed. He told us to pull over to the side of the road if we thought we were in trouble. He used less traveled country roads leading us to Elgin. We arrived at home and parked the car in the front driveway. Since the driveway sloped down, I knew to secure the car by setting the parking brake.

Now it was time for us to take a ride on our own. Dad and Mom watched as we drove out of the driveway and headed to Barrett and Pat's to show them our car. We inadvertently chose the route with the only incline in town. As we rose to the top of National Street, both Kerry and I implored the light to stay green. It did not cooperate. It changed quickly to yellow and red. We stopped at the top. We were the first car at the intersection. A car arrived behind us.

"What do we do now?" Kerry said.

"I don't think I can do it myself without rolling backward into the car behind us," I said. "We've got to work together. I will stay in the driver's side and hold on to the wheel and the shift."

"OK. I will move over so my foot will go on the gas."

"And I will put my foot on the clutch," I added.

Kerry moved to his left and came close to me. He put his left foot on the gas pedal. We stared at the traffic light. It changed to green.

"OK, here we go. I am shifting and I've got my foot on the clutch."

"Jeez. I am pressing on the gas pedal. 1-2-3," Kerry said.

Like two of the Three Stooges we clumsily coordinated our efforts. We lurched our way into the intersection and continued to Barrett and Pat's house.

Our parents added novelty and fun to their decisions in creating milestones for Kerry and me. We traveled on to more and more autonomy.

Dad supported further independence and guidance in ways more serious than driving a stick shift vehicle. I conversed with Dad as a youngster and through the years of adolescence, young adulthood, and up to his death when I was thirty-four. We talked about topics including friends, our family, marriages, divorces, and fatherhood. Reading Dad's letters, I am reminded that he encouraged me in many ways. When I was considering joining a fraternity, he offered this advice in a letter dated October 24, 1969:

"Just want to tell you how glad I am that you are thinking fraternity again because I always feel it was partly our fault that you didn't join last year. It would be all over now, and you wouldn't have to be worrying about this year being a pledge, etc. when last year you were practically in if we had helped you make up your mind and encouraged you to go in."

He offered advice about travel opportunities in a November 1, 1970, letter:

"Remember what I told you, that even if you have to eventually borrow to finish your college education, it is better to make the best of all your opportunities over there in Italy and not pass up anything that seems like a 'once in a lifetime opportunity.' Like going to Greece. If everyone else is going, don't pass that up due to a couple of dollars. You're young and have a long time to pay back loans. It's warm in Greece until December the airline ads say."

Support and encouragement continued into later years after I had finished college, established myself in a teaching career, and moved back to the Elgin area from Oakland, California, in 1978 with my first wife, Sheila. I felt comfortable confiding to Dad that I was going to counseling therapy. As close as I had been with Dad throughout my life, the counselor said comments I had made during our sessions revealed aspects of what he considered my uneasiness with my father. I recall my revelations had to do with discovering my own identity. While appreciating the way in which Dad exhibited a maleness I thought of as acceptable, I let myself be troubled by the contrast of qualities of design, maternal care, and household chores not in other fathers' repertoires. I had some of those same qualities in myself. I was happy to hear people say, "You are so much like your father," while also guiltily questioning "What kind of male am I?" How was I to reconcile this gender identity confusion in myself? My therapist encouraged me to talk to my father. I phoned Dad one morning and asked to meet him. He eagerly accepted my invitation. I arranged for a substitute to take my fifth-grade class at Edgebrook School in McHenry.

We met at Floyd's Restaurant in West Dundee. I talked about my perceptions of him, the appreciation I had of our relationship, the confusion I was feeling about male/female gender attributes, and my marriage. Although I had feared the conversation, my trust in Dad was readily reconfirmed. I started uneasily in conversation but quickly switched to easy dialogue with him. I let him know Sheila and I were open and honest with each other. She was an excellent listener when I told her I was concerned about my attraction to men. Dad did not look surprised or judgmental. He encouraged me to continue talking. He made it comfortable for me to reveal a physical relationship I had with a male friend at Loyola during the spring of my first year of college. I told Dad what it was like to come home for that summer with a secret about the relationship and how I kept my feelings inside me until I spoke to Sheila and now to him seven years later.

Dad, as always, was an exemplary listener. He conveyed an understanding and said he wished I had spoken to him about my feelings when they were occurring. But he appreciated I was sharing with him now. As fearful as I was about inquiring what he and Mom thought about this aspect of my life, Dad was supportive. He was noticeably and intentionally interested. He spoke and let me know that he loved me. He talked about his perception of several people he knew having a range of feelings about "sexual orientation," although we did not use those words. He expressed no disdain. He encouraged me to keep on going to counseling.

I do not recall asking him not to talk to Mom about our conversation. Perhaps I asked him, "What do you think Mom will think?" I don't recall Dad and I talking about the topic again in the next five years prior to his death. I do not know if he talked to Mom. I assume he did. Twenty-seven years later, the seed of identity I had planted with Dad bloomed. I discussed my sexual orientation with Mom after my second wife and children's mother, Gina, and I separated and headed to eventual divorce. I have been out since 2005 and in an ecstatically happy marriage with my husband, Leon. From 2011–20, I worked in Broward County schools as an advocate for LGBTQ youth, parents, and staff. When students asked me to tell my story, they often queried why I did not come out when I was younger. They told me about their parents and the difficulty they have with talking to them about their sexual orientation. I told them the story about my conversations with Dad and Mom. I let them know understanding and healing is possible. I was there to support them no matter the outcome of their conversations they were hoping to have with their parents. My work with these students reaffirms my continual gratitude for Dad's love and support and the equally supportive position Mom embodied when I spoke to her many years later.

Mom and Dad were champions to me with their support, encouragement, and listening throughout my life. In my earlier years, whether it was my musical interests, doll play, or educational pursuits, they propped me up through their inquiries and openness. In my teens and twenties, they showed their support through the letters they wrote to me. When I was a junior-year college student in Rome immersing myself in Italian culture and language, Mom took it upon herself to learn Italian words and vernacular. She typed the following heading on a letter dated Monday, September 8, 1970:

"Lunedi, Settembre Venti-Oht."

I wrote in my response dated October 6, 1970:

"Mom, your letter has a bit of Italian in it. Did you buy a dictionary? I'll write one of the next letters in Italian, so you can translate it."

As a result of the letters I was composing to them, they supported me in my writing, as evidenced in this letter from Mom on November 9, 1970:

"This is strictly a mother's pride, but I'm almost tempted to see about getting your letters published or something."

She provided further written commentary on February 9, 1971:

"I think you should concentrate on being a writer. Your letters are good."

In the years that followed, I experienced the joys and challenges of parenting and navigated through the stress of two divorces. My parents may not have understood all that I was experiencing in my life. Yet, I did not fear abandonment or exclusion from them. I am ever grateful to Dad and Mom for supporting, encouraging, surprising, conversing, and fostering the sustained brotherhood I have with Barrett and Kerry.

To a family life treasured.

These are the only two photographs taken of Marion and Bill and my brothers and me with just the five of us. The first was taken in 1952. The second picture was taken in 1981. I wished there were more. Families, remind yourselves to take the time to have photos taken together. Each family needs more than two pictures to chronicle a lifetime of togetherness.

CHAPTER 9

Cousins Living as Brothers and Sisters

I am not sure if it was intentional on the parents' part to treat the six of us as brothers and sisters. There is a twenty-year age difference between oldest Maureen and youngest Kerry. This type of span occurs only occasionally in a two-parent or single-parent family. Maureen, Kathleen, and Sharon referred to us as their younger or little brothers. In the time I have been writing this book, the 1950 census has been officially published. In that document, we are listed as siblings. Is there a more official type of verification?

Barrett looked up to the girls. He was interested in their activities when they attended elementary and high school. He liked to go to the sporting events at the schools. His earliest sports heroes were the athletes on the St. Edward teams who came to the house to socialize with the girls. In 1954, Sharon graduated from St. Edward, and Barrett entered as a freshman the following September. He graduated in 1958, and I entered the same high school six years later. There was no break in attendance at St. Edward in our extended family—from Maureen's entrance in 1945 to Kerry's graduation in 1969. We had some of the same teachers. When I shared stories about my friends with Barrett, Sharon, Kathleen, or Maureen, we found a connection spanning our years and histories. In turn, many of my friends were siblings or cousins to classmates with Barrett and my cousins.

The St. Edward connections provided me with a relatability to learn about my "sisters." They stored their high school yearbooks on the second-from-bottom shelf of the bookcase behind the entrance door to their bedroom. I sat on the floor next to the shelf or on the bed nearby to page through the yearbooks, beginning with Maureen's in 1946 and continuing to Sharon's graduation in 1954. My review of their yearbooks was like a research project to learn about my cousins, to see into their lives in the years before I was born or was too young to recall. I became acquainted with the building, history, and culture of the high school before I started my own attendance. When I read a name or saw a picture of a friend of theirs, I connected the name to someone else I knew. In addition to yearbooks, I read through the collection of books with Nancy Drew, the Bobbsey Twins, and the Hardy Boys as lead characters. I retreated to these shelves to discover imaginary worlds in these stories. Reading the books intensified the connection to my cousin "sisters."

Maureen married Bill Osborne in June 1952. I did not know her when she grew up in our house. Maureen was my adult older sister. When she came to Elgin to visit her parents with her family, she came upstairs to the third floor soon after her arrival. Her kids usually followed her up. She wanted to spend time with Dad and Mom. The flow and interchange of the families germane to her as a youth and teenager continued with her into her adult years.

In some summer months, Maureen and Bill invited me to stay a few days at their house in Clinton, Iowa. I played with their daughter, Kathy, and her younger siblings as they came into the family. I was closer in age to them than I was to Maureen. I read their collection of magazines including *Reader's Digest*, *Look*, *Life*, and *Redbook*. I spent time going through the pictures and stories and got a further idea of what it was like to be part of a husband-wife family involved in yard and construction projects, decorating a house, and following recipes.

Maureen and I talked on the phone frequently as I came into adulthood and through the years to her death in 2014. With the advent of cell phones, I would often call her while driving. These conversations strengthened our relationship with each dialogue.

Kathleen remained at home in Elgin through her early twenties. I was aware of boyfriends who came in and out of the house. When I was home during the day as a preschooler, she came home from work and joined us upstairs. We enjoyed each other's company. I was fascinated with her skiing activities. One winter, she broke a foot or leg in a skiing accident. She spent time in the hospital and was released to stay home and not go to work. She passed the time doing paint-by-number kits at the kitchen table. I loved to sit and watch her dip the mini brushes into the tiny paint containers. She allowed me to paint in the larger areas of her canvas, not the small areas. After all, I was just learning to color with crayons on coloring books. I was dangerous with a crayon. I did not stay in the lines. If I messed up a small area with paint, she may have limited her chances in the imagined paint-by-number derby. She helped me to print numbers and letters. We formed a bond during these times at the kitchen table with one of her legs propped up on a chair. We talked and talked. Kathleen was never at a loss for words. She loved to talk. As I got older and understood our shared concept of being a middle child, she chided and teased me about our position in each of our families. Our bond remained unbroken.

After her recovery from her injury, Kathleen told us she was moving to New York City. As daunting as her skiing lessons seemed, moving to New York City was like skiing the Olympic Slalom track. Courageous. After having office and secretarial jobs in Elgin, she wanted to leave Elgin and discover something new. In New York City, she moved into a boarding house for single women. Mrs. Finneran was the housemother. Kathleen found an office job. If you have watched any episodes of *Mad Men*, you have a feel for her work environment and her attire of skirts, blouses, sweaters, and jackets. No pants. She joined a parish and made friends in a young people's group. Check out the movie *Breakfast at Tiffany's* with Audrey Hepburn for a story about young women in New York City in the 1950s.

Kathleen met Frank Martino in 1957. They married in January 1958, at St. Mary with surrounding days of activities hosted by Lawrence and Mildred for Frank's large New York Italian family, speaking two languages and contributing to the fun. In the weeks before the wedding, boxes arrived each day containing presents purchased at department stores and gift shops. Mildred set up folding tables covered with white tablecloths in the master bedroom to display gifts arranged by categories including tableware, bowls, and appliances. I learned about martini sets. I watched Kathleen open gifts in the days prior to the wedding. She showed me how to write a proper thank-you note. A blizzard greeted the dawn and continued through the wedding day. In the few pictures I've seen of the wedding, Kerry and I are in winter tweed sportscoats with bow ties, and Barrett is dressed in a suit and tie styled for a high school senior.

After the afternoon wedding reception, guests came to the house. The party lingered into the night hours. Frank and Kathleen departed for their first apartment in Mt. Kisco, New York. They moved from there to homes they bought in Farmingdale and Babylon. Her letters and cards with postmarks steered me to view state maps in the encyclopedias on the bookshelves in the second-floor living room. This shared set of encyclopedias represented a financial savings, which was another advantage of being a two-family house.

The set was purchased during the girls' elementary years in the mid to late '30s. Mildred ordered annual updates each year through 1970. The set was continually put to use by Barrett, Kerry, and me. On some of the encyclopedia pages I saw key passages the girls and Barrett had marked in pencil. This was before highlighters. Only pencil was used. Mildred considered these books of learning as sacred as the Bible, so she was understandably not keen to find ink in the books. After her girls, she expected us to follow their lead in showing respect for these books.

My learning and writing were enhanced in letters I wrote or typed to Kathleen, Frank, and their family. The following letter is one of the earliest in the collection of written interchanges between me and our family. Cousins Stephen and AnneMarie Martino found this correspondence from September 23, 1959, in a box of memorabilia saved by Kathleen. I typed in all capital letters:

"DEAR MARTINOES; [working as a 4th grader on plurals, punctuation, and spelling]

LAST THURSDAY WE WENT TO TAKE BARRETT TO COLLAGE. HE HAS ONE OF THE NEWER HALLS. IT IS VERY PRETTY. AFTER THAT WE WENT TO AUNT CECILS AND UNCLE MIKES. THEY ARE REMODELING THEIR HOUSE, AND IT ISN'T EXACTLY A MESS BUT IT IS OKAY. MY DAD AND I WERE THERE FOR ABOUT FIVE HOURS AND ALL MY FATHER WAS DOING WAS CHANGING FURNITURE AROUND. AUNT CECIL IS STILL TEACHING FIFTH GRADE AND I DON'T KNOW IF SHE IS A HAVING A HARD TIME WITH IT.

MY MOTHER IS GOING TO START WORKING TOMORROW DOWN AT THE WATCH FACTORY IN THE

OFFICE AND THIS IS HER SECOND JOB THIS WEEK. HER FIRST JOB WAS AT WOODRUFF AND EDWARDS BUT SHE DIDN'T LIKE IT AND ONLY WORKED TWO DAYS.

IT IS VERY HOT IN ELGIN AND SCHOOL IS JUST TERRIBLE BECAUSE OF THE HOT WEATHER. WHEN YOU RUN AND PLAY OUTSIDE YOU GET ALL SWEATY.

LAST WEEK I SIGNED UP FOR CUB SCOUTS AND KERRY SHOULD BE ONE THIS YEAR TOO.

TODAY I SIGNED UP FOR ALTAR BOYS AND SO DID KERRY AND I SHOULD BE SERVING BY CHRISTMAS.

KERRY THINKS HE HAS A VERY NICE SISTER BECAUSE ONE HOT DAY SHE TOOK THEM FOR A WALK AROUND THE BLOCK AND THEY SING FROM 11:15 TILL TWELVE O'CLOCK.

I PLAY UP AT THE OLD CEM DURING NOON HOUR BECAUSE IT WOULD BE TOO CROWDED ON THE PLAYGROUND NEXT DOOR TO THE SCHOOL. I HAVE LOTS MORE FUN THERE BECAUSE IT IS MUCH BIGGER. ONE DAY WHEN I WAS PLAYING UP THERE WE FOUND A GRAVE STONE.

SCHOOL IS GOING ALONG PRETTY GOOD AND SISTER IS PRETTY NICE. I HAD TO STAY AFTER SCHOOL TONIGHT TO MAKE UP WORK FOR LAST THURSDAY WHEN WE TOOK BARRETT TO SCHOOL.

MY MOTHER IS TYPING THIS LETTER BUT I TYPED THE FIRST PART. SHE IS PRACTICING FOR HER JOB SO SHE WON'T GET FIRED THE FIRST DAY.

I WILL HAVE TO CLOSE THIS LETTER NOW AND I WILL TRY TO WRITE TO YOU DURING LETTER WRITING WEEK.

LOVE, KEVIN" [signed in my penmanship]

My written and verbal communication with Kathleen, Frank, and their children has continued throughout our lives, providing a continual conduit between the second- and third- floor families.

Kathleen was four years older than Sharon. Sharon was four years older than Barrett. She was finishing eighth grade and starting high school when Kerry and I were born. She babysat for us. As I did with Maureen and Kathleen, I glimpsed at Sharon's life through her yearbooks. During her college years, she was at the house on some weekends and in the summers. I relished her company. She advised me not to bite my nails saying, "What will girls think about a boy with chewed nails?" She taught me how to fold the sheet and blanket at the bottom corners and tuck them in between the box spring and top mattress. I still think of Sharon when I make a bed. She told me how important it was to know how to drive a stick shift car long before I was of driving age. She conveyed it was especially important for a girl like her to know about stick shifting and the clutch. She would say, "What if I am on a date with a boy in a stick shift car and something happens to him? I have to know how to drive a stick."

After graduation from Mt. St. Mary College in Milwaukee in 1958 with a degree in social work, Sharon started her first job with Catholic Charities in Rockford. Kerry and I visited a few times at her apartment with its tucked away Murphy bed that ingeniously dropped down from the wall behind a hidden door. I'd never seen a bed like that before. At night she made popcorn and read stories to us. She had no TV.

After a year or two, Sharon longed for change. She moved back to Milwaukee. She continued working in social work and earned her master's degree. I knew about a bachelor's degree, but this was my first awareness of higher degrees. On one of her weekends at home, I listened to her as she sat on Mom and Dad's bed and talked to them about her classes and work. Her stories gave me one of my first inklings of wanting to do well at school and go to college. Knowing all three girls and Barrett eventually departed Division Street and Elgin, I realized my future plans could include leaving home after my years in school finished. I had choices.

In Milwaukee, Sharon met John Safar. They married in Elgin in November 1964. We visited their apartment in Wauwatosa and the home they later purchased in Menomonee Falls. Sharon and I stayed close through letters, phone calls, and visits to her house. We had a shared interest in social services and education. In May 2003, we shared what was to become our last time with just the two of us. It was during a weekend memorial service for our Uncle Ed and Aunt Rosanna in Minocqua, Wisconsin. During the middle of the first night, I was awakened with pain. A cousin, Dr. Mike, drove me to an emergency room. I was diagnosed with a kidney stone, medicated with Valium, driven back to the hotel, and escorted to the bed in my room. I slept for six hours or so until awakened by Sharon's knock on the door.

"You look like you are reviving. Let's get you out of here," she said. "You need to be ready for the memorial service in two hours. You are singing 'The Irish Blessing.'"

"What do you have in mind?" I asked.

"Put on some pants and a shirt. We will find something."

We drove away from the hotel. We happened upon a Perkins Restaurant and Bakery and decided this was the perfect place for us. I had not eaten and was feeling the glowing effects of the Valium and the subtle pain of the kidney stone.

"You've got to get something in your system," Sharon said. "What appeals to you?"

"Cherry pie and a milkshake," I answered.

"That's good for starters. What else?"

I ordered a bacon, lettuce, and tomato sandwich. Sharon ordered pie and coffee. We sat, ate, and talked for more than an hour. I was experiencing marital problems. She encouraged discussion without advising. I talked about my sons in college and high school. She shared stories of her children and grandchildren. Time with her was what I needed. We drove back to the hotel without pausing in our conversation. She escorted me back to my room. Outside the door, we gave each other a strong hug.

"Think you will be okay?" she asked.

"Yes, thanks," I said. "It was fantastic to have this time with you."

"Take a nap. See you in an hour."

These older sisters provided a lifeline to me as I navigated through life with travel, dating, marriages, becoming a father, career activities, and divorces. When I was planning my return home in June 1971 after a year in Europe, Kathleen helped me coordinate an earlier return to surprise Mom and Dad. They thought my return was going to be six days after I actually arrived. Unbeknownst to them, my flight was from London to JFK, not Chicago. I arranged with Kathleen to pick me up at JFK. I spent a few days with her and family in Babylon. When Dad happened to call her, she did not let on that I was there. He said how much he and Mom looked forward to my arrival. I flew from JFK to O'Hare, arranged for transportation to Division Street, and walked in the door days early. Kathleen pulled off that surprise.

Maureen and Bill supported me through challenging parenting dilemmas and shared in the joyful milestones of child rearing. When working through problems I was having with my sons, all three of the girls talked me through tough situations. In a particularly hard time, in 2003, I happened to be driving past Mt. Hope Cemetery in Elgin. I drove in and went to the family plot, where Lawrence, Mildred, and Dad were buried. I called Maureen on my cell phone. Shadowed by the gravestone containing our parents' names, she listened, talked, and guided. A few months later at a family gathering she took me by my arm, and we walked outside. She checked in about how I was doing.

In 2006, I called Maureen to tell her I was gay. She was the first person in the family after Mom, Barrett, and Kerry with whom I shared this information. We had a long, supportive conversation followed by a call to Kathleen. Sharon was then deceased, but I wish I could have called her, too. Throughout my life, my second-floor sisters impacted me with a continual source of love, care, and support. The relationships my brothers and I had with them only served to intensify the uniqueness of the bonds between the families of the second and third floors.

Keep on appreciating your brother and sister relationships.

PART III

CULTIVATING A CULTURE OF ONE FAMILY

Although many funeral home owners lived in residences above, attached, or near their businesses in the mid-twentieth century, few were in situations of two families living together. The design of the apartments coupled with the unspoken yet accepted direction to navigate our lives as a singular unit contributed to the creation of one family coming from two.

We came together during the difficulties of World War II, the insecurities of miscarriages, the fear of health challenges, the increase of offspring in the midst of Catholicism, the undercurrent of Dad and Lawrence's tensions, and the navigation of opinions about the Vietnam War. Through these key times and others, we steadfastly joined in our appreciation of music and maintained environments of privacy and camaraderie.

CHAPTER 10

Impact on Families During World War II

When Dad and Mom joined Mildred and Lawrence in business during the summer of 1940, complications leading to World War II festered in Europe. Four days before Barrett's first birthday, the Japanese attacked Pearl Harbor on December 7, 1941. Sharon was a preschooler. Kathleen, a fourth-grade student, and Maureen in fifth grade. Under the direction of President Franklin Delano Roosevelt, the United States Congress declared war on both the European and Asian fronts.

During the war years, the families navigated and cohabitated in settings common to other families. The radios on each floor were likely tuned to programming such at Franklin Delano Roosevelt's (FDR's) "Fireside Chats" and his wife, Eleanor's more frequent broadcasts. The families kept informed through these programs and the local and Chicago newspapers delivered to the house each day. Life during World War II created shortages of items such as rubber, metal, and clothing, as the production of those materials was prioritized to the military. Food was also in limited supply for reasons including lack of imports for products such as coffee and sugar, limited trucking and train transportation, and the military's demand for canned goods.

As a result of these shortages, the US government created a system of rationing to distribute goods equitably to families and households not in battle zones. Most single or married adults used the ration books issued to them. Mom, Dad, Mildred, Lawrence, Maureen, Kathleen, Sharon, and Barrett each had their own ration books. I have the ration books Dad and Mom used. Each book contained removable stamps to purchase meat, sugar, cooking oil, canned goods, and other items.

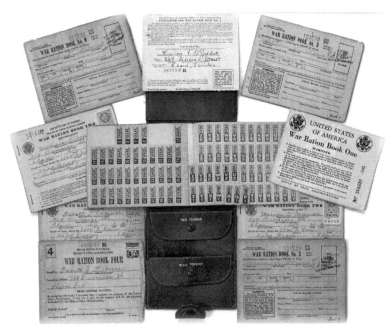

WWII Ration Books for family, 1940s.

Mom and Mildred planned and prepared the meals for each family. Although each apartment contained kitchen cupboards and pantries, they inventoried each of their supplies and worked together to create meals to adequately feed everyone. Each family ate separately. However, the items for their menus came from either one of the kitchens. The sharing of rationed items allowed each family to make the most of the stamps allotted to them. The two families worked together for the benefit of all.

The families came together throughout the years of the war to adapt to day-to-day adjustments and life-changing events beyond grocery supplies. Dad and Lawrence's oldest nephew, Mickey Dermody, was killed attempting to save his colleagues in a Jeep accident on May 16, 1944. He was eighteen. He'd enlisted less than a year before. Uncle Mike and Aunt Cecil received what was to be his last letter to them on the day before they knew about his death. Two days after, Aunt Cecil received the flowers he had previously arranged to be delivered for Mother's Day. My middle name, Michael, is in honor of Mickey and his father.

Mickey's death resulted in the collective grief of the family. Grandpa Dan O'Connor died Christmas Day, seven months after Mickey's death. The family felt his demise was due in part to a mournful heart. Uncle Lawrence signed the death certificate. His funeral was at Burns Funeral Home, the business in Hammond where Lawrence got his start. Grandpa was buried in Calvary Cemetery in Gary next to his wife and grandson.

Further personal involvement came from the enlistment of Bob Allanson who married Dad and Lawrence's youngest sister in 1940. Mom's sister, JoJean, left Elgin in June 1944, moved to California, and married her high school boyfriend, Malbert. He was one of the youngest survivors of Pearl Harbor in 1941.

The two families experienced social, emotional, and personal changes considered inconceivable in prior years. During these years, Dad and Lawrence conducted funerals for military casualties. The effects of the war intertwined in both their business and personal lives, further bringing our families together.

CHAPTER 11

Miscarriages: Personal Griefs Shared

My parents experienced miscarriages between Barrett's birth and mine that intensified the concerns of the entire household.

I first learned about miscarriages from a story on *Dr. Kildare*, one of two shows that premiered in the 1961–62 television season. The other show was titled *Ben Casey*. These medical shows were forerunners of later popular shows *St. Elsewhere*, *E.R.*, and *Grey's Anatomy*. *Dr. Kildare* was based on a radio program and movie of the same name from the 1930s. Richard Chamberlain was the young star of the TV show. At twelve years old, I recall watching an episode titled "Solomon's Choice." Afterward, I walked from the back room where our TV was located to talk to Dad in the living room. He was dusting tables and poised close to the vacuum. Mom was not home. Barrett was away at college. Kerry was elsewhere in one of the two apartments. I sat at the end of the couch positioned on the longest wall. My memory allows me to capture the context of our dialogue:

"Dad, I just watched *Dr. Kildare*. The show talked about a lady who was not able to get pregnant. Another character was going to have a baby she did not want."

"Tell me more about the story you watched," he encouraged.

"They mentioned a word. 'Miscarriage.' I am not sure what that is."

Dad removed the dust rag from his hand and placed it on the nearest table. He walked over to the couch and sat next to me and responded to my inquiry.

"The story about the woman who was unable to get pregnant was like what happened to Mom and me. Do you know why there are nine years between you and Barrett and only a little more than a year's time between your birth and Kerry's?"

"No."

Dad began to explain.

"After Barrett was born, we wanted to have more children. Do you know how it happens?"

"How what happens?"

"Do you know what happened between Mom and me before you, Kerry, and Barrett were born?"

"I have an idea, but I am not sure."

Dad went on to explain about the functions of the male and female bodies and the physical nature of how conception occurs. As a Catholic parochial student, I had no instruction in these topics. An exception to this was our parish priest who informed seventh-grade boys about masturbation. He didn't use the word masturbation, but he explained enough for us to know to what he was referring. He instilled fear when he let us know masturbation was a mortal sin. Once we masturbated, we were doomed to hell for our sin. My friends and I decided that fear of hell wasn't enough to halt our practice, though after his talk, I did go to confession every Saturday to confess my sin of masturbation to the same priest who had lectured us. I had a hard time picturing myself in hell for an act that was pleasurable enough to keep repeating.

The talk from the priest about masturbation was the only lesson about sex in my schooling. Fortunately, during my recent final six years employed in public school education, I designed and instructed seminars for kindergarten through twelve grade teachers about age-appropriate curriculum referred to as "Family Life" or "Human Sexuality." I trained the teachers how to incorporate "Family Life" topics in their teaching. These opportunities gave me satisfaction knowing I was slapping my own elementary education in the face while helping students learn about the changes in their bodies as they were experiencing them.

Fortunately, my father was not hesitant to talk to me about my own body changes and the topic of miscarriages. He sensed my uncertainty while presuming I talked to my friends about perceptions of sex.

"We wanted to have a brother or sister for Barrett," Dad continued. "Some married couples have intercourse because they want to experience the pleasure. Some couples have intercourse because they want to have children. I mentioned to you about women's monthly cycles and why mom has Kotex in the bathroom cabinet. When a woman has what is called a 'flow' every twenty-eight days or so, the flow of blood-like fluid goes in the Kotex pad. This flow is called a 'period.' Mom places the pad in a container and puts it into the wastebasket. This usually happens once a month. When there was no flow around the date Mom expected, it meant she may be pregnant. She went to our doctor. He examined her and confirmed if she was pregnant."

"Is this what happened when you found out Mom was pregnant with Barrett?"

"Yes. And Mom stayed pregnant, and Barrett was born."

"A little over nine years before I was born. Right?"

"Yes."

"Why did it take so long for me to be born after Barrett? I don't have any friends who have almost ten years between their birth and their brother or sister."

"It's a long story. When Barrett was about a year old, Mom missed her period. She went to the doctor, and he told her she was pregnant. She came home and told me. We were so happy. This was the same feeling we had when we realized mom was pregnant with Barrett. We thought she would follow this pregnancy the same way she had with Barrett. We didn't tell many people about it, but we did let Lawrence and Mildred know."

"Why did you tell them?"

"We wanted to share our happiness. We asked them not to tell people in the family—not even Maureen, Kathleen, and Sharon. We thought it was too early to tell. In January or February of 1942, Mom started feeling sick to her stomach. This went on for a couple of days. Mom's pain did not go away. One day, mom noticed bloody fluid coming from the area of her vagina, the word I used a little bit ago."

"Did it hurt?"

"I think Mom might say she felt uncomfortable. She called the doctor and made an appointment for the next day. When she went to her doctor, he examined her and told her she'd had a miscarriage."

"What does that mean?"

"It means the baby was not able to stay in the uterus in Mom's body. When the baby is in the uterus, it's called a fetus. The fetus released itself from Mom's body. It's called a miscarriage."

"What happened?"

"The doctor advised Mom to stay in the hospital for two nights. Her doctor told us to keep trying."

"Huh?"

"Keep trying means a month or two after the miscarriage, we continue having intercourse and hopefully get pregnant again."

"So, what did you do?"

"Mom got pregnant again. I think sometime in 1943. Mom was feeling good. She was working in the house, taking care of Barrett and helping me with the funeral business. She was pregnant for about five months and then she started getting sick. She lost the baby."

"What do you mean? *She lost the baby*?"

"Lost the baby is what people say when they have a miscarriage. Lost means the baby you thought you were having dies in the womb or shortly after birth. The baby is no longer alive."

"What happened then?"

"We were nervous after this second miscarriage. We went back to the doctor. He told us to keep on doing what we were supposed to be doing. He knew Mom didn't have a problem getting pregnant. He encouraged Mom and I to keep trying. In 1945, Mom became pregnant again. The doctor advised her to be careful with lifting anything. He said for her not to play tennis or golf. He let us know what types of food to avoid. Lawrence and Mildred knew what was happening. They told Maureen, Kathleen, and Sharon. When Mildred or one of the girls saw Mom getting out of the car with a bag of groceries, one of them went downstairs to help her carry whatever was in her hands."

"Did that help?"

"We thought so. The third pregnancy lasted a few months. But then it happened again—another miscarriage. Mom knew the symptoms. Sometimes, the baby aborted itself right at home."

"Aborted?"

"Abort means the pregnancy stops."

"What did you do? Were you scared?"

"Yes. Mom was scared each time it happened. We took the tiny fetus and brought it to the hospital."

"Did you give the fetus a name?"

"No. Oh, we would talk about names for babies, but we didn't get to the point in the pregnancy where we gave the baby a name. The hospital took the fetus. Maybe they called it 'Baby O'Connor.' After that, Mom suffered two more miscarriages—one in early 1947 and again in the summer of 1948."

"Five miscarriages?"

"Yes. It was one of the hardest parts of your mom's and my lives. We loved your brother and being parents. We wanted him and us to have a bigger family. Your Aunt Marge and Aunt JoJean had babies during those years. Your cousins Jon, Wendy, Cheryl, and Terry were all born. Your Uncle Ed and Rosanna had Deniece and Roseann. Aunt Lillian and Uncle Bob had Lani. We were so happy for each of them, but we felt left out. Each time we had a miscarriage I felt a sick feeling, like a punch in my gut. It's like the sadness I felt when my father and mother died. We got excited each time we knew we were pregnant, but we did not share our joy with very many people. It was like we needed to keep it a secret."

"Why?"

"Because each time a miscarriage occurred, we were filled with sadness. Everybody downstairs was sad every time Mom didn't hold on to the pregnancy."

"What did *you* do?"

"I was sad with Mom. She was so discouraged and kept thinking it was something she was doing wrong. I reminded her I was there for her. I wasn't able to feel what she was feeling in her body, but I felt it in my heart. I was frightened of what would come each time. I would do my best to keep up our spirits. We enjoyed our times with Barrett. We just kept on going. The doctors thought of ideas about what was happening. Her miscarriages happened sometime between the second and fifth month. The doctors recommended Mom have a surgery."

"For what?"

"The surgery was inside of the uterus and the areas around the uterus. They hoped the surgery would strengthen the muscles in mom's body. Mom and I talked a lot about the surgery. She gave the final say to go ahead and have the procedure. The doctor said Mom was healthy in so many ways; he didn't think the surgery was too much of a risk."

"What happened?"

"Mom did well with the surgery. They used stitches to close the area near her belly button where they cut into her body. The stitches stayed in for about ten days. The doctor said to try to get pregnant again after three to four months. In the summer of 1949, Mom stopped having her period again. We went back to the doctor, and he confirmed she was pregnant. Like I said, Mom didn't have a problem becoming pregnant; the problem was holding on to the pregnancy. The months went by—August, September, October . . . each day, week, and month were tense. We kept thinking she might miscarry again. By the time Christmas of 1949 came, Mom was finishing the sixth month of her pregnancy. Her body didn't show any signs of being pregnant. She didn't look like other moms do when they are pregnant. Her body looked the same. Lawrence, Mildred, Maureen, Kathleen, and Sharon all knew she was holding on to this pregnancy. On Christmas Eve, we hung a stork ornament on the Christmas tree. A stork is a symbol of a bird symbolizing a person is expecting a baby. When people came to the house to visit for the holiday, they either saw the stork, or we pointed it out to them. We told them Mom was pregnant and holding on. You came along about three months later."

"March 16."

"Your due date was March 17. Our aunts and uncles were excited our baby was coming on St. Patrick's Day. You came a day early."

"After I was born, what happened?"

"Mom felt fine during the time she was in the hospital with you. She felt fine after she came home. She was feeling good. Barrett was so excited to have a brother. He helped to take care of you right from the first day you got home."

"So, what happened with Kerry?'

"Everything was going so well. Mom was feeling wonderful. We wanted to have another baby. We decided not to wait and started to do what we needed to do to get pregnant again. When you were about six months old, mom realized she was pregnant. We went to the doctor. He told us to do everything we did when she was pregnant with you. Kerry was born with no problems on June 17, 1951. It was Father's Day. He was a special gift."

The content of the conversation was a lot for a twelve-year-old to take in. Dad did not bring up the topic again. Neither did I. The only time I recall talking to Mom about the situation was in the last twenty-four to thirty-six hours of her life when she was in the cardiac care unit. One of the nurses asked her about the scar in her abdominal area. She looked at it and said, "Gee, I don't remember where it came from."

"Mom, maybe the scar is from the surgery in 1948 or 1949 to stop the miscarriages you had. After the surgery, you became pregnant with me and then Kerry."

"Yeah, I think you are right. I did have a surgery."

I am not sure why the topic was not brought up prior to the time. After my conversation with Dad, I didn't feel I needed to know more. Maybe I sensed Mom didn't want to talk about it. Interpreting my conversation with

Dad affirmed he and Mom wanted to grow their family. There has never been a time in my life I felt Barrett, Kerry, or I were unwanted.

CHAPTER 12

Passages and Pipelines Invigorate Interactions

The effects of Mom's miscarriages were just some aspects of coincidental lives of both families resulting from the intersections of our shared spaces in the house. Our connections were ritualized as we came together via intersecting routes from the outside to inside, making our crossed paths inevitable. When I made an entrance to go inside our house, I walked up six outside steps to a porch where the back door entrance was located. When I opened the door, I looked up twenty-two steps to the back hallway. The middle third of each step was covered with a different colored carpet piece. The carpet pieces were secured with tacks. Perhaps we could not afford one piece of the same carpeting and opted for these remnants from the carpet salesperson. Friends and I turned the steps into a game by announcing the color we planned to go next. In declaring a color, each of us counted the number of steps to the color and extended our legs over the interval.

I had two additional ways to reach the second floor from the ground level. One way was through the canopied front door on the south side of the house. Another entrance was through the first-floor office door on the porch at northwest side of the house, eight steps above the driveway. I walked those stairs leading me to a broad porch. We stored rakes, a lawn mower and yard equipment under this porch. We played in this area to create forts and hiding places. The wooden spindle gate and railing under the porch provided privacy in the damp, musty underworld, while sunlight sometimes cast shadows of the spindle's design. We occasionally found a stray cat, rabbit, or raccoon looking to establish a home. They scampered away and allowed us our time in the space. We used this play area until we became too tall.

The door to the office was at the center of the wall of the house. Entering the door took me directly into the office and front foyer area. I turned right to start up the four-sectioned, angled stairway enhanced by a wooden railing coordinated with the stately architecture of the house. Climbing twenty-two steps, I reached the broad landing space overlooking the stairway and twelve-foot-high windows. I usually turned left at the top of the stairs and walked past a closed drop-leaf dining room table positioned against a wall covered with a mural painted during the time of previous owners. The mural depicted people from colonial times dressed in the clothing of the era and standing next to carriages and horses. The landing area doubled in function as Mildred and Lawrence's dining room. They sat as many as sixteen people when the table was open.

Directly past the mural, I took a right turn into the hallway also accessed via the back stairs. When I reached this area, Mildred or Lawrence often acknowledged my presence with a "hello." When others congregated in the hallway, I might have stayed and involved myself in ongoing discussion. This space where the third-floor stairs met the second-floor hallway allowed the conversations, music, and lives of the residents of both floors to be interconnected. The conversations focused on the happenings of the day, reports from family and friends, and sharing ideas about parenting and recipes. The area was a central point for the families to come together with a frequency and intensity of the central desk area at a hospital emergency room.

Sometimes, I wandered into the kitchen to be part of meal preparation or join Mildred at the table. There, she was reading the newspaper, cutting out and reviewing recipes from magazines, or typing letters to her daughters, family, and friends. She let me look over her shoulder as she was typing and allowed me to put paper in the typewriter. I used a one finger approach to type my spelling words or letters to my cousins. When I made an error, she coached me as I erased with a round rubber eraser attached to a stiff miniature broom-like brush. I blew my breath to scatter the eraser crumbs off the page. White-out tape or liquid had not yet been invented.

While in the kitchen, I might have checked to see what was in the oven when a meal was being prepared. Seeing and smelling the meal, I may have been enticed to consider asking her to eat dinner with them. This request was especially valid if I knew I didn't want to eat what was being prepared in our third-floor kitchen. Liver and onions come to mind. Living as a part of two families, I savored the opportunities for meal options not available to my friends in their homes.

Mildred, Mom, and Dad allowed me to participate in baking and cooking. They taught me about how to measure items for recipes and how to prepare food. Mildred's specialties included apple dumplings. We made the dough together and rolled it out flat. We cut it into sections big enough to wrap around each peeled and cored apple. We placed them in a white porcelain nine-by-twelve-inch baking pan rimmed with a red band. We sprinkled the dumplings with sugar and cinnamon and placed the pan in the oven. Juice from the apples bubbled through the dough, creating a red syrup. Every ten minutes, she guided me to open the oven door. She pulled out the rack containing the pan. I watched her dip a tablespoon into the sauce capturing hot syrup to drizzle over each of the dumplings. The aroma of the dumplings wafted its way up the stairs to the third floor and continues in my lifetime of olfactory memories.

Mildred was a baking and kitchen aficionado. She delighted in her skills. In her letter of December 29, 1970, she wrote about her experience with preparing bourbon balls:

"I found myself being much confused in attempting anything this year. First off, I attempted some fudge, WHICH JUST NEVER FAILS. But after putting in most of the ingredients, I re-read the recipe and realized I had just put in half of the necessary sugar. So, I proceeded to add the sugar and natch, the fudge was grainy. All five pounds of it. Then one day I thought I would be really extravagant and make some bourbon balls. Not ever having made them, I used a recipe I saw printed in the newspaper, which calls for 2 ½ cups of vanilla cracker crumbs, ½ cup bourbon, confectioner's sugar, cocoa, etc. Then the ingredients are to be formed in balls and rolled in more powdered sugar. Mine just wouldn't stick together. THEN I looked over some other recipes for bourbon balls, and they took most of the same ingredients EXCEPT there should only be ONE cup of crumbs. I did manage to get a few of them stuck together by using more bourbon, so now when one is in need of some 'heart medicine' we just open the box of bourbon balls and inhale! What incense!"

When a wake or funeral was occurring downstairs, baking was done with the kitchen door closed and an open window. Otherwise, the aroma might find its way down to the funeral parlors, a pleasant but out of place distraction for the mourners.

I often spent time on the second floor. I watched TV, fell asleep on the couch, laid on the floor to read, listened to music, or practiced piano lessons. I felt equally comfortable on the second floor as I did in our living spaces on the third floor.

Shared stairs, hallways, and rooms became ever-present aspects of our lives with us being unaware of the amount of exercise sustained in daily life while we routed ourselves through the house. I imagine some of you exercise on stair climbers at your gyms or homes. We climbed the steps of our house six to ten times daily from ground level to second and third floors. Imagine if we had a watch or "smart" device recording and analyzing our health data. We championed our cardiovascular health by virtue of the house we inhabited.

In addition to routes through the house bringing us together, the demands of water on our pipelines gave opportunities for further family collaborating. Our families had limited bathroom accommodations compared to what many now have in homes and living spaces. During one year from the time of Kerry's birth to the following June when Maureen married Bill, eleven people lived in the house. In addition to our two families of five, Mildred's mother, Grandma Kruzan, resided on the second floor. Many of you now live in residences with two, three, or more bathrooms for your families. We had just one bathroom per floor.

Maureen's departure was followed by Grandma Kruzan's death in 1956 and then Kathleen, Sharon, and Barrett's exits for jobs or college attendance over the next eight to ten years. The house was emptier, but a steady flow of family and friends continued their visits for either overnights or shorter social get-togethers. The second-floor family had access to a bathroom with toilet, tub, and shower. Prior to the late 1950s, those of us on the third floor used a bathroom tub, a sink, and a toilet, but no shower.

In addition to limited bathroom spaces, the water heater was in the basement. If the shower or bath on both floors were used simultaneously, the hot water in any given faucet turned colder. If dishes needed hot water at the same time as baths or showers, hot temperatures disappeared, and cold water took over. Water pressure lowered throughout the house when one of the two toilets on the residential floors or the one toilet in the funeral home flushed concurrently. Based on their previous family experiences in residences with many individuals, the two sets of parents were accustomed to these situations.

During one third-floor remodeling period, our bathroom area was redesigned to include a tub with a shower. In spite of the small area of the room, most of our family of five often occupied the bathroom at the same time. Dad may have been sitting on the toilet. Mom may have been at the vanity and either Barrett, Kerry, or I were in the tub or shower. Privacy was not an element of our lives in the space. We learned during Mom's bath times to allow *her* the privacy she sought. Due to the layout of the bathroom, we were not in each other's line of vision while we used the toilet and she took her bath. When we entered through the bathroom door, we announced ourselves to Mom who was unseen to us. When it came time to wash our hands, we did not use the bathroom sink where her privacy would have been compromised. Instead, we went to the kitchen sink.

I think of those days with a bit of laughter on how we maneuvered. Picture my dad entering or being in the bathroom as I was sitting on the toilet. When I heard him say, "Flush," I knew he was notifying me the odor I was emitting needed some attention. He may have followed with, "Get the smell out of here," or, "Show some consideration for the others who are in here." To this day, I am aware of the power and effect of a good flush when defecating.

It was more convenient for a third-floor resident to seek the use of the second-floor bathroom than the other way around. In most of my elementary and teen years, only Lawrence and Mildred resided on the second floor. Their bathroom was more available. If our third-floor bathroom door was closed and occupied, I retreated down the stairs and looked to the right to see if their bathroom door was open. If it was, I entered and closed the door. I closed the second entrance to the bathroom connected to my cousins' bedroom.

This bathroom was a haven of Victorian design with white and black tiles in patterned design on the floor. The wall area from the floor to ceiling was covered with white subway tile. This tile was matched in the tub and shower area. A radiator in this bathroom and an indented square area in the tiled wall housing three bare light bulbs gave off exquisite heat. This warmth was especially appreciated in the winter months. The bathroom was supplied with *Reader's Digest* magazines. I did a lot of reading while sitting.

If I was having a real emergency while both third- and second-floor bathrooms were occupied, I went down the flight of stairs to the single bathroom on the first floor used by client families or to a toilet in the basement, in a room next to the embalming room. In 1961, an addition was built onto the first floor that included additional parlor areas and men's and women's restrooms in the basement below. These facilities provided two additional sources for our family when no wake or funeral was occurring. The men's room had a urinal. Revolutionary. Sometimes, I walked to the basement just to use the urinal. None of my friends' homes had a urinal. Oh, the benefits of being a funeral home kid.

Laundry also brought us together. Mom, Mildred, and Dad taught me the laundry process. I never saw Lawrence near a washing machine. When the families first moved into Division Street, one wringer washer was placed in the basement furnace room. Mom and Mildred both used that machine for their laundry chores. When I was around kindergarten age, I traveled with Mildred from the second floor to the basement to do the "wash." She was small in stature and frame, but this did not diminish her strength or tenacity. We carried bags and baskets of dirty clothing and linens down the front hall stairway. This led us through a door at the bottom and into the casket room. We maneuvered our way past caskets to a thick, purple velvet curtain covering the basement walls. A door was behind the far-right end of the drape. I pulled back the drape and reached for the doorknob. When the door was opened, we entered the section of the basement where the preparation room was located. An immediate right turn took us into the furnace/laundry room.

The machine's wash basin was smaller than the size we know today. Four metal, two-foot-long legs supported the tub on the sides extending from the bottom of the tub to the floor. A wheel inserted into the bottom of each leg allowed movement across the floor. A double cast-iron sink installed during the construction of the house stood to left of the machine. These sinks had depths of utility sinks in homes today. Four metal legs supported the sink above the floor with pipes and a faucet at the top center. The knobs on either side of the faucet controlled the flow of hot and cold water. This sink and faucet arrangement was a luxury in 1887, an accoutrement adding to the original grandeur of the building.

Mildred picked out items to be scrubbed prior to washing. My earliest remembered tactile experiences come from taking a soiled piece of laundry and rubbing it against the rounded, serrated grooves on the side of the sink basin or on a separate scrubbing board standing upright in the sink. I applied flaked soap to the material. I rubbed the stained area of the fabric on the grooves until it was evident, with her approval, the soiled area was removed.

We rolled the washer next to the sink and faucet. She attached a garden hose to the faucet and helped me to extend it into the washer tub. I turned on the handles allowing the water to flow through the hose. Only cold water was used with dark items. We used both the cold and hot water faucets with white items. Mildred preferred as much hot water as possible for these loads. As the water entered, steam rose from the basin.

She added a bit of the soap flakes stored on a wooden shelf above the sinks. The electric cord for the machine was now plugged into the socket between the sink and the room entrance door. I pressed the start button. The agitator inside the bin began to move circularly back and forth. She directed me to place one item at a time into the basin. I was tall enough to peek in over the top of the basin to watch the process. I was fascinated by the sloshing of the soapy water and the items shifting from side to side and top to bottom. The whooshing sounds combined with the feel of sprays and mists of water on my face and hands. Mildred reminded me not to put my hands in the basin.

In the absence of timers, Mildred decided when the wash process was complete. She directed me to press the red button marked "STOP." The agitator stopped. I connected a black hose, wider in diameter than the hose used for filling, to the bottom of the machine basin. The other end of the hose was placed into one of the sinks. Once the set up was finished, I pressed a button imprinted with the word "DRAIN." The soapy water drained into the sink. I placed a round rubber cover over the drain as cold water filled one of the sinks. We transferred the items from the washer basin into the cold water for rinsing. We twirled the items around in the water. Each item was lifted up and down as the soap suds rolled off, and the clothes were placed into the adjoining sink also filled with cold water. The rinsing process was repeated.

The washer did not have a spin cycle function for water to be extracted from the items. We pulled out each item and placed it in a device with a space between two wooden or rubber rollers hung on the side of the sink basin. I turned a crank to move the rollers together on their spindles. The saturated article traveled through the rollers to squeeze out the excess water. This came with a continual reminder from Mildred, "Keep your fingers away from the rollers. Be careful."

Each wrung out item was placed into one of the straw baskets. These wet items were heavier than the dry ones we transported to the basement. The soapy, dirty water remained in the basin until Mildred or I emptied it through a hose attached to the outside of the machine and extending to a drain on the floor. Gravity helped to push the water through the descending hose.

At the completion of this process, we now continued our work to hang the items to dry. On days when the weather was warm or hot, we climbed the basement stairs with full baskets to hang the wet pieces with clothespins on ropes stretched across the back yard. This drying process was not done on days of a wake or funeral. People attending may not have desired to be reminded the undertakers' families wore underwear, pajamas, and bras. When not hung on clotheslines in the backyard, we took the items to the back rooms on the second and third floors where hooks screwed in the walls held the lines stretched across the room. During these inside drying times, the laundry hung on clotheslines above our heads while we played a game on the floor, sat and read a book or newspaper, worked on our homework, or watched TV. Mom's niece resided with us during her senior year of high school in 1954–55. Her bed was in this area. When she got in and out of bed, she positioned herself around the clothing and undergarments hanging above her head. Mildred and Mom arranged their laundry schedules so as not to compete for available drying line space.

In the early 1950s, Mom and Dad installed a top loading washer in the bathroom area of the third floor. Eventually, they installed a dryer not needing a vent to the outside for the hot air and lint. About the same time, Dad created and installed a pull-out hamper in a cabinet below linen closet shelving. The hamper was divided into sections for dark, light, and sheets/towels. My brothers and I learned readily how to sort clothes for washing. We all helped with laundry chores while watching TV or doing homework and playing games. As clothes came out of the dryer, Mom put full baskets in our laps with items for us to fold. We also put our wet, laundered pants on devices called pants stretchers. We pushed these stretchers inside the leg of each pant. The springs of the stretchers expanded the material to create a crease down the front and back of the pant. We knew how to make the crease neatly and securely. We positioned the pant stretchers along the stair railing in the hallway dining area. The pants dried overnight. In the morning, we released the dried pants from the stretchers, now ready to wear or rest on a hanger in our closet.

In the 1960s, Mildred and Lawrence placed a unit with a singular basin for both washing and drying in the closet area which was originally the location of the pull-chain toilet. I could view the wash and dry process through the windowed door of the machine. I was fascinated. Of course, those types of front-loading appliances are now common. I have one in our condo.

Plumbing in general presented a problem in the house as explained in a letter written by Mildred in October 1969:

"The folks upstairs had a cat-ass-tro-fee when the kitchen sink stopped up completely. It happened Sunday night, and yesterday your Dad worked for hours until 1:30 a.m. today to get it unplugged. He finally succeeded, but now Bill will believe that plumbers earn their money and won't hesitate to pay whatever is necessary. His hands are a sight— swollen and raw from plunging them into the water loaded with Liquid Plumber, which is basically lye. Tonight, he is scrubbing the bathroom rug and generally cleaning up."

Another plumbing catastrophe occurred during the 1979 Thanksgiving Day celebration. The holiday family dining was planned for the third floor, with preparations and ovens involved in both the second and third-floor kitchens. The plumbing for the third-floor washing machine was in the interior wall between the kitchen and laundry area. Those in charge of preparing the potatoes filled the bottom of the sink with peels. They turned on the garbage disposal. The peels went down the sink with a whirring sound. Less than a minute later, a shout came from the TV area near the laundry room. The washer filled itself with water and the wash cycle began. Strange. I opened the lid and was astonished to discover potato peels sloshing around in the basin. I pressed the stop button. We delayed dinner preparations as we scooped the peels from the water, scraping them from the sides of the basin and depositing them in buckets and pans. We turned on the spin and drain cycle, watching as water flowed through the basin and into the pipes. We gazed at the cleanest potato peels of any Thanksgiving Day celebration. We missed an opportunity for a side dish of potato skins.

More than sixty years later, with the modern conveniences of large washers and dryers and improved plumbing, I still keep alive the memories of sponges, rags, buckets, pipes, potato peels, and wet times from Division Street. Plumbing brought us all together.

CHAPTER 13

Confronting Childhood
Viruses and Diseases

In the midst of our personal intersections within the walls of the Division
Street house, our parents encountered the challenges we children experienced from the threats of childhood viruses. During my childhood times,
parents worried about the impact of chickenpox, mumps, measles, and polio.
Smallpox had essentially been eradicated by then. My parents bore scars from
their inoculations given in their younger years. From the time of Maureen's
birth through the 1950s, our two families talked and worked together to
navigate procedures to prevent and treat viruses prior to immunizations. I
lived through these viruses.

Polio was discovered in the US in the late 1800s. The first epidemic occurred in 1916, the year of Mom's birth. Public health officials recorded approximately 27,000 cases and 6,000 deaths. Cases peaked in 1952 when I was two years old. Polio was presumably transmitted through feces and airborne droplets traveling from person to person. It took six to twenty days to incubate and remained contagious for up to two weeks after contraction.

Franklin Delano Roosevelt brought the disease to the forefront. He suffered polio paralysis in his legs in 1921 when he was thirty-nine. He became governor of New York in 1929 and president in 1932. He served as a role model for the many thousands who contracted the disease. In contrast, his staff and the press photographed him above the waist without his crutches and wheelchair. Government entities did not want him to be portrayed with what was viewed by some as a weakness impairing his ability to be effective in his position. Eventually his polio was recognizable in photos and films, and the public realized the condition was not detrimental to his pursuits.

The virus was often found in children. The reach and outbreaks of polio expanded as World War II ended in 1945. Some attributed the spread of the virus to car exhausts. Since the cases increased in summers, other people thought flies and mosquitoes bore responsibility for the spread. This belief resulted in extensive spraying of DDT to eradicate the insects. Trucks made routine passes spraying chemicals on Division Street and all over town. We ran or rode our bikes behind the trucks ingesting the spray into our lungs. We thought of this repellant process as lifesaving, only to later discover the harmful effects of DDT on people, birds, and wildlife.

I became familiar with headlines and pictures of polio victims in the Chicago and Elgin newspapers. Many of the pictures showed children using crutches and canes or confined to wheelchairs due to full or partial paralysis of the arms and legs. Some victims suffered paralysis of their urinary tracts resulting in catheterization. Fevers from the virus caused delirium and night-mares. Hospital wings saw increases of large metal canister-shaped iron lung machines with the heads of youngsters poking out of the top. The iron lung was a negative pressure chamber assisting the breathing process for severely paralyzed patients. The children were quarantined away from their parents.

Similar to the ways we are approaching COVID-19, the Elgin area and many parts of the country closed swimming pools, lakes, and movie theaters in the hopes of lessening the advance of the virus. Our four parents feared polio might limit their children's chances of living a life without physical disability. Dad and Mom warned us not to drink from public water fountains. Citizens disabled by polio, birth defects, and afflictions had little to no support until the American for Disabilities Act (ADA) was passed in 1990.

Our parents lived through the Great Depression and WWII as they experienced the success of the funeral business. Now, they faced the threat of polio directly affecting their children. They helped with the March of Dimes, an organization that campaigned to fund the development of a vaccine. We saved dimes in containers at home and took them to stores to make donations. Dad and Mom volunteered to go door to door collecting dimes.

In 1954–55, Dr. Jonas Salk led the development of a vaccine for polio. We learned mosquitos and flies were not responsible for the transmission. When the vaccine became available, I received my first shot at our pediatrician's office. The second dose was developed as an oral vaccine by Dr. Albert Sabin. To accommodate all those who needed the vaccine, a distribution center was established in the gymnasium at Elgin High School, two blocks from home. Kerry and I walked with Mom and Dad to receive our second doses. We stood in a line that extended throughout the gym and outside onto the street. After the second dose, we did not worry about polio. Since the vaccine was developed, the worldwide incidence of polio has decreased by 99 percent.

In addition to polio, most children of our time contracted measles, mumps, and chicken pox. We approached these viruses like most other families. When we contacted the virus, we stayed home from school, experienced the symptoms, took the medications, and rested until we had clearance to return to school. Parents treated these situations as a matter of course. They knew once we survived the passage of each virus, we had immunity. Mom and Dad even looked for opportunities to expose us to the virus. When a cousin or friend of the family contracted, for example, chicken pox, our parents put us together with them. Within a known incubation period, Dad and Mom watched for symptoms and set up a system of care for us. These viruses established themselves in our schools. Half a class may have been absent during a period until a virus ran its course. This approach was seen as the remedy. Now, with the discovery of vaccines for each of these conditions and inoculations scheduled within the first two years of birth, children and parents do not have to make these viruses a part of their lives.

Our families lived through twenty years of fear of the viruses. They connected through their discussions about the viruses and the actions they took. They operated as a team in ensuring that we maintained our health. They compared information from their pediatricians and friends. Maureen's and Kathleen's first children were born during a time before the availability of immunizations. My own children were able to receive immunizations in the first two years of their lives. I am grateful to the lessons learned by my family that protected my children and the generations that continue.

CHAPTER 14

Catholic Influence in Our Families' Lives

The Catholic religion was an influence in our families for decades prior to my birth. Mom, my brothers, cousins, and I shared connections to St. Mary Church and School. Mom was an elementary student when the new school building across the street from the church opened in the mid-1920s. She recounted how she carried her school possessions three blocks on Prairie Street from the former St. Mary School to the new building. Coincidentally, the old school building was located next door to the original O'Connor Funeral Home at 118 Villa Street. She graduated from eighth grade in 1930. Maureen followed as a first grader in 1937.

Mom's parents married in St. Mary Church in 1910. When Lawrence and Mildred moved to Elgin, they joined the parish. Mom and Dad were married there. Maureen, Kathleen, and Sharon were also married in the church. Two of Barrett's children married there. Our family was connected to St. Mary Parish like the tentacles of an octopus are connected to the head. Inseparable.

Mildred's strong faith was combined with her comical views on religious interpretations and practices. This was evident in her writing of October 28, 1969, when she was referencing one of my Jesuit instructors at Loyola:

"Saw where Father Powell was speaking of 'Human Sexuality and Human Loving.' I can say that when Auntie was a girl, all I knew about sex was that it came after FIVE! Oh me ... "

On December 29, 1970, she wrote in her characteristic sardonic phrasing about the hymns she heard at Christmas Mass:

"I only recognized one carol. 'Silent Night.' No one said, 'Christ the Savior is born!' I did learn that MARY HAD A BABY—all ten verses, and I still didn't know who the obstetrician was."

Lawrence ushered at Sunday masses, joined the Knights of Columbus, and volunteered for Catholic Charities. He sang in the choir. When Dad came into the business, he too joined the Knights and ushered. Mildred was a member of the Catholic Sodality. All four parents participated in the parent groups for our parochial schools. Dad used his creative skills to help with Christmas decorations. When the church needed funds, our parents helped with phoning families to encourage them to contribute. Dad performed in plays and musicals at the school gym to help raise money for parish expenses. Their involvement was done to help the church, but also to keep a presence among the parishioners. When they volunteered, they did not intentionally recruit clients, remind them of the services they provided, or hand out matchbooks with the O'Connor Funeral Home logo and phone number printed on the cover. Rather, their presence as volunteers may have influenced a family to seek our funeral home service when the need arose.

During the first thirty years of the business, Dad and Lawrence provided funeral and volunteer services to the three Catholic parishes in Elgin. In the late '50s, a fourth parish, St. Thomas More, was established on the west side of Elgin. From the earliest years of the business, all in the family knew the names of the priests stationed at each parish. When a newly assigned pastor or assistant pastor came to town, Lawrence and Dad reached out to introduce themselves and offer support. They may have visited them at the rectory or taken them to lunch or dinner. They wanted to meet the priests prior to the ever-unpredictable time when a family needed the funeral home's services.

Assistant pastors changed positions and came through town with the frequency of shifting passenger lists at a Greyhound bus depot. It seemed a new assistant was always arriving at one of the four parishes to take a position. They stayed two years or less before transferring to another parish in the diocese. When pastors or assistants transferred to a different parish, Lawrence and Mildred stayed acquainted. The Christmas card mailing lists included the names of priests scattered in a fifty-to-sixty-mile area mostly west of Elgin where the Rockford Catholic Diocese extended. They gave the priests holiday gifts, usually alcoholic in composition, placed in gift boxes wrapped for the occasion and delivered by Lawrence or Dad.

Being acquainted with so many priests added to the requirement of attending Mass. The rules of the Catholic Church made it essential to attend Mass each Sunday. The nuns and priests instructed that if we did not attend mass on Sunday, we committed a mortal sin. Not attending Mass was as grievous as murder and adultery. If we skipped Mass on Sunday and died prior to going to confession, we ran the risk of being sentenced to eternity in hell by a god who to me in all other cases seemed to be forgiving. It wasn't until I went to college that I started to have less fear of going to hell when I did not attend Mass on Sunday. I have no reports from those who have predeceased me about suffering from the fire of hell for lack of attendance. I am happy to have put the fear aside.

It was in part from fear that I attended Mass with Mom, Barrett, and Kerry every Sunday. Dad usually went with us to church but stood in back as he greeted and ushered. We always sat in the same section to the left of the main altar, facing a side altar dedicated to the Blessed Virgin Mary. Sometimes we sat in the same pew each service. "Our" pew was about two-thirds of the way toward the back. I assume this section was rooted in Mom's upbringing with her own parents, aunts, uncles, and cousins who also positioned themselves in this vicinity. No one from our family sat in the center sections or on the opposite side of the church. On the few occasions I sat in those locations, I felt like I didn't belong. It wasn't our spot. I don't know where Lawrence or Mildred sat. They went to Mass at a different time than us. Rarely, if ever, did I attend Mass with them. Someone always needed to be home to answer the phone.

During each of many times sitting in our side of the church, I looked around and saw friends and their families in other pews. Each family put themselves in their regular placement. I tried to get the attention of friends to wave, make a face, or signal a message. During Mass, I regularly familiarized myself with the representations on the stained-glass windows and the names of the donor family from the 1800s etched into the glass. I imagined our family name on one of the windows. The first seven of the fourteen stations of the cross hung in between the windows with the remaining seven stations on the opposite wall. On my seventh birthday, I reached the "age of reason," the time in Catholic life when a child was deemed responsible for knowing right from wrong. After instruction from the nuns and assistant pastor, I was eligible for confession, a milestone in Catholic upbringing. I confessed my sins in the confessional on our side of the church.

Lawrence emphasized the importance for Barrett, Kerry, and me to serve as altar boys. This was not a requirement for all the boys in our classes. In

Lawrence's eyes, it was essential for us. Lawrence was our guide and sponsor as we took a series of after-school trainings in the fall of 1959. He took it upon himself to tutor us and keep up to date with our training. He told Kerry and I he was doing this exercise as a surprise to Dad and Mom. I am not sure if this was true, but I was motivated by thinking it was secret. We sat with him at the scheduled time to memorize prayers in Latin. He said a phrase. We repeated. As much as I wasn't sure if I wanted to be an altar boy, I knew there wasn't a choice. I was fond of these close times with Lawrence.

When it came time to serve at our first Mass at a 6:15 a.m. weekday service, Lawrence came upstairs to awaken Kerry and me and make sure we dressed. We still believed it was a surprise for Dad and Mom, so they purportedly slept through our morning preparations. Lawrence drove us in the morning darkness to St. Mary. We went to the sacristy and attired ourselves in black cassocks and white surplices taken from hangers in a wooden closet. We busied ourselves with the preparation tasks of lighting candles on the altar and pouring water and wine into matching glass cruets and placing them on the glass tray. We heard people walking into church and taking their places.

When it was time to start Mass, the priest instructed us to walk out to the altar in front of him and take our positions. As we turned to face the few people in the congregation, Dad and Mom sat with proud smiles. They knew all along about what was happening. I rarely knew them to come to weekday Masses. Mildred wasn't there, because, of course, she needed to be at home in case someone called on the phone to tell of the passing of a client.

Attending Mass regularly and serving as altar boys were two expressions of participation in Catholic practices. Keeping with other traditions, many in our family were selected as godparents to babies born into the family. As soon as a baby was born or before, the parents made the decision about who was to be the godparent. The baptism date was usually two to four weeks after the birth. In Catholicism, baptism is essential. A baby who died before being baptized was believed to go to an eternal place called Limbo. This is not a place where people bend backward and dance or scuttle their way under a bar held by two onlookers. It's not the Limbo Rock. In our elementary Catholic catechism instruction, Limbo was portrayed as a peaceful place between heaven and hell. The souls who go there are not condemned to punishment. They are simply deprived of the existence with God in heaven. It's a holding area. I envisioned Limbo as enclosed with no way out.

The concept of Limbo is a bit of quirkiness amidst a collection of unfounded or unproven theological ideas. Nevertheless, a baby needed to be baptized. The babies not baptized were sentenced to stay in Limbo until the end of the world or when God decided to open the door to welcome them through heaven's gates. In an emergency when an infant's life was in danger, a baptism was conducted by anyone with the wherewithal to get a cup of water and pour it over an infant's head and say a prayer. These kinds of emergency baptisms counted in Catholic teaching.

Limbo was not perceived as a bad place. But it was preferred to not put a baby there through lack of baptism. Baptism day was conducted in a church at the altar with the baby wearing lace finery previously worn by a relative or purchased new from a store. The church service was led by a priest and attended by the parents, godparents, and assorted relatives and friends. The ceremony was followed by a food and music fest, usually at the home of the parents or grandparents.

O'Connor and Division Street babies were often god-parented by someone in the immediate family. My godparents were Mildred and Uncle Mike Dermody. Dad was Maureen's godfather. Lawrence was Barrett's godfather and later served as godfather to Barrett's daughter, Kelly. Dad and Mom were godparents to Maureen's daughter, Anne. Dad and Mom departed from tradition when they selected their friends, Bob and Margaret, as Kerry's godparents. Bob gave Kerry a silver dollar on each of his birthdays. Following that example, I give a monetary gift to each of my godchildren: niece Erin, nephew Riley, and cousin David. Barrett and Kerry were godfathers to other Division Street offspring. Being a godparent was considered an honor. We all did our part to be witness to the newborns' reprieve from Limbo. We enjoyed a dance or two under the limbo bar at the parties following the baptism.

I found myself in my own Limbo state of religious questioning and uncertainty when I was in my twenties and finished with sixteen years of Catholic education. I was getting into questions about my upbringing and understanding about Jesus Christ. When I was a student at Loyola Rome in March 1971, I took a music appreciation class entitled "History of Music" taught by Professor Mo (short for Maestro) Feist. He introduced us to the recently released recording of *Jesus Christ Superstar*, which has now been produced on film, theaters, and TV. I wrote to Dad and Mom about my first impressions when I saw the film in a letter dated August 2, 1973:

"I want you to go see *Jesus Christ Superstar*. Wow—what an experience! It's directed by Norman Jewison, the same guy who did *Fiddler on the Roof*. I went through so many emotions and feelings during the whole movie. It's the first time I've seen Christ portrayed so humanly. Maybe too humanly. I mean he didn't portray enough of his God side. But I went through so many questions like: 'I believe in this guy?' and 'How did he ever get so many people to follow?' and 'If he hadn't died like he did, would he have had as much effect?' and 'Was he stupid or just a little farfetched?' and 'What kind of ego trip was he on?' At one point I told myself I'd never go to church again. But by the end, I was a believer again—a little shattered, but once again a believer.

Jewison has tied in modern-day events with what's going on in the film. He uses the same fifty people rather than the typical cast of thousands, so that lends a real personalness to it. And Mary Magdalene gives Christ a humanness that most of us have cheated him of. The story was all there in the lyrics, but I never really put the WHOLE story together in my mind. The scenery is deserty—dryly beautiful (filmed in Israel), and some of the techniques are great. At one point everybody is singing. They say 'Jesus, will you die for me?' The camera just stops right on his face. And I suddenly thought that he wasn't really that sure about what he was doing. The story is taken from Judas's viewpoint. I didn't like Christ at first. He almost seemed too gentle, and his anger forced. ENOUGH. GO SEE IT. TELL ME WHAT YOU THINK."

Looking back through the letters from Dad and Mom in the weeks that followed, they made no reference to having seen the film.

I do appreciate the practices and experiences growing up in a Catholic household. I adhere to the feelings of tradition, closeness, and participating together. I now find the aspects of faith and the rigidness of Catholic rules difficult for me to sustain. I do treasure my memories but not enough to sustain my relationship with Catholic ideology.

The "Little Church" is one of my religious memories. When Dad first joined the business, he wanted a way to have the funeral home be visibly present and acknowledged during the Christmas season. He joined with a family friend to build a replica of a church about the size of an outdoor playhouse. The design and structure included white siding, a pitched roof, steeple, and stained-glass windows on either side of the structure. He placed a half-moon window on the front and back walls. The inside of the structure contained an altar with communion rail, red plush carpets, and rows of pews scaled to the size of the structure. He installed a sound amplifier in the steeple. A portable Victrola, concealed behind the altar, played "Oh, Holy Night." After Thanksgiving weekends, Dad positioned the little church in the front yard next to the large wooden sign with O'Connor carved in raised white letters. As dusk fell, an electric candlelight glow whispered through the window openings. Spotlights attached to the trunk of the tall pine tree in the front yard highlighted the display. One picture from 1940 showed the church with two small evergreens on each side of the front steps. Sharon was standing next to the church in a snowsuit with a puff ball adorning the hood on her head. She was four years old.

MINIATURE CHURCH

William O'Connor built this model church on his lawn to provide Christmas music for his fellow townsmen. Exquisitely modeled, it has tiny pews, an altar, red plush carpets and stained glass windows. It is wired for sound with an amplifier in the steeple. A portable victrola, concealed behind the organ, plays "Holy Night." Visitors come from miles around to look and to listen to this realistic expression of the spirit of Christmas.

"Of all the things I've made," says Mr. O'Connor with a happy smile, "this little church pleases me most. I guess it's because my neighbors enjoy it too."

Little church picture and article, approximately
1940. Publication unknown.

The church was displayed each year through the mid-1950s. As I looked out from our living room window, I saw families parking their cars on the street or on our driveway. They rolled down their windows and listened to the music.

They walked from their cars up to stand near the little church. Children and families posed for pictures, both during the day and night times. Dad took deserved pride in the structure. He told me of his numerous woodworking pursuits, the church pleased him the most. He liked it because it brought enjoyment to neighbors and others who passed by the house during the holiday seasons.

Dad stored the church in the garage after the holiday seasons concluded. In later summers, the structure was placed in the backyard. At age five and above, maybe as old as ten, Kerry and I crawled through the entrance of the Little Church placed in a backyard area. By this time, the dollhouse size furnishings had gone missing. We played in the inside with our own imaginations. Our friends joined us in play. Some summer nights, Dad and Mom let us sleep in the church. I woke up to bright sunshine and heat penetrating through the roof. We outgrew the structure. The church fell into disrepair. My aunt and uncle asked to use it on their rural property west of Elgin. They converted it to a chicken coop with perches and nests to hold the eggs. We used the original window openings to reach in and collect the eggs.

Consistent with the way in which our families intertwined life with death, our collective Catholic practices combined the physicality of a model 'little church' eventually becoming a place where eggs were laid, eaten, or naturally warmed to evolve into new chickens. Like the hatching of eggs, births were equally as common in our family.

CHAPTER 15

Our Families Grow

S tarting with my birth in 1950 through the early '70s, cribs were set up at various locations on the second and third floors. Depending on the occasion, as many as four to eight children under the age of ten may have been in the house.

When Maureen and Bill welcomed their first child, Kathy, in 1953, Kerry's and my lone distinction of "diapered" ended among the two Division Street households. All combined, Lawrence and Mildred and Dad and Mom became grandparents twenty-three more times over the next thirty-one years. Maureen visited from North Carolina with Kathy. Their second child, Marie, died at birth in November 1954. Eileen came in April 1957. When Mildred told us in the fall of 1958 Kathleen was pregnant with a baby due the following March, I took it upon myself to walk through the neighborhood and knock on doors.

When someone answered, I announced, "Kathleen is going to have a baby." I didn't know some of the people on whose doors I knocked. When I arrived back home, Mildred stopped me by the kitchen door and asked, "Where have you been?" I told that I went and told the neighbors. A scolding followed.

"News about her pregnancy is only for us in our family. For now. I know you're excited, but you can't go knocking on doors and telling people."

I then comprehended about expectant-baby-announcing etiquette and discretion. Mary Beth Osborne was born in February 1959, followed a month later with Kathleen and Frank Martino's son, Stephen. His birth brought the count of Division Street second cousins to five. Lisa Martino was born in 1960, Jim Martino and Anne Marie Osborne in 1961, and Anne Carmel Martino in 1962. In May 1963, Barrett and Pat became first-time parents with the arrival of Kelly. John Martino came six months later. Sean O'Connor followed in 1964.

January to April of 1966 were banner months for births. Each woman of childbearing age in our two families gave birth to babies. We welcomed the additions of Shannon Safar, Erin O'Connor, Michael Osborne, and Vincent Martino. In 1967, David Osborne and Lynn Safar were added to the roster, followed two years later by Scott Safar and Brian O'Connor.

Kerry and I lived a distinct experience becoming brothers-in-law at ages eleven and twelve and uncles less than a year later. When it was time to bring Kelly home from St. Joseph Hospital, Barrett and Pat did not go directly to their one-bedroom apartment. They stayed with us to benefit from Mom and Dad's assistance. For a week or so, they took up residence in our bedroom. The cradle and crib on the second floor used for the visits of Lawrence and Mildred's grandchildren was moved upstairs to our room. Kerry and I moved to one of the second-floor bedrooms or to the back room.

After Barrett and Pat felt physically and emotionally ready to move back to their own apartment, Kelly initiated our years of continued participation and care for Barrett's children. Kerry and I became hands-on uncles, accustomed to the frequency of new grandchildren on the second floor, folding diapers, and warming milk filled bottles in boiling water on the stove tops. Kerry and I became babysitters, as my cousins and Barrett had done for us. We babysat at our house or went to their apartments and houses. Dad and Mom also helped at every opportunity. Dad remarked in a letter dated June 30, 1972:

"Sunday, after supper, Pat took Barrett to the airport. Kelly and Erin went to stay allnite [sic] with Cease and Joan. Saen [Dad's spelling of Sean at the time] stayed here, and Brian ended up staying with his mother. Saen wasn't ready to go home, so he stayed Monday nite, too. Tuesday, we got going and went to Wing Park and golfed, after we picked up his clubs at home. You should see him. We played with two other guys. Saen shot an 80. He doesn't miss any. It was fun. Went to lunch. Too bad Barrett and Pat and kids are moving 'cause I've analyzed and maybe I'd be a better grandfather than I was a father. Saen was fun and easy to have around."

I wished I probed this remark further with Dad. I wonder why he felt the way he did. Another mystery.

The frequency of visits on the second floor of grandchildren, coupled with the accessibility of Barrett and Pat's children in Elgin, kept me knowledgeable of how babies grow and their developmental progressions. I overheard Mildred's phone calls with her daughters. Mildred gave me the telephone to talk to whoever was on the line. Just as the girls referred to us as "little brothers," we became the older brothers/cousins/uncles to the babies expanding our family size.

Kerry and I assumed caretaker roles before our teen years. I have always been comfortable with children. My experiences with caregiving contributed to my earnestness to learn about child development. My learning and fascination in being with those younger than me led to my interest in an educational career. I have always loved being an uncle, cousin, caregiver, teacher, and principal.

CHAPTER 16

Harmonizing

Some in my family have shared memories of the music they heard coming from the third-floor apartment. It was an invitation beckoning them to walk the stairs to visit whoever was at the top. Music played a significant role at affairs for friends and family and a comfortable refuge from the families experiencing their grief in the funeral home below. Dad and Mildred played the piano on the second floor. Most of us children took piano lessons. Dad played the organ on the first floor. This was one way for him to relax.

Lawrence was a practiced, dedicated, and proud tenor-baritone singer. His singing was good and often requested by others at family events and church occasions. He was a featured soloist in chorus groups. He practiced his vocalizing with humming or bellowing the musical scales. When I walked up either of the stairways from the first floor, I often heard "Do-Re-Mi-Fa-So-La-Ti-Do." He used a reel-to-reel tape recorder to record a few rounds of the scales going from low to high ranges. He rewound the tape and played it back to critique himself. The process repeated. After giving himself the starting note at the piano, he sang unaccompanied. Lawrence was very happy when he was singing. He did not allude to a secret ambition, but I think he may have pictured himself a renowned singer like Nelson Eddy or Irish tenor John McCormack. He listened to their recordings on a regular basis. He was a soloist in the church choir. He sang at weddings, including the marriage ceremony of Gina and me. He passed on his singing skills to me. Just as he sang at my wedding, I sang at the weddings of my nieces and nephew.

I knew better than to offer criticism to him. On the other hand, we in the family talked about his singing. Maureen, always playfully reminded me, "It's okay to talk about your own." Dad commented on Lawrence's singing in a letter he wrote on January 3, 1971. He referenced a recorded tape Dad was sending me. The tape included a solo of the hymn "Panis Angelicus" at Christmas Midnight Mass. Dad wrote:

"Lawrence has been wanting to get his Panis off it. Frankly it was lousy—the accompanist!!! I hope he has removed his singing by now. We have plenty of good organists in our church without being ecumenical to the point of bringing in a Methodist who had no musical ear."

Mildred also commented on a typed aerogramme dated a few days earlier on December 29, 1970:

"LS sang but it was really off-key, which of course I couldn't say to him as he would just DIE. The whole spiritual Mass was off-key, especially when the trumpet would blast off, so really it wasn't his fault. He was only able to practice once with the organist who was so confident he didn't need practice."

Both apartments provided space for a record player also known in the 1940s and '50s as a hi-fi. That is short for the two words "high fidelity." The hi-fis were contained in furniture cabinets. When I wanted to play more than one record, I stacked four to five records on the thin metal spindle. Each record dropped down the spindle when ready for playing on the turntable. When all records completed their play, we picked up the stack through the spindle, turned them over, and dropped them into place to play the tunes on the opposite sides. We put the most recent album purchases on the top of the cabinets. Additional albums remained stored inside the areas in the console cabinet between the radio dials and the turntable. Record albums traveled from floor to floor. If someone was looking for an album, it was no doubt in the other apartment.

Mom, Dad, Lawrence, and Mildred listened to the recordings of big band conductors Fred Waring, Cab Calloway, Duke Ellington, and George Gershwin. They listened to singers Fanny Brice, Bing Crosby, Kate Smith, Tony Bennett, Lena Horne, Doris Day, Peggy Lee, Dinah Shore, Frank Sinatra, and Rudy Vallee singing songs like "Brother, Can You Spare a Dime?" "On the Sunny Side of the Street," "In the Mood," and "All of Me." The songs on the albums represented the music of their dating and early marriage years. These songs continued to be played on the record players, sung by Uncle Lawrence in his performances, and played by Dad on the piano.

Their interest in musical performances continued throughout their marriages. Mildred wrote to me on November 12, 1970:

"We went to the Blue Moon Ballroom to see and mostly hear Wayne King and his orchestra. There were male and female singers with the orchestra, and believe me, all the mammas and grandmammas were oooohing and awwwwing over the male crooner. He was REALLY adorable—REALLY Kevin. I don't believe he was hired to sing but just to smile and get the gals swooning. Afterward we decided to get a sandwich someplace, but all the dining rooms were closed. So guess what? We ended up at Masi's (in Dundee). Guess it has a 4–5 a.m. closing. It was jumping, and we got the usual cries of 'grandma and grandpa' but in a fun kind of way."

In addition to albums from orchestras and singers, the record collections included such Broadway scores as *Annie Get Your Gun, Carousel, Cabaret, Kiss Me Kate, My Fair Lady, South Pacific, Camelot, The Music Man,* and *Man of La Mancha.* I knew the melodies and lyrics to many songs from these scores. I still know them.

Barrett purchased many of these cast albums. Listening to "Officer Krupke" from the show *West Side Story*, I expanded my vocabulary and concepts with lyrics including "social disease," "neuroses," "my mother wears a mustache," "my grandma pushes tea," "marijuana," "bastard," and "S.O.B." Mildred once shouted over the volume of the music up the stairs to the third floor, "How can those words be in a song?" Her remark gave me all the impetus I needed to listen and uncover the meaning of lyrics with words new to me. Gratefully, I had the opportunity to sing the Krupke song in a musical review in Woodstock in the 1990s. Being part of the rendition harkened me back to my seven-year-old self on Division Street.

Barrett and Sharon provided melodic connections with the record players in their bedrooms. They exposed the family to music popular in the 1950s. Kerry and I were aware of rock and roll singers before our peers who did not have older siblings. Barrett and Sharon purchased and played 45 RPM records. In addition to Elvis Presley, other popular artists included Brenda Lee, Frankie Avalon, Buddy Holly, Bobby Vinton and groups such as the Kingston Trio, Everly Brothers, and Bill Haley and the Comets.

During his teen and college years, Barrett developed an interest in the Columbia Record Club. I followed in his footsteps. The club lured buyers into opportunities to receive an initial collection of six to ten albums for the price of one $1.99 album. The albums were mailed in a box the same size as the album covers. An order of ten arrived in a form-fitted cardboard container. After the initial purchase, the customer was expected to purchase at least one album a month until reaching the quantity of albums received in the initial plan. Sounds easy, huh? It was a thrill to receive the box and play the records one by one or stack them on the spindle of the player.

Membership in the record club came with problems. At least once a month, the record club sent out a catalogue with available records and a reply card. The card indicated the name of the record available for the month in a particular genre of music Barrett or I selected with our individual memberships. If either of us neglected to mail back the selection card by a date two to three weeks later, the record was automatically mailed to the house and charged to the account. This album counted toward our album commitment agreement. The record club was both enticing and potentially punishing to my limited financial resources. Mom and Dad held us to the financial responsibility of our errors.

As Kerry and I developed interest in music in the early 1960s, we begged Dad and Mom for a stereo record system in our room. They agreed to the idea but insisted that we find the funds to purchase the equipment. We sold our electric train set, advertising through local newspaper want ads. Dad and Mom guided us through the negotiation of prices. We found a buyer, procured the cash, and went to Sears to purchase the stereo record player we selected. Dad built shelving to store the record player, our album collection, and 45 RPM record purchases.

Kerry and I shared musical tastes in pop songs played on teen radio stations. Most nights we fell asleep to the sound of radio programming. When Kerry and I listened to our selections while the family system was playing something else, we closed our bedroom door and played our selections at a lower volume. Dad and Mom became acquainted with our evolving music interests. From time to time, numerous systems and radios in both apartments played concurrently, creating discordant sounds if I happened to be standing in the right receptive position.

Beyond the music shared via records, radio, and TV played on both floors of the house, our families encouraged us to see live theater. The first production Mom, Dad, Kerry, and I saw together was *Oklahoma* in the late 1950s at St. Mel's High School in Chicago. The show was directed by Jerry Sullivan, a high school friend of Maureen and Kathleen. We sat in one of the front rows with the proscenium of the stage just above my viewing position. I was fascinated looking up and watching the story unfold. Whenever I now listen to songs from the show, like "Oh, What a Beautiful Morning" or "Poor Jud is Dead," my mental vision immediately returns to this first viewing vantage.

Next, we went to see *The Sound of Music* in Chicago. Barrett had bought the original cast Broadway album in 1959. The family knew the songs, and I had taught myself music scales on the piano from the song "Do-Re-Mi." The supporting role of the Baroness in the production was played by Kathleen's friend, Lynn Brinker. After the show, Lynn invited us backstage to visit in her dressing room. She took our programs to be signed by Florence Henderson (*The Brady Bunch*, anyone?), who played Maria. Over the following years, Mom and Dad took us to see *Hello, Dolly!* with Carol Channing and *Mame* with Angela Lansbury. In the late '70s, Dad and I took a trip to Chicago to meet funeral home vendors and spontaneously went to Arie Crown Theater for a matinee performance of *Sweeney Todd* with Lansbury.

Dad and Mom relished the lyrics of songs. Dad in particular was fascinated with the words and musical poetry of Rod McKuen. Dad commented in a letter written on October 24, 1969:

"Our house has been neglected, so I took down the awning, washing windows and cleaning and playing Rod McKuen. Keep wondering why kids like him because really they haven't lived long enough to understand all his recitations. Aunt Lillian calls some of it 'earthy,' and I think it's great because it's all so lifelike, but he was smart enough to put it in words and make money from it."

I connect music with history. Andy Williams was a popular solo artist with numerous albums and a TV variety show. The songs from *The Andy Williams Christmas Album*, released in 1963, are holiday standards played each year. Per Dad's direction to me on Friday, November 22, 1963, I walked fifteen minutes to Ryburn's Record Store in downtown Elgin to purchase the album. I was in eighth grade but not in school because the teachers were conducting parent-teacher conferences. After purchasing the album, I decided to stay at the store. As I was perusing its vast collection, an announcement came through the store's radio. US President John F. Kennedy had been shot in Dallas. I froze there, not believing what I had just heard. The first announcement stated he was rushed to a hospital. A short time later the announcer said Kennedy died. Having been a supporter of Kennedy and collector of his campaign buttons, I froze with the first phases of grief and shock and then exited the store and walked home. I found Dad, Lawrence, and Mildred listening to the radio with their vision glued to the TV screen in the second-floor living room. The album stayed in the bag for days until we felt the delayed urge to share in the joy of Christmas music. Now when I hear Williams's holiday songs, my mind immediately returns to Ryburn's Record Store and my stunned walk home.

CHAPTER 17

Gimme a Head with Hair

The title of this chapter comes from the opening lyrics of the song "Hair" included in the score of the musical of the same name and popularized by a group named Cowsills. Have you seen or heard the song or the production? It was first produced on Broadway in 1967 then made into a movie. It has been revived numerous times. The theme and songs of the musical focus on the revolution of social and political thinking occurring in the country in the 1960s. Boys' and men's hair grew longer with the showcasing of The Beatles and other influential musical groups and singers. Hair length was displayed readily in pictures and stories about youth involvement in politics. The attend- ees at Woodstock Musical Festival in 1969 sported long hair cascading over necklines and shoulders adorned with ribbons, hair bands, and jewelry. This contrasted with the short crew cut styles of the NASA astronauts and ground crew viewed on TV.

In your families you have your own individual hair styles. During our Division Street years, the families commented on each other's hair, the beauticians in town, and the styling Dad and hairdressers created for the deceased. Dad even used the skills he acquired in mortuary school to cut and style Mom's and Mildred's hair. I watched as he gave them permanents or rolled their hair in rollers and positioned their heads under the dryers available in both apartments. They held bobby pins and clips in their hands, ready to give to Dad as needed, as they bantered similarly to what is heard at a salon. They didn't sit as still for their stylings as Dad's deceased clients.

Mildred experienced periods of hair loss and thinning, so Dad helped her with special treatments massaged into her scalp. Her hair kept thinning. Dad advised her how to brush her hair from the back to the front to give style at the top and sides of her face. After a while, she decided to wear wigs to save time from the treatments and styling. Dad again helped her to select wigs and fitted them in a way she felt comfortable.

My parents, Lawrence, and Mildred observed as the length of the younger generation's hair reached longer lengths. Although not adamant in their comments about the length, they insisted we keep our hair clean and combed when involved in work for the funeral home. They reminded us we represented the business and our hair presentation may be seen detrimentally. Mom referenced hair length in her letters with an acknowledgment when we made the effort to change our hair to what she considered acceptable. Mom wrote in a typed aerogramme dated October 28, 1970:

"Had my hair done and no longer wearing a beanie of dark hair. Liked it really well, and it is quite light without using any bleach. Speaking of hair, Kerry had his hair cut. It looks good, not very short. After his cut, somebody asked him how much weight he lost, and he said 'About 130 lbs. I got my mother off my back.'"

She followed up on November 9:

"Here's a sample of my hair. Just cut it off and you might be able to see the color. Kerry got his cut with just a little pressure from us—it was too long, but he didn't get it cut very short—just styled better."

Mom probably did not realize she referenced Kerry's hair in two letters dated twelve days apart.

Mildred wrote about hair in a letter dated January 9, 1971:

"Well dear—be a good boy—say your prayers and cut your hair, and I'll miss you always until you get back in the US."

She wrote again a month later on February 8, 1971:

"I guess IF you get around to seeing a barber, you will be able to stuff a pillow. Lots of love, Auntie M."

Kerry's hair made an impression yet again as conveyed in Mildred's letter dated March 1, 1971:

"Kerry looks real sharp, as he got his hair styled. I don't know what got into him, but believe me, he looks HANDSOME."

After Dad and Mom spent three weeks with me in Italy, Austria, and Germany, she wrote on April 29, 1971:

"Am sending you a check for $15 but the extra $5 is for AN ITALIAN HAIRCUT! Really, you shouldn't leave Italy without getting one. Dad and I both thought all the Italian men had real neat haircuts, and then too Grampa Ciraulo was a barber, so you should get one. Another reason, you should let all the girls see how really handsome you are when your hair is neat—and besides, I would like you to get one. ENOUGH REASONS!!! Mom"

I did get a haircut a couple of weeks later. Kerry was visiting me in Rome. The haircut cost eighty cents. I wonder how I spent the additional $4.20 Mom had provided. Perhaps on bread, cheese, and wine in the Italian tradition.

Hair brought our families together in stories, in laughter, and practicality. Keep on stylin'.

CHAPTER 18

Smoke Got in Our Eyes

The name of this chapter is adapted from a song recorded by The Platters in 1958. Although the lyrics have limited application to our family stories, the funeral home and apartments' atmospheres were characterized by the presence of smoke, ashtrays, and silent butlers (containers used for holding ashes emptied from ashtrays).

Dad, Mom, and Mildred all smoked. I assume they started smoking in high school or shortly after. Maureen and Kathleen started smoking in their late teens. There was little to no knowledge about the addictive effects of nicotine or consciousness of smoke odors. Smoking was socially accepted. The aroma of cigarette smoke was prevalent throughout the apartments, in the furniture, and on clothing. Dad, Mom, and Mildred held cigarettes in their hands in many family pictures. Most TV shows advertised commercials from cigarette brands. Those commercials stopped in the early 1970s when cigarette packages started labeling warnings about the health hazards of smoking.

One of Kerry's and my jobs was to check for lit cigarettes in ashtrays. Mom was concerned about the possibility of a fire in the apartment and realized a burning cigarette might be the culprit. When we started to go downstairs with Mom, she might turn around and say, "Go into the bathroom. I think I may have left a cigarette burning in the ash tray when I was at the sink."

"Do I have to?" I'd reply.

"Go and put it out. You better check in the kitchen and my bedroom, too."

One or both of us followed the routine and dutifully checked per Mom's request. Sometimes she *had* left a cigarette burning. Mom was conscious of her smoking habit and possible consequences to all of us.

Mildred was the first to break the habit in 1965. Dad knew smoking was not healthy but had little success with quitting. In 1969, Pat developed conditions preventing her from walking after Brian's birth. Dad was a prayerful person. He asked God to help Pat find her way back to health. He offered to God to give up smoking so that her health would improve. He quit immediately without a support group or the yet-to-come nicotine patch and gum. Who is to say Pat's recovery was not the result of Dad's prayers, sacrifice, and change of habit? A nurse friend of the family helped Pat with Vitamin B injections she took from the hospital where she worked. Illegal? Yes. But the shots helped restore Pat's mobility. Dad may have extended his own life by quitting his smoking habit as well.

Mom continued to smoke. Dad did not find fault with her. He knew the tenacity of the addiction. She quit four months later. In a letter dated November 13, 1969, she lamented:

"Have been reading in the paper about the people attending the clinic down at the Y to quit smoking. I really feel for them and almost think it wouldn't hurt me to go down and get in on the sessions just to make it easier. Although I am certainly over the hump—it has been since September 21 since I smoked a full cigarette—I would still like to have one, and the withdrawal symptoms are horrible. All I can say to you kids is don't start the stupid habit, and you will never have to go through the ordeal of quitting. Last Friday night we were with my class reunion group over at the Elks for dinner. There were seven couples, and only one girl smoked, and she only had one after dinner. One other man, her husband, smoked a pipe.

I think the funny thing about my quitting was that I had been off them for about two weeks, and JoJean did not know I had quit. I guess, Kevin, you did not know about this, but I quit the nite we were in to see you and afterward went downtown to see *Funny Girl*. I had such a sore throat. Dad suggested I quit for a couple of days. I threw away the cigarette I was smoking. It was the last full cigarette I smoked. My friend, Mary, called the other night, and she started out by asking me, 'Is this Smoking Anonymous?' Seems she had been off them for eleven days and just had to talk to someone else who had quit. We had a good talk and compared notes on how we felt and what we were going through."

They started their first full year as nonsmokers on January 1, 1970. Dad was fifty-seven and Mom was fifty-four, concluding almost forty years as smokers. They no longer smoked among friends. When guests came to the house who smoked, they did not detain them from doing so or put away the ash trays prevalent in the décor of the apartment. We had yet to learn about secondhand smoke.

Even though they all expressed a momentary longing for the puff of smoke, they did not indulge. They succeeded in conquering an addiction identified during their lifetimes.

Smoke may have gotten in my eyes and the aroma of nicotine in my nostrils in my childhood environment. I thank Mom and Dad for their recognition of the detriments of smoking and the tenacity modeled to me for them to quit. I'm forever grateful for not indulging in the smoking habit.

CHAPTER 19

Parents as Entrepreneurs

While Dad and Lawrence earned enough income from the funeral home to make the payments to sustain the business and households, Mom, Lawrence, and Mildred all endeavored to combine their creative and business skills to potentially generate additional income.

Mom and two friends developed a harness-like product designed to keep babies from climbing out of their cribs. They called the item Stay-Put. The harnesses tied up the front using thin roping similar to shoelaces. They sewed four lengths of ribbon to the harness. The ribbons were long enough for the baby to move about the crib but short enough to keep them in the crib. The other end of the ribbons attached to the rails of the crib. The inspiration for the design came from the harness Kerry wore in his hospital bed when he was recuperating from leg surgery.

They named their company BeMar Sales and created a logo. The "Be" represented the name of one of the partners, Bernadine. The "Mar" was the first three letters of Mom's name and their friend Margaret. They designed stationery and envelopes for invoices and business letters. They packaged the product in a cellophane bag with a folded cardboard label and directions stapled to the top. Mom and her partners arranged gatherings of friends to box and ship the product to customers who found the items in advertisements placed in newspapers and magazines targeted to mothers and families. They arranged to have the product displayed and for sale at children's clothing stores and in gift shops at local hospitals.

Stay-Puts were the forerunners of infant and children's car seats. It's unfortunate I was not wearing one in the early '50s when I was riding in the 1949 Chrysler with Mom. She was rear-ended near a stop sign. The force of her braking and the car hitting us from behind propelled me forward from my place in the front seat, hitting my head solidly enough on the windshield to crack the glass and thrust me back over the top of the front seat to a landing position in the back seat. I recovered quickly with a bump on my head.

In the 1980s, I secured my two sons in car seats. I thought of Mom's team and their invention. Their lower-than-desired sales prevented them from continuing their venture. In today's world, Stay-Puts would be outlawed as dangerous for the welfare of the child. In hindsight, it was to our advantage the product failed. Just think of the lawsuits! However, we had stationery and boxes of the product in storage areas until Mom discarded them in one of her reorganizing times.

In addition to Mom's business venture, Lawrence managed a foray into a business creating cold cream, makeup removal products, and a brown tinted cream he called mask, which was reputed to have ingredients to help with adolescent complexion blemishes and unwanted facial ailments. I was allowed to watch but not participate in the preparation process. He poured water corresponding to the amounts listed on the recipe into pots on the stove of the second-floor kitchen. Steam filled the kitchen. He precisely measured the materials for the creams using scales and weight devices positioned on the kitchen counter. He didn't have a lab coat but wore a white shirt or sleeveless T-shirt. The consistency of the cream became eventually thicker with the heat. At a finishing point, he ladled the ingredients into two-ounce white glass jars. When the ingredients cooled, he screwed black lids onto each jar and secured printed adhesive labels with the name and directions for the cream's use on each jar. I was allowed to place the jars into boxes with cardboard slatted dividers sectioned into a dozen spaces.

During our teen years, Kerry and I used the mask daily in a nightly routine of rubbing the product into our complexion. We let it sit and ferment for a few minutes and then rinsed it off. We added spirits of camphor and an additional thin layer of the mask before going to bed. I am not sure if the mask worked any better than Clearasil or the products my friends used. Through my mid-twenties, I was never without a jar of mask. I used it in the years after college when I started my first teaching job. As my age increased, the concern about acne dissipated. I do believe Lawrence's cream kept my skin relatively blemish free.

I don't know what happened to the last of the jars or to the recipe cards written with words, numbers, and fractions. He mentioned on occasion the recipe was from a neighbor or family member in Hammond. He kept making the product to honor her legacy. He talked about his vision of marketing the creams and using the profits for college tuition for Kerry and me. Mom was going to help with the sales and bookkeeping. These plans did not happen. I am not sure why he didn't give the product to my friends or market it through the high schools. This was in the years before street fairs and neighborhood craft markets. His scientific and laboratory skills came from his training as an embalmer and what he knew about caring for the skin of the deceased. The word "derma" was on the label. He took his recipe to his grave.

Mildred, too, wanted to branch out on her own in the mid-1950s. She received her first driver's license and then purchased a used sedan with an automatic transmission and a front bench seat, but no AC or any kind of accessory power. She took the courses for her real estate license. She started a job at Reinert Real Estate and began listing homes.

She supported the work of the funeral home when answering the business phone and providing the household responsibilities that kept Lawrence ready for his work. But real estate *was her* job. She showed her excitement with stories about her office work, listing houses, and showing properties to clients. These experiences highlighted her skills of organization, positive outlook, and the socialness with which she engaged people. She talked of price differences and commissions. She was an evolving professional woman—proud of what she was doing beyond her role as housewife, volunteer, and ambassador for the funeral business. She used the spirit of adventure she exhibited in the move to her new home in 1930 and turned it into her professional quest. Her secret ambition may have been to be a realtor at her own agency and be recognized in her own right. When she sold her first house, I heard her voice resonate from the bottom of the stairs to the third floor: "The sale went through. I sold my first house. What do you think about that?!"

On some occasions, she took me with her to inspect a house for a possible listing. When we got in the car, she pulled the seat up as far as it went to accommodate her short reach. I barely saw over the dashboard and through the windshield. On one trip we drove to Meadowdale, a residential development of small ranch houses six miles north of our house. It was a prime market for Mildred, the newly licensed realtor. She opened the door to the house. I held her keys and purse as she took her clipboard and completed the needed documents. She used a tape measure to get the dimensions of the rooms. When she was finished, we got back in the car and headed back to her office. I sat in one of the waiting room chairs. I ate the snacks available in the office kitchen. I felt especially included and supported in the relationship with her.

Mom, Lawrence, and Mildred endeavored to make lives better for themselves and our families. They honed their skills and interests. To all who explore opportunities in careers and interests, keep on entrepreneur-ing.

CHAPTER 20

Tensions Exposed

Despite what's been expressed so far about how we got along with each other, not everything between the families was perfect. Dad and Lawrence did experience tension in their relationship. I did not experience their strain in obvious grimaces, words, or expressions but rather as an undercurrent to the public persona they presented as brothers in business together. The business was successful. They each did what was needed without a display of arms around shoulders, hugs, handshakes, or other signs of camaraderie and support. They did not argue in my presence.

Was the tension I perceived in their relationship from Lawrence's position as owner and Dad as employee? Their birth order? Differences in personalities? The reality of one of them always having to be available at the funeral home, precluding them from going out and socializing together? Dad maintaining the illusion of co-ownership when he was an employee?

Answers to these questions are rarely discussed and at best interpreted with little to no analysis. Lawrence's first business venture was successful. Dad's venture in Aurora did not fare as well. I did not sense jealousy from Dad. He needed the job he had and the apartment that came with it. Lawrence needed Dad's skills and abilities to run the business. Although I didn't hear Lawrence acknowledge Dad, I know there was unexpressed appreciation from him. I know they loved each other and their immediate and extended families.

My brothers and I had relationships with each of them. Lawrence was not a paternal substitute, while at the same time he respected and treated us like sons. Dad had a similar relationship with the girls. In contrast to my observations of the distance between Lawrence and Dad, my brothers and I consistently communicate and share time together. We have assumed the best of what Lawrence and Dad offered and taught us, melding into the strength of our brotherhood.

I was once involved with Dad in an incident where he expressed his frustration with Lawrence, alerting me to the dynamics of their business and personal lives. Dad and Mildred were friends in addition to being in-laws. He met Mildred when Lawrence and she dated in the late 1920s. Their relationship strengthened when they first moved to Elgin. He experienced the entrance of his three nieces into the family. Dad and Mildred shared common interests and talked about the business, their families, children, news, cleaning projects, and decorating. They developed friendship and understanding, bridging the families together with ideas and support. Mildred was like Dad's older sister.

The family became aware of Mildred's health situation in July 1966. I was pulling weeds and raking debris from the side driveway area planted with lilies of the valley when I heard the phones inside ring. I was customarily aware of the business phones ringing on summer days when the office door and some house windows were left open. Whenever a call came in, I heard and felt the vibrations of the pulsating phones on all three floors. The phone demanded to be answered within the first three rings. I raised my head and caught a glimpse of Dad opening the door of the car he'd just parked in the driveway. He sprung up the office porch steps.

Within a second or two, the ringing of the phone stopped. I kept raking, sweeping, and depositing debris into the bin positioned next to my work area. A few minutes later, Dad came out the office door and hurried over to me.

"I ran to the phone because I thought it might be Lawrence. He's been gone since yesterday. Or was it the day before? Who leaves town for a day or two or three and doesn't let us know where he's going? That's Bruhth. I am used to that."

Dad and Lawrence called each other "Bruhth," an intonation like the sound of the first syllable of "brother." Actually, all of the four O'Connor brothers referred to each other as "Bruhth." Their two sisters referred to each of them with the same nickname. When all the siblings came together, it was difficult to determine to whom one of them was referring when they mentioned, "Bruhth." Back to the story at hand.

Lawrence was independent, to a point of frustration regarding his departures from the house. Sometimes, he told Dad or Mildred he was going to get away for a day or two. Other times, he did not make any announcement before leaving. A phone call from him would come after the fact, announcing he was gone. Dad came to accept Lawrence's spontaneous departures as one aspect of their relationship. He truly didn't mind having sole responsibility. As well as they maintained the business, Dad perhaps relished the times he was not, as I heard him say, "under Lawrence's thumb."

Dad continued his story.

"The call was from your Aunt Cecil. It was a collect call. Of course, I accepted the charges. She and Mildred were on their way to Elgin from Dyer, Indiana, and stopped at the Hinsdale Oasis overpass on the tollway to eat. Mildred collapsed. An ambulance came to pick her up, and Aunt Cecil rode with her. She's now at Lutheran General Hospital in Park Ridge in the emergency room. Mildred is on a breathing machine. I'm driving to the hospital. I told George [a worker at the funeral home] I am leaving, but you know George will leave at five. It's two o'clock now."

"Is she okay?" I asked worriedly.

"I don't know. She said she wasn't feeling too good last week, but she wanted to be at Aunt Cecil's to help out after Uncle Mike's funeral. She thought maybe she wasn't feeling good because she quit smoking."

I think Mildred told Dad things she didn't tell Lawrence. The intricacy of her health situation may have been one of those instances. Dad and Mildred opened up to each other in ways they may have not to friends or family. Dad listened without judgment and offered advice when asked.

"I am worried about Mildred. She is all by herself. I'm going to the hospital in Park Ridge. I want you to stay in the house and listen for the phone. Kerry is upstairs. Let him know what is happening. Mom will be home around five. I called her and told her to come right home after work. If Lawrence calls, tell him where I went. Tell him to get to Lutheran General."

I started to put the rake and broom away under the porch.

"Leave those here outside on top of the flower bed. Get inside. When the phone rings, let George answer. I told him if Lawrence calls, he should find you or Kerry to talk to Lawrence. Do not answer the phone in Mildred's kitchen in case it's Maureen, Kathleen, or Sharon calling to say hi. I don't want them to know anything for now. Aunt Cecil said she will call them from the pay phone at the hospital. I'm leaving."

He slid into the driver's seat and backed quickly out of the driveway. Lawrence eventually called in, and we told him what happened and where Mildred was. He drove there from wherever he was. She remained at the hospital for at least a week. Maureen, Kathleen, and Sharon came to Division Street, and we all took turns visiting during her hospital stay.

Mildred was diagnosed with angina, a coronary disease where the arteries supplying blood to the heart are narrowed with a buildup of fat. Mildred told us later that she had felt pain in her shoulders, arms, and neck—some of the symptoms of angina. She tolerated the pain and kept busy in her activities to help Cecil. In 1966, few public service announcements or TV ads alerted people to the symptoms she was experiencing. There was limited access to the statins and medications available today.

When she arrived home on Division Street, a team of ambulance drivers, assisted by the family, positioned Mildred in a chair and carried her up the front steps to the second floor. She was instructed to restrict her movements and motions and not leave the apartment. Her daughters took turns assisting her. Some of their kids stayed in the house, too. Both apartments were full of activity.

The sounds of grandchildren added frivolity to the house, but Mildred was not permitted to get on the floor and play games with the kids. She took the prescribed medications and followed a diet absent of the knowledge and sophistication we now have. If the medical profession knew then what is known now, Mildred may have lived longer than the five years after her diagnosis.

Mildred resumed her real estate work and activities at home. She took short and long trips on her own and with Lawrence and friends. Dad kept himself aware of how she was doing. He made reference in a letter he wrote on November 12, 1970:

"Don't know what to think about Mildred, as she's had about three or four sick spells this past month. She went to Dr. Hoban last Thursday for her appointment, and he didn't put her into bed. She claims she gets these awful pains that tie her up for five to ten minutes and they go away. I've been with her at such times. Must be an ulcer cuz no one could survive that much heart attack and a lot of it could be nerves. The more one thinks about pain the worse it becomes. That would be the joy of Christian Science religion or belief that says there is no such thing as pain or doctors or medicine etc. Anyway, don't say anything in your tapes or letters unless she says something about being sick. The next day, she's at everything again, cooking, baking, and out in the car driving. She deserves a lot of credit for not lying around, complaining, or feeling sorry for herself. All for now. Have fun. See the world! It will be a long winter next year, but you'll have your tapes, letters, pictures, and memories. Love, D"

Dad and Mildred's closeness mitigated some of the tensions each of them experienced with Lawrence. They were allies, while not being adversarial to Lawrence. Mildred observed the manner in which Lawrence occasionally treated Dad as an employee. As the owner, Lawrence felt that he could make decisions independent of Dad, with an unspoken acknowledgment that Dad would take care of business when he was either spontaneously absent or had planned in advance.

Lawrence was attentive to Mildred as her health encountered more negative turns. Sometimes when there is tension in a family, people tell me there is an atmosphere akin to walking on eggshells. This wasn't the case. The tension between Dad and Lawrence was not discussed by them. They communicated enough to maintain the business. For me, the tension was conveyed in the lack of warmth between them in contrast to the ready communication and hugs between Dad and Mildred. Where was Mom in the mix of these everyday proceedings? She was not just an observer. She and Dad talked often. She checked in on Mildred and maintained a supportive relationship. She didn't ignore Lawrence. Reflecting on this many years later, the interplay of the adults was tethered on their reaction or lack of reaction to Lawrence's control. The dynamics and interplay between the four adults did work to maintain our joint households and the business.

CHAPTER 21

Student Unrest Becomes Personal

Connecting our family to politics referenced by presidential terms, Uncle Lawrence and Mildred were born during Teddy Roosevelt's presidency. Dad was born when William Howard Taft was president and Mom during the presidency of Woodrow Wilson. When the four of them attended elementary and high school, Taft, Warren Harding, Calvin Coolidge, Herbert Hoover, and Franklin Roosevelt served their terms. Lawrence and Mildred's marriage, the start of the business in Elgin, and Maureen and Kathleen's births happened during the Hoover presidency. Mom and Dad's wedding, and the births of Sharon and Barrett came during the first and second terms of FDR. Kerry and I came along during the Truman years. In the years after Truman, the births among our extended offspring continue through these Biden years.

The presidential practices and programs of administrations influenced the lives of our family. I became politically interested as a six-year-old watching the Democratic and Republican conventions on the second- or third-floor TVs. During those two weeks in the summer of 1956, the adults watched as President Eisenhower was redesignated as the GOP nominee and Adlai Stevenson from Illinois was nominated by the Democrats as his challenger. Four years later, my interest intensified. I was intrigued with John Kennedy. As in 1956, the conventions on TV stayed on into the night. I fell asleep long before the broadcasts ended.

I was in fifth grade when the campaigns went into full swing after Labor Day. Kennedy made a stop in Elgin, but we stayed in school. I wonder now why the teachers didn't walk us the three blocks to downtown to see him speak. One of my teachers, Sister Marlene, wore a Nixon button. Her influence may have something to do with why we stayed in our classroom. David Carey was my other teacher in fifth grade and also the following school year. He made references in class about his Democratic Party affiliations. Through his influence, I became increasingly interested in Kennedy and other Democratic candidates in state and local elections. Mom and Dad encouraged my interest and gave permission to Mr. Carey to show me the Elgin Democratic Headquarters and accompany him to some political events. On the morning of Kennedy's inauguration on January 20, 1961, Dad and Mom allowed us a morning absence from school to watch the event on TV. Dad wrote notes to give to our teachers when we walked to school for the afternoon. He wrote about the importance for us to watch history.

Other than their support for my interest and watching the conventions and daily election updates on TV, minimal political banter or discussion happened in the house. My parents, Lawrence, and Mildred were not outwardly involved in politics. This may have been due to the business. Conveying clarity about their support for a party or candidate may have influenced potential clients not to patronize the funeral home. In contrast, their interest in candidates may have influenced potential clients to use our services. Hard to say.

After Kennedy was elected, comedian Vaughn Meador and his colleagues created a humorous recorded portrayal of the Kennedy family and Presidential cabinet. The record album was ranked #1 in sales. Our family listened to the recording and laughed out loud. I assume the voters in our house supported the first Catholic president. Beyond the 1960 election, they declared few preferences.

My parents' encouragement coupled with Mr. Carey's influence led me to any class connected with government studies. Civics was my favorite class in eighth grade. I was president in the class of twenty-four students. I do not recall how the vote was conducted. Nor do I recall my responsibilities, if any. I stayed active in student government through high school.

In the first six months of 1968, my senior year, the political climate was in upheaval. Lyndon Johnson announced in March he was not seeking reelection. This decision was based partly on US involvement in the Vietnam War. Additionally, two Democrat Party Presidential contenders, Senators Eugene McCarthy and Robert Kennedy had gained in their challenge to Johnson. On April 4, Martin Luther King was assassinated. Protests erupted across the country. Kennedy was shot on June 5, 1968. He died the next day.

The Democratic National Convention was planned for August 26–29 at the International Amphitheatre in Chicago. I was accepted to do volunteer work as a clerk within the convention hall. As the months and weeks of the convention approached, groups opposed to the war announced plans to protest during the convention. Although working at the convention fit into my own political interests and aspirations, Dad and Mom told me I was not to take part in the work. My challenges to them did not sway their thinking.

Most of the news of the convention focused on the activities and protests outside the Amphitheatre and not the proceedings happening inside. Groups such as Students for a Democratic Society (SDS), the Chicago 7, and others claimed responsibility for the protests. Protestors chanted, "The whole world is watching," as confrontations occurred with the Chicago police. The street scenes were broadcast side by side with video and pictures of Mayor Richard

Daley yelling at TV cameras inside the convention. There was division among people about the war, civil rights, and the actions of the police. These divisions were similar to what has been happening currently in the country with disagreements about demonstrator and police behaviors.

The convention nominated Hubert Humphrey, Johnson's vice president. He was defeated in the November election by Richard Nixon, which was unacceptable to me. I was in my first freshman semester at Loyola. The voting age in the US was twenty-one. My voting voice was yet to be acknowledged. I was elected Freshman Class President in September. I was zealous during the campaign. When Nixon won the election, I felt a disenchantment with politics. I lessened my attendance and participation at meetings.

As the allure of student government waned in the remainder of my freshman year and continued into my sophomore year, my political interest continued to be fired by my opposition to the United States' involvement in Vietnam. One of my favorite instructors at Loyola, Mr. Greenwald, was suddenly not present for class one day. Rather than be drafted, he declared himself a conscientious objector and moved to Canada.

I became involved in the student movement at Loyola as an editor for the university newspaper. I was concerned about the welfare of my friends being drafted and sent to military action. Although I understand the purpose of World Wars I and II, I've never been one to believe war or militarization serves much purpose.

I became more outspoken in writings to Mom and Dad about my feelings regarding the war and the Nixon administration through my involvement with the newspaper and interactions with other students on campus. My relationship with Mom started to show stress in February 1970. She and I came head-to-head in phone conversations as well as our letters. Dad kept a neutral position with me although I know he and Mom talked about the stress of what was happening. Our letters conveyed our differing opinions. In a letter dated February 18, 1970, she wrote:

"Read your letter and well said. I am sure the generation gap is getting wider, and that is good. No doubt when I was a child (I was once) I didn't agree with my folks. In fact, I was probably the most obstinate of all three of us, but that is in the past, and now we are the older generation. I could argue with you, and maybe someday when you are home, you can tell me more of what is wrong with the people our age. But I want you to think of the school you are attending, the things you have always had, and remember that it is people our age who gave them to you. Your group is smart, and you will probably do great things too, but not with dope, taking the law into your own hands, and always wanting to do just as you darn please ["not you" handwritten in the margin of her typed letter]. Our laws, some of them, probably should be revised, but we must have them, and they must all be obeyed. The trial in Chicago was trying to change all that, and they did their best to make a mockery of our judicial system … Enough said … [She types inquiry about what is happening with my driver's license renewal and then continues with her commentary.] Was just rereading the first paragraph, and believe me, Kevin, I wasn't referring to you about breaking the law, taking dope, etc. We have and are sure will always be proud of you and your ideas. We can be proud of the young people who are doing something about pollution and housing and all those other things that we have neglected. I am sure you wouldn't want Dad and me to change and to act like your generation or to have the same ideas because if we did, Dad wouldn't have a job because Lawrence wouldn't have him around. And if I expressed myself at work, like the people you saw in *Hair*, I, too, would lose my job. That would be sad, as you and Kerry would then have to quit school and go to work. Mom"

Dad, Mom, Lawrence, and Mildred lived through World Wars I and II. Perhaps, they favored our country's participation in international conflicts.

Those of our generation, without the earlier generation's experiences with war, displayed less support for the war in Southeast Asia. Student unrest continued throughout the country. At a rally held on May 4, 1970, at Kent State University in Ohio, police fired gunshots, killing four students. A movement began to call for student strikes throughout the country. As was customary, I called Mom and/or Dad two to three times a week. Many of the calls made to Mom at work came through her WATTS line, a way to make long-distance calls from Chicago to Elgin without being charged for the call. I was honest with Mom about what I was doing. On some occasions, she hung up the phone. This was the first time I felt rancor with her.

After we had spoken in a phone conversation on Sunday, May 10, 1970, I wrote a letter in green ballpoint ink on both sides of fourteen half sheets of typing paper. My letter included the following excerpts:

"Dear Marion and Bill [intentional salutation, not Dear Mom and Dad. I now recognize this as a bit of adolescent disrespect]:

Have just returned to my room after our vocal confrontation of an hour ago. To tell you the truth, I put off making that call. I wanted to wish you a Happy Mother's Day, but I knew what would follow. Mom, you're the only person that really ever causes me to argue. That's why I called Dad on Friday and why I asked Dad to come to the phone tonight. I can talk to him, explain my stand, and then he offers his comments. Mom, you fly off the handle when anything the least bit distasteful to you is mentioned.

Mom, you said you can't figure out why after being so seemingly happy for so long, I changed so much. I am changing. I won't say I'm content, but that all has to do with the change that's going on within me and around me. Our society is perhaps going through one of the biggest changes it has in a long time. The war, pornography, films, and sexual mores have brought on new ideas concerning freedom, morality, and reality.

So, too, with the strike. It's part of a change in ideas. Last Wednesday night, there were close to 1,500–2,000 kids in the union when we decided to march to the Broadway Armory seven blocks away. I decided that by going, I could answer a few questions for myself. I'd be running away from making any kind of decision if I didn't try to see both sides. If I remember nothing else about what you did for me, I'll remember Dad telling me not to run away. Just ask questions, try to explain yourself. That's why I went Wednesday night. I'm really glad I did. There's nothing more 'impressive' than seeing a fifty-year-old man drive by on Sheridan Road, roll down his window and yell, 'You dirty fuckin' college kids.' Or seeing people throw firecrackers and water balloons from the high rises. Even more impressive is seeing all the kids keep their cool. Just keep marching PEACEFULLY because if nothing else has been stressed, it's that violence will do no good at all.

That's what Wednesday night taught me. Thursday, I had thoughts I would study, but I ended up talking to kids and adults all day trying to formulate ideas of my own. There was all kinds of talk about what was to happen, and I began getting a little scared. Not because I was afraid of violence, but I could tell there were some big changes taking place, and I was right in the middle. At four o'clock I began leafletting at the L station on Sheridan. For the first time, I was sure that the strike might be of some value. People came off the buses and trains, took the flyers, and talked. The flyers explained our stand and invited people to come to a rally on Thursday night in the gym. One lady came up to me. She was about sixty or so and said she was behind us all the way. She saw the strike as the first constructive, positive denial of the legality and reasoning of the war. I've seen and talked to her at the rallies and Masses held in chapels and gyms. She plays cards and plants small vegetable gardens and has grandchildren who she cares for just as much as you care for yours.

Thursday night I went to the rally at the gym. There were 500 chairs, and they were filled. There were about 2,000 students in the gym. Ideas were presented by various speakers. Many of the ideas were given ovations by the students. Not many of the older people stood up and cheered like the students did. They had questions and came looking for answers. One woman stood up and spoke. She had a thirty-year-old son and an eighteen-year-old son (sound familiar?). She could see the strike as necessary to get some answers and to try to get some commitment from the nation. For so long, the nation has complained but never done anything. This is the first time that there was nationwide support (50–60 percent of all American universities observe the strike) and 'togetherness.' Nobody was worried about race or ethnicity or clothes or hair. We all cared about our future, young and old people alike. Together we could work to do something about the war. So, this woman stressed the point of informing and educating the community.

The walk to Northwestern was now planned for the next day. Friday, I went to Mass on the steps of Mertz Hall. When crisis strikes, Mass means so much more than the 'have to' clause for Sundays. I guess this non-meaning is what keeps me from Mass on Sundays. After Mass, I went to another meeting. The big question was whether to march to Northwestern or not. The leader of the Northwestern movement came to talk to us. There would be no violence and police escorts would be available. That made me feel a lot better. The rally began at Loyola at 1:00 p.m. with students from other colleges and high schools. By 2:30 p.m. there were close to 5,000 on the field. I'll never forget that march. I went because I wanted answers. The march and rally at Dyche Stadium would hopefully give me the answers. The walk along Sheridan Road was impressive. Neighbors looked from windows. Some met us with water. There were police at every corner and student marshals on the periphery of the marchers. As we approached Evanston, the Northwestern students marched with us. We were now close to 10,000 strong. We got to Dyche and sat on the football field. We listened to speaker after speaker present his or her side. I stayed until about 7:30 p.m. and came home, got a few more answers, and became more committed.

I came back and watched the Nixon conference and news. What impressed me about the news was the scene on Wall Street where the students were demonstrating quite peacefully until a group of construction workers broke through the police lines and beat the students to the point where students couldn't do anything. Do you call this a victory for your generation? After seeing that and remembering back to Thursday night when the man screamed at us from his car and we were showered with water and firecrackers from the apartment buildings, I just wonder who incites the riots? It would have taken just one more firecracker for one impulsive student to touch off a melee. That might have caused all kinds of violence. Perhaps if your generation would have a little more respect for the freedom to assemble and dissent, there would be no violence.

There is something about the past five days that has made me want to learn. It's really a wonderful feeling to want to learn without worrying about a grade. Wednesday, Thursday, and Friday became my education. I learned more there than I ever could have learned in a book. I learned a lot about myself. Am I willing to lay my grades, a semester's work, a future on the line for something I feel to be unjust and unfair? I learned how to deal with people and how to accept each other and every one of their ideas and think it out and apply it to my own philosophy. One of the more important things I learned was to learn to deal with change and that it is up to me to decide to accept change or deny it. Somebody put it well today: 'Your conviction to your ideas may lose friends, but it gains them, too.'

I can now see importance in the strike. Education is when you learn to apply what you learn in the classroom to the world outside the textbook. It might even hurt because it causes you to think and decide. The strike may not end the war. We are just trying to let people (that's you) know why, what, and for what reasons we feel the war isn't quite necessary. Part of our education is accepting your opinion, and who knows, we just might change our minds. So might you. The strike is a different kind of education. It's a strike against 'business as usual.' The education is switched from campus to community. We've got to learn. You've got to learn. Everyone must learn what the war is about. The strike is intended to INFORM because so many people are unaware of what goes on or why we are doing what we are. Sure, Nixon wants to end the war. Once again, his political career is crumbling and that's happened to him more than once already in his life. Maybe he can end the war in eight weeks, but that isn't any reason to quit striking.

People are talking again. People seem to care. People are coming together. A teacher friend of mine said that for once, many of the teachers are beginning to see that they think a lot like the students. A gap is being closed and trust, a virtue sorely needed in our society, is being received. The strike is providing the learning, the interest, and concern that was perhaps lacking among many people.

So now to bring this down to a more personal level. Mom, you sounded disappointed in me, really upset. You probably just don't understand me any more than I can understand you. At Mass tonight, the priest brought up the point that no mother has ever understood her children. Mary never understood Christ, but she gave him a pat on the back when he needed it.

I would hope you wouldn't be disappointed in me. If you think you failed in any way, you're wrong. You shouldn't be disappointed in me. You would if I was going along with the crowd, not knowing or having any idea what I was doing. But if college has taught me nothing else, it's to make my own decisions. I'm doing the best I can with this life. I have no idea about my future, but I'm willing to try new things to find a purpose in life.

You called me immature. If I was immature, I'd be running to you constantly for advice, asking for money and maybe sympathy. Maybe I'm still too young to be utterly independent, but I know I'm sensible and rational to stand on my own two feet. I may be disappointing to you, but you'd be even more disappointing to me if I knew you weren't trying to find some answers because no matter if you're twenty or fifty-six, every day becomes an education. I hope you and your friends and my relatives won't respect me any less for trying to come to a self-concept.

So, tomorrow is Monday. The strike is optional for students who want to continue. As I told you before, I'm not sure of what I'm going to do. I'll go to classes tomorrow to try and get some things straightened out to see where the teachers and I stand. I just wanted you to know what's been going on in my mind the past few days. I just want you to know how and why I feel because I know you care. See you in a few weeks. Kevin"

The next morning I added the following to my letter, prior to mailing:

"It's now Monday at 5:30 p.m. I'm really confused now. The students had a 12:00 p.m. meeting. About 2,000–3,000 kids were there. Everything was clarified about the status of classes. I had two classes today. I can get out of both of those with B's. The classes will still be conducted but more on a basis of what's going on now. All discussion will be centered on the strike and its implications. The administration has decided to back us, admitting that after what's gone on, the university will not be the same. Teachers and students are to meet and decide what to do in each individual situation. At the second student meeting, some students felt that this partial strike wouldn't be effective enough. So tomorrow, even after the students voted to have the partial strike, there's a group of kids who desire the full strike. So, they're going to sit in at Damen Hall and try to convince kids not to go to class. Wednesday there are both faculty and student meetings, and more will be decided and voted upon. As I said in the original letter, things are changing from day to day. But the change is important if it progresses to some conceivable end. I can't say at all how I'll feel twenty-four hours from now."

Mom was typing a letter on her company letterhead from work on May 11, 1970, a few hours after I wrote the letter that I had yet to send. Unbeknownst to either, we were corresponding simultaneously. She typed:

"Kevin, about all this student dissent. If I said I agreed with everything, then I would be a hypocrite. I do believe you kids have a point, but you are sure going about it the wrong way. You have so much to lose and so little to gain. Of all the kids I have talked to (you included), you can't say what you want. Yes, I know to end the war, pollution, and overpopulation can't be done overnite. Kevin, take a good long look at your leaders. Make sure you are following the type of people you can look up to. Don't become just one of the crowd. I would like to come in for one of your rallies. Let us know when. Oh, with all the extra work, they finally gave me a raise. Love, Mom"

On the morning of the student march to Northwestern, I called and spoke to Dad. He asked if I still planned to march.

"Yes," I answered.

Dad responded. "I understand what you are doing. Mom and I are both worried. We know what happened at Kent State, and we ache so much for the parents and families of those kids. Be careful. Be safe. Call when you can. I do love you."

I hung up the phone with a feeling of relief yet regret knowing that Mom was not as supportive as Dad. On the other hand, I was enthralled with the feeling of independence and declaration of who I was. Dad mailed a note card dated May 12, 1970, with this handwritten commentary:

"Dear Kevin, If you were at 10 p.m. Mass Sunday, they may not have used the same Communion verse as we did at 10 a.m. Mass. I'm sure it went over many peoples' heads, but it hit me right between the eyes. Look it up in your church readings for May 10, 7th Sunday after Easter (I brought the book home!): "People: Father, while I was with them, I kept them whom you have given me, alleluia. But now I am coming to you. I do not pray that you take them out of the world but that you keep them from evil, alleluia, alleluia."

There was no further writing from Dad. I know he cared not only about me. He cared about Mom, too. My letter adolescently juxtaposed the feelings for him and for Mom. Fifty years later in reading it, I know how my words doubtlessly hurt both of them with my youthful petulance. He wished me no harm. He expressed his love.

In a later typed note dated May 14, 1970, after Mom received my long letter, she responded:

"Dear Kevin, So sorry about everything. Sure hope you stay safe and get all your answers. We will be gone all weekend. Marion (a.k.a. Mom). P.S. This sounds like I don't care. I do and did read everything you sent."

I get tears in my eyes when I read and re-read Mom's words. The tears are from the recollections of the strife experienced on campus with my friends, the remembrances of conversations between my friends and their parents, and the way so many verbal and written expressions were charged with emotion and immediacy.

The tensions in the country, combined with the conflicts in our writing and discussions, embedded context for an incident with Kerry, Mom, and me. In the summer of 1970, Kerry and I worked at a manufacturing facility near the offices where Mom was employed. Mom drove us to work in the morning and picked us up in the afternoon. It was about a fifteen-minute drive from our eastside Elgin home to the southwest side of Elgin. During one after-work trip to a Piggly Wiggly grocery store parking lot, the words and tensions of our discussion escalated as quickly as a fan's excitement when a successful three-pointer by Michael Jordan vaulted the previously losing Bulls to a game buzzer victory. "Fuck" was uttered by either Kerry or me in the discussion we were having with Mom. She vehemently let us know of her disapproval. She pulled the car into the parking lot and slammed the door with the force of a Muhammad Ali punch. Hard. Deliberate. She marched into the store. Kerry and I may have considered joining her in the store. We both, without speaking to one another, remained in the car. I do recall laughing a bit. We dismissed the laughter when she returned to the car and drove in silence on the ten-minute ride home.

In a letter Mom wrote on March 10, 1971, as a follow-up to a tape I had recorded and sent to the family, she remarked: "I laughed when you mentioned the episode in the grocery store parking lot, as I have certainly never forgotten it and never will. But I had never told Dad anything about it and he wondered what you were talking about. So, after your tape was finished, I told him. He laughed and thought it was funny. Maybe it is now, but it wasn't then."

Dad was writing a letter on the same date and same time as Mom's letter and commented:

"Mother and I listened to your latest 'joyous' tape last night in bed and sure enjoyed it. This morning I am getting ready for a 1 p.m. funeral, and I sure have laughed because last night was the first time I had heard the four-letter word story at Piggly Wiggly, and I roar when I picture the scene between you three. Love being your father, Dad"

Mildred partially conveyed her political thinking in a letter typed January 9, 1971, on thin onion skin typing paper (using both sides):

"Did you hear from anyone about the retired former judge? On December 15, he was arrested and released on bond because it had come to light that he had helped himself to a check for $12,000, which wasn't his. I guess in his retirement he has practiced law and was the lawyer for a couple getting a divorce. The man in the case had given him a check for $12,000, which he was to turn over to the man's wife, but when she didn't receive it, though it had been cashed (forged), the judge was arrested. In an article in the newspaper a couple of nights ago, the reporter wrote he admitted his guilt and made restitution, but of course his license was revoked. I really feel sorry for him and his family, as Kathleen said when she was working for him, he more or less robbed Peter to pay Paul, but I guess this time he couldn't repay Peter. Maybe I am just naïve, but I sorta think he really wasn't a thief, or he couldn't have practiced for thirty-eight years without getting caught. He was so active in Boy Scouts and many civic affairs, it seems a shame to have this spoil his reputation. That, coupled with our deceased Secretary of State Paul Powell scandal, is quite sickening. Maybe you've read since Powell's death, about a million and a half dollars (in cash) has been found stashed in shoeboxes, evidently to avoid taxes. Don't you think you are aspiring to the wrong business?" [I was a political science major with aspirations to be involved in politics.]

I wrote to Dad and Mom sometime in May 1973 as the story of the Watergate break-in was unfolding. I was finishing my first year as a resident of San Francisco and making plans to attend UC Berkeley in August:

"What do you think of Watergate? I thought Nixon's speech really avoided the issue, but at the same time, I don't think he really knew that much about it. It was just all those guys under him trying to make a bigger and better impression to get a bigger piece of the pie. It will be interesting to see how it turns out . . . to see what the press itself has blown up, who was framed, what was framed. It's a scar, and I can't help but believe that it really all occurred, but I still think there are a lot of implications that have yet to be uncovered."

Two months later on July 25, 1973, Mom referred to what was unfolding regarding Nixon and Watergate:

"Big question. Who is lying in the Watergate deal? Have you been watching? I do like Senator Ervin and really think he is the most honest of the whole bunch. He is too old to have political ambitions, so maybe he will keep pursuing til he gets the whole truth. Just heard on the radio that Nixon won't give up the tapes."

She was referring to the hearings occurring in the US Senate. During the next year, the tapes were released and implicated Nixon. Journalists Carl Bernstein and Bob Woodward investigated the story, connecting the break-in of the Democratic Party offices directly to Nixon. Their reporting led to a book and movie adaptation entitled *All the President's Men*, released in 1976 starring Dustin Hoffman and Robert Redford. I invite you to read this book and watch the movie.

Although political party preferences were not readily acknowledged within the personal and professional lives of the Division Street funeral home during most of my childhood, the continual influx of newspapers, magazines, TV news, and radio programming provided the influence to nurture an interest in political affairs that I continue to maintain. Political stresses in the family prior to my birth are unknown to me. I am grateful to the objective atmosphere provided by my parents that allowed discussion. The turmoil of the '60s and 70s brought our differences to an apex that was resolved with time. The political communication between Mom and me was positive in tone in 1973 compared to 1970. I am grateful for the next thirty-seven years until her death, when we captured opportunities to discuss political topics objectively and understandably. She told me she voted for Clinton in 1992 and 1996. She was a Hillary supporter in 2008 and then voted for Obama.

I encourage offspring to remain open to ideological ideas that are every bit as challenging as earlier turbulent times. I continue to seek to understand.

CHAPTER 22

Togetherness: Reflections from Maureen, Kathleen, and Sharon

This chapter provides a closing to this part of the book about how our two families carried on lives together in a living situation perhaps considered by some as unusual. Our success at togetherness was summarized best in writings by Maureen, Kathleen, and Sharon.

My brothers and I planned a surprise party for Dad and Mom's fortieth anniversary held on Memorial Day weekend in 1979. When we mailed the invitations, we provided a piece of paper and a self-addressed stamped envelope to the invitees for them to write a recollection of Dad and Mom. We included the responses in a book we gave them at the party.

185

Maureen, Kathleen, and Sharon each wrote on behalf of their own families. Their writing conveys much about our life together as one joined family on Division Street:

MAUREEN: "Forty years is a long time for memories, however—an extra set of parents—three 'brothers'—a godfather and 'tattler of my youthful indiscretions—borrowing up and down—a wedding without a hitch—rhubarb pie and Heath bar cake—a round kitchen table and a milk jug bought in Delaware—a Clinton, Iowa weekend—"Chloe and My Hero"—much talking over a glass of wine—moving a chair an 'nth of an inch—godparents to Anne—stretching clotheslines in the back yard—piano music—parties—never an empty house and—and . . . Love, Maureen, Bill, Kathy, Eileen, Mary, Anne, Michael, and David"

KATHLEEN: "There are of course many memories. As a 'child' I can recall Dad yelling 'Virg' in the a.m.—can recall baking cookies with Kevin and Kerry and taking Kevin on a trip to North Carolina and visiting Kerry at St. Joe's when he was in a cast—he always smiled for me! I can recall Mother taking me to the hospital to see Barrett—telling the head nun I was sixteen (I was twelve and chubby!). Now since living far away and being married, I vividly recall "Mr. Goodbar" on a trip to Elgin and especially with your family and my own. I especially recall BOSTON and Barrett and Pat's—locking ourselves in Kendall's at night—nice tour of the plant!—a trip through downtown Boston—losing and finding Erin and returning home to celebrate with four gallons of 'wine tasting' (who bought the best wine?), a ziti dinner and Ping-Pong til around 3 a.m.—kids n' all. Much fun and laughter! Love for a lot more. Kathleen, Frank, Stephen, Lisa, Jim, Anne, John, and Vincent (should you forget names!)"

SHARON: "I was asked to put on a sheet an event or two that I specifically remember of shared memories or events. How can I do that when your marriage has been almost as long as my life? I distinctly remember:

- Bill's spontaneous organ playing, which brightened many quiet hours.
- Helping Bill move furniture whenever he had a whim 'to change things.'
- Babysitting with Barrett during the long-awaited birth of Kevin.
- Trying to plant grass with Marion in a mutual attempt to be creative.
- Helping Marion rescue Kevin and Kerry from the third-story pigeon coop in the barn.
- Sharing worry over the disappearance of Checkers.
- Sharing the worry over Kerry's broken leg and Barrett's accident.
- Christmases, weddings, and lots of 'good party times.'
- And, especially, just a lifetime of borrowing and sharing and consistent respect for privacy that miraculously always existed between the second and third floor of 364.

So—please—accept my thanks for a wealth of 'things' too numerous to mention . . . for providing me with three handsome 'almost brothers' . . . .

And thanks for providing me with many of the shared good times . . . .

And for being there to give me much needed support though many of our shared bad times.

Happy Anniversary. I hope you have at least 140 more.

Lots of love, John and Sharon, Lynn, Shannon, and Scott"

Many of the events about which they wrote are referenced in prior chapters or chapters to come. I purposefully didn't explain their words or phrases. I intend for you readers to interpret a sense of two families as one.

PART IV

THE CALLING, CRAFT, AND SERVITUDE OF THE MORTUARY BUSINESS

Fifty-four is the number of years (1930–84) the family business existed at the Villa Street and Division Street locations. After Lawrence's purchase of the Division Street house and the work he, Dad, Mildred, and Mom put in to create business and living spaces, they attuned themselves to the clients with whom they worked. They showcased their personalities of care and empathy. Their business started in a funeral home industry experiencing changes in customs and traditions. Fewer families were choosing to have funeral services in their own homes. They found it convenient to be assisted in a "funeral home," where undertakers conducted the proceedings. I assume families made this decision to remove their own home from the physical aspects of grieving.

In the first ten to fifteen years of the business, Lawrence and Dad did conduct some funerals in family homes. They prepared the body using the preparation facilities at the funeral home. The coffin with body was driven to the family's home. Dad and Lawrence cleared a space to display the casket. They set up lighting and floral arrangements. They acted as the host in their client's homes as the family attended to those coming to pay respects.

Viewing their work retrospectively, whether done in families' homes or the parlors of the funeral home, I realize Dad and Lawrence wanted to help families transition through the death and services and into lives after the rituals. Their attention was on the survivors referred to in obituaries. They relegated their own emotional needs to a secondary position to devote themselves fully to the grieving families.

Like other public service workers, their work was done beyond a desire for income. The business sometimes lost money. Our families made sacrifices when the business was not providing income. We lived simply.

To support our living arrangements, each of us played a part in maintaining the structure of the house, the landscaping, and the overall operation of the business. As children we made expected contributions, completing the jobs assigned to us and tasks we took on ourselves. Our uniqueness as funeral home children separated us from the jobs done by our friends. We took out the garbage, walked the dog, and pulled weeds like most of our peers in their homes. We also folded the sheets for the ambulance, vacuumed flower petals from the back of the hearse, and were reminded that our presence in our school, social, and work activities had the potential to reflect positively or negatively on the business. We were responsible ambassadors.

Dad, Lawrence, Mildred, and Mom intertwined their personal and business lives, demonstrating an awareness to my cousins, brothers, and me of how a funeral home business was maintained. I learned lessons of servitude and sacrifice that I carried with me through my part-time jobs, educational career, and volunteer activities. I received a foundation proven to be as strong as the ashlar stone that supported the structure of the house on Division Street.

CHAPTER 23

Casket Experiences: Lifting, Rolling, Pushing

Within the Division Street house, the topic of caskets, an essential part of the business, was difficult to avoid. Lawrence and Dad ordered caskets as needed. Upon arrival, they positioned them in the casket display room. When families came to make arrangements, Dad or Lawrence guided them from the office area to a winding open staircase in the front foyer accented by an expansive half-moon window. The stairs led to the casket room. The family of the deceased was not aware of doorways connecting to other areas of the basement, as Dad and Lawrence installed floor-length, dark drapes to conceal these doorways and the pointy edges of the rock foundation wall.

The lighting from the ceiling, wall, and floor lamps cast a mix of soft hues highlighting the features of both the inside and outside of the dozen caskets on display. When a client entered this room, Dad or Lawrence guided them in choosing a casket suited to their situation and price. If a family did not care for the caskets on display, Dad made calls to Elgin undertakers or casket suppliers to determine options for the family. Plans were then made to have it delivered in time for the wake and funeral.

Once a body was embalmed and dressed, it was placed in the casket chosen by the family. First, the casket was wheeled next to the white porcelain preparation table where the body was laying. If the body was under a hundred pounds or so, Dad or Lawrence alone maneuvered the body into the casket. When the body was heavier, an additional person helped facilitate the process.

Getting the body into the casket was just one of the tasks. The weight of the casket with the body inside ranged anywhere from 100–300 pounds or more depending on the size of the corpse. Two or more people were needed to carry the casket from the basement to the first-floor parlor. It was essential not to dent or scratch the casket as it traveled. Once the casket arrived on the first floor, they placed it on a wheeled cart and moved it to a display area in one of the parlors. The actual display area varied. If they knew the visitation or wake was predicted to have a large attendance, they placed the casket in front of the window in the main parlor. If they predicted the attendance to be lower, they placed the casket in a different location to create a more intimate setting for the family.

In the late 1950s, Dad and Lawrence worked with contractors to install a casket lift to ease the process of getting the body and casket from the basement to the first floor. It was an eight-by-four-foot platform built on top of a motorized system like an elevator. This lift was constructed above the steps of the outside entrance to the basement. The contractor designed the lift with three levels on which to stop for entrance and exit. The middle level was at the ground level with a door to the back driveway area. When a body came to the funeral home in a hearse or similar vehicle, a wheeled gurney was rolled off the back door of the hearse and onto the lift. Using a control facilitated by a levered handle, the lift was powered down to the basement level where the gurney with the body was wheeled into the preparation room.

When it was time to move the body and casket to the first-floor level, stairs no longer needed to be used. The casket with body was placed on a wheeled cart and pushed onto the lift. Dad positioned himself on the lift to control the motor. This control handle was nearest to the outside door. Lawrence fit on the opposite end of the lift when a casket or gurney was on board. There was no room for a person to stand alongside the casket. The width of the lift platform was barely wide enough for the casket.

Once the casket was placed on the lift, Dad controlled the lever handle. He went past the level of the outside entrance and up to the next and highest level. This level was approximately eight steps higher than the outside/driveway entrance. A double-door wide entrance was cut into the side of the house. Once the lift reached there, the wheels of the casket cart or gurney became flush with the floor level of the back parlor. Dad or Lawrence or both of them wheeled the casket from the lift to the parlor where it was placed. Dad and Lawrence were understandably elated with the installation of this lift. It was now much easier to move the caskets from floor to floor.

The casket lift also provided Kerry and I with some adventures. At an age probably younger than ten, Dad allowed us to take the controls. We helped with wheeling the caskets onto the lift and taking them up to the first floor. As we got older, we helped when a body came into the funeral home or when furniture or supplies needed to be moved. In the absence of bodies, caskets, and furniture, we played or practiced our control skills. These sessions happened with or without Dad and Lawrence's knowledge. We heard and often ignored requests like, "Do not play on the casket lift." Neither Kerry nor I dabbled in employment as elevator operators. But based on our experiences, we were qualified.

CHAPTER 24

Always Ready for the Next Funeral

Living in a house used by the public, as well as providing a home for two families, presented unique challenges for upkeep and updating.

Consider the foot traffic. Dad and Lawrence knew the business thrived nicely with about fifty funerals a year. Ten or less people attended some wakes. Other wakes had a turnout of five hundred or more. The average number of attendees in a year's time was somewhere around 12,500.

How many of you have 12,500 visitors to your house any given year?

Overall, Dad and Lawrence took the responsibilities for cleanup. After a funeral, they returned the parlors to readiness for whenever the next funeral was to occur. Sometimes, there was a stretch of days without funerals. Or they may have conducted five or more funerals in a given week. Regardless, it was necessary to have the parlors ready for whatever came next.

When there was a break between wakes, they folded chairs and stacked them against the walls or in closets. They dismantled flower stands and stored them in the closets along with the casket trucks (the wheeled platform/cart on which the caskets had been placed).

They used a heavy commercial vacuum manufactured in the 1940s or '50s. As elementary students, Kerry and I pushed it using both hands. In addition to this task, we dusted the tables and mantles. Dad instructed us to put lemon oil on a cloth and wipe the woodwork. The smell of lemons still takes me back to this chore. We didn't get paid or receive an allowance. When we told them we had places to go and friends to play with, they let us go.

Mildred and Mom did not clean the funeral home. Not at all. Dad was the one of the four parents who crossed over from business to apartment cleaning. This was especially true when Mom started working outside our home. Dad was fastidious with decorating, design, and housework. He left his mark on the funeral home areas with continual cleaning and keeping all the hung artwork, sculptures, and other decorative elements in order. He knew to be ready when a death and ensuing funeral occurred. Later, when business allowed additional financial resources, he hired two employees—Mabel and her sister, Maude—to spend a full day once a week to keep everything in order.

Cleaning was one essential aspect of the business. The business phone was also necessary to initiate and maintain contact with families, the community, service organizations, police departments, and government offices. Because the business was ultimately concerned with helping others during the time of someone's death, sickness, or injury, the adults at home gave their immediate attention to each incoming call.

In the initial years of the Villa Street location and later on Division Street, there was one line for the business phone. The number was 1400. The phone book listing for the second-floor kitchen was 6242. The third floor was 7682. Each of those numbers connected to a party line. Phones at that time did not have dials, buttons, or a keypad. When a phone was answered by someone in the house, the voice of an operator announced, "You have a call from" and she indicated the number of the caller. When Dad or anyone in the house wanted to make a call, they picked up the receiver. A signal was received by an operator, letting her know Dad wanted to make a call. The operator identified Dad by name. He asked the operator to be connected to a particular name and number. The operator put Dad's call "through" to the recipient he intended to reach.

This process continued until a dial system was instituted in the mid-1950s.

Dad and Lawrence installed business phone extensions throughout the house for ready access. In the basement, a phone was located on the outside wall of the preparation room. The first-floor phone was on the desk in the office. The second-floor phone extension was located at a counter below a window in the hallway dining area near the top of front stairs. The third-floor phone resided on a table in the living room near the door to Dad and Mom's bedroom. As phone systems improved, Dad and Lawrence added extensions throughout the house and in the front entrance and lower level of the new addition to the funeral home. The newer models of the phones came with two multiple lines. When Dad was talking on the 1400 line, an incoming call rang on the second line designated as 1401, allowing one to put the current call on hold with the push of a button and answer the incoming line.

We had numerous phone extensions throughout the house. A phone was always within 10–20 steps. If any of us found ourselves on the toilet while assigned to phone duty when the phone rang, we rapidly finished in the midst of our toileting and walked swiftly to the phone while pulling up our pants or readjusting a skirt or dress. We had to get to the phone. There were no answering machines or voicemail for a caller to leave a message. Lawrence and Dad were tied to this essential aspect of the business. I recall hearing Dad exclaim "damn phones" in an exasperating tone more than once.

Even after our voices changed, Kerry and I rarely answered the business phone. We waited for one of the adults to answer within four rings. If no one answered, only then did we take the call at the extension nearest to where we were.

When a call for the business came in, the ringing was heard throughout the house. When these calls occurred while I was sleeping, I adapted to waking up briefly. I'd hear Dad's voice on the phone in the living room. Before he concluded the call, I was back asleep. Or, I became so accustomed to these calls I slept right through the ringing, Dad's conversations, and the sound of his steps going down the stairs. The ringing of the phone was part of our lives—at any time, night or day. Dad referred to the phone aspect of the business in a letter he wrote to me on January 28, 1971, indicated with a time of 1:30 a.m.:

"I went to bed and to sleep, but was awakened by a death call, so naturally came back home wide-awake—after writing this much to you, I'm relaxed and can now go to sleep—will continue later . . . Dad."

We all had to be ready for the next funeral. Always.

CHAPTER 25

Youthful Tasks in Requiem Environments

I absorbed the meaning of the words "death call" early in my life. It's the term used when the undertaker is called to remove the body of the deceased to its next location, usually the funeral home. When Kerry and I reached our teen years, we rode with Dad or Lawrence in the hearse to hospitals, accident scenes, rest homes, or family homes.

On one particular trip, Dad and I went to a house where the body was on the second floor of a small house with a narrow winding staircase. The family greeted Dad and me at the door. Dad recommended the family wait for us in another part of the house. He knew it was disconcerting for family to see their loved one escorted out of their home.

With him on one end of the gurney and me opposite him, we lifted the cart up the stairs and into the room where an overweight, elderly, deceased man was lying in bed. To get the cart close to the bed, Dad instructed me to help him move a dresser and chair to another part of the room. This provided the clearance to wheel the cart parallel to the bed. He directed me to unzip the zipper on the body bag, open it fully, and then pull back the sides of the bag. Next, we rolled back the blankets and sheets covering the body. Transferring a body respectfully from bed to bag is a task similar to moving your bed partner to one side of the bed so you have enough room to get in on your side. Of course, the advantage in moving a deceased is you eliminate the concern you have in awakening your bedmate. The height of the cart was adjusted using handles and pedals with our hands and feet. We rolled the cart to the height of the bed. We pushed the cart snug against the bed and locked the four wheels to stop movement. We moved the body to the edge of the bed by tugging on the sheet under the person and pulling the body as close to the cart as possible. Dad positioned himself at the head and put his hands under the deceased's shoulders. I was at the opposite end with my hands under each leg above the ankle.

"Are you ready, Kevin? When I count 1-2-3, I want you to lift the body from the bed to the body bag. Okay?"

"Got it, Dad."

"1-2-3."

This was my first and last experience lifting someone of this weight. We positioned the body in the bag and closed the zipper. We rolled the cart to the top of the stairs and adjusted the height to its lowest level. Dad directed me at the foot of the cart to walk backward down the stairs. Dad guided me from his position at the head of the cart. I took one backward step at a time, making a turn after three steps on a landing. I continued to the main floor, Dad coaching all the way. We paused at the bottom. Dad instructed me to guide the cart out the front door and down the few remaining porch steps. We raised the cart back to higher level and continued wheeling to the single back door of the hearse. We rolled the cart inside the hearse and locked it into position. Then we closed the door and returned to the house to reposition the furniture. Afterward, I walked to the hearse as Dad said his goodbyes to the family before driving us to the funeral home.

Dad and Lawrence executed a litany of responsibilities. For each death, they needed to embalm and prepare the body, meet with the family to make plans for the wake and funeral, prepare the parlors for viewing, and compose and submit an obituary to the newspapers and radio station. This preparation was ongoing. One of my jobs, which I shared with Kerry, was to set the furniture for the viewing. Kerry and I placed chairs at spots along the periphery of the viewing room, leaving an open area for mourners to stand during a wake. With dust rags and furniture spray in hand, we polished the woodwork. We placed Kleenex boxes on the tables. We put lecterns at the entrance of the room.

When Dad involved me in the set up for a wake, he directed me to bring a floral or plant display from the back room where florists had earlier delivered them. He positioned each display to fit into the design for the viewing area. The casket was placed between two tall floor lamps in front of the wall or window. A single bulb in each lamp cast its light through a frosted glass bowl to the sides of the casket and up to the ceiling. The light bounced back from the whiteness of the ceiling, highlighting the casket and the countenance of the deceased.

Each funeral display was different because the quantity and appearance of flower arrangements differed from wake to wake. Metal floral stands came in varying heights. We placed taller, broader pieces in the back with smaller baskets in front. The full display was symmetrical. Most families arranged with a florist to design a spray of flowers to place on top of the casket with a banner indicating a significant role of the deceased: "Father," "Mother," "Son," "Daughter." I placed ceramic or glass bowls containing green plants on tabletops in the room. I made sure the gift card was clearly displayed with the plant or floral display. Dad wrote a brief description on the back describing the display. Guests saw the name of the donor as they gazed at the displays.

The family used the written information when they wrote thank-you cards. As my printing and handwriting improved, Dad instructed me what to write, helping me to spell any unfamiliar words. "Chrysanthemum" is one flower word I added to my speaking and writing vocabulary.

A wake usually concluded by nine o'clock. Dad or Lawrence rearranged the furniture in preparation for the funeral the following day. The periphery's chairs and couches stayed in place. They converted the open middle section into six to eight consecutive rows of folding chairs facing the casket with three to four chairs on each side of the aisle. When this task was delayed until morning, Dad occasionally requested we do the work. He estimated the number of chairs needed based on what the family told him, the number of people who came to the wake, and what he heard from attendees about their intentions to come to the funeral service. With all this information, Dad let us know the importance of his estimation. If we set up more chairs than attendees, this might cause the family to be disappointed in the attendance. If we set up too few chairs, we set up additional seating as people arrived. Dad usually opted for an arrangement of too few chairs. If more people came than available chairs, the family's reserve was strengthened in knowing so many people came to pay respects. Chair setup was a delicate balance.

The service at the funeral home usually began between nine and ten in the morning and lasted fifteen to thirty minutes. When the service concluded, Dad or Lawrence took position at the front of the casket, faced the audience, and made a statement: "On behalf of the family, we thank you for your attendance. We invite you to walk by the casket to pay your last respects and proceed to your cars. We will drive to (the name of the church and/or cemetery). Our funeral directors will direct you. For this final viewing, we will start at the back row."

Dad walked to the back and instructed those in the last row to walk up, proceed by the casket, and walk out. The immediate family of the deceased in the front row, watched as each person passed. After the last person, the family stepped forward to face the casket. They said their final goodbyes and made their own exit to awaiting vehicles.

When the last family member departed, Dad or Lawrence placed any item the family wanted in the casket, folded up the sides, pulled the cover down, and latched the cover in position. The casket was on a wheeled cart. This was wheeled to the outer hallway where previously assigned pallbearers waited. Dad or Lawrence instructed them to line up three on each side, guided them to walk downstairs outside to the hearse and slide the casket inside. Dad or one of his colleagues opened the driver's side door of the hearse and slid behind the wheel. Most times, a police escort vehicle was in front of the hearse. The undertakers directed the funeral procession to a church for additional services or directly to a cemetery.

While these procedures occurred in the front driveway, assistants simultaneously transported all or some of the floral displays from the coffin area to a station wagon or van in the back driveway. Once they loaded vehicles with flowers, they exited the property through the side driveway. When all was proceeding smoothly, the flowers arrived at the church or cemetery before the funeral procession. Kerry and I sometimes helped in this process. Funeral processions usually proceeded with few complications or interruptions. When the lead police car approached a stop sign or stop light intersection, the officer slowly moved through, followed by the hearse. This signaled those cars in the cross street to come to a halt. A "short funeral" of five to ten cars may have taken less than a minute to go through the intersection. A "long funeral" of 10–20 cars or more took longer.

If the procession arrived at a church, the hearse pulled up to the curb of the pre-designated entrance, and the cars either stayed in a line or drove to spots in the church parking lot or street. After the church services concluded, the casket was reloaded into the hearse. The cortege then proceeded to one of the cemeteries in Elgin.

One time Dad was driving the hearse and leading the procession for the funeral of the mother of our next-door neighbor. Their family, like ours, all lived together in one house. Dad looked continually in his mirror to make sure the cars were behind him and getting through each intersection. He drove through the cemetery gate with all other vehicles following in order. As he was routing himself through the cemetery road, he did not see a tent and chairs set up by any grave.

His first thought was that the cemetery had forgotten to prepare for the funeral. Then he realized he was at the wrong cemetery. He kept driving through the circular road and went out the exit. Every car followed as he drove a short distance over city streets to the intended cemetery and led the procession to the grave area. The procession halted. Mourners departed their cars to walk to the grave site. As the family gathered, Dad went to them and said, "Sorry the ride took longer. I knew your mother so well, I just thought she might like to drive by her friends and family at the other cemetery." He stood by his story. The service continued. Later, he let them know what happened. They laughed together.

Most funerals occurred in the morning and concluded by noon. Dad and Lawrence came home to eat lunch and follow up with duties. Kerry and I helped with the reverse procedure of the chair setup. Each chair was folded and stacked upright along a back wall of the funeral home or closets. We then transferred any remaining floral displays from the viewing area to vans for delivery to places designated by the family, Dad, or Lawrence. The area near the display area was often littered with petals and residue from the floral displays, so Kerry or I pushed the vacuum, watching the petals get sucked up into the bag. Once we finished, the parlor was ready for the next wake or funeral.

When I started to drive, I was assigned the job of delivering flowers and plants to waiting rooms at the hospitals, common areas of rest homes, churches, or to the client's home. In addition to plants, I delivered a box or basket to the grieving family containing the cards from the floral displays, the register book showing the names of those who attended, a box of thank-you cards, and the donation envelopes left in a rack at the entrance to the viewing area. Dad was careful in keeping lists and inventories for the families. It was all part of his customer service. He caught himself one time in an indiscretion. After the funeral of Mom's brother-in-law on the morning of New Year's Eve, Dad and I worked on the post-funeral duties. We loaded the station wagon. Before I left, he stopped me.

"Wait. Let me take one plant. Mother and I can use it to put on the buffet table for the party we are having tonight. They received so many plants, they won't notice. I will take it over to them tomorrow."

I drove to my aunt's house. My cousins came to greet me and help take plants and materials inside. I stayed for a while and shared in food and conversation. I announced my exit and headed to the front door.

"Hey, Kevin, where's the pretty plant with the green leaves and a few yellow flowers? It was on the table at the front near the casket."

I looked up, caught my cousins' attentions, and laughed like I was being tickled, stuttering on my first word.

"D-Dad thought you wouldn't mind if he and Mom used it for their party tonight."

They joined in my laughter and agreed that Dad's attempt would not be forgotten. By the time I arrived home ten minutes later, I heard him on the phone laughing right along with them. The plant did make a beautiful centerpiece.

In addition to our chair and flower duties, Lawrence sometimes asked us to be greeters at the front door when wakes occurred. Kerry and I would stand at the door dressed in long pants, collared shirt, and necktie. Sometimes we wore a white collared polo shirt and khakis. We watched people approach the front doors after they exited their cars parked on the street or lot. The entrance opened into a hallway with eight wide stairs leading to a landing. When they arrived, we opened the doors.

"Welcome to O'Connor's. I am Kevin O'Connor," I'd say. "Which family are you here to see?"

We then instructed them which way to turn when they reached the landing. Later when people exited the parlors and came down the stairs, we aided those who appeared to need it or simply thanked them for coming.

Kerry and I readily adapted ourselves to the role of pallbearers when needed. Dad and Lawrence also employed our friends to be pallbearers for the funerals of people who had no family or friends. These people may have lived alone or made pre-arrangements with Dad to take care of them when they died. Other situations occurred when someone discovered a dead neighbor, tenant, or homeless person on the street. When police discovered a body, they contacted the funeral home. Dad and Lawrence worked with the police and other agencies to discover and confirm the deceased's identity. In dire cases, there was no identity. Or even when identified, no one claimed to know the individual. In all these cases, Dad and Lawrence provided a funeral. A local minister assisted. The body was embalmed and placed in a modest coffin. The night before or the morning of the funeral, Dad let us know he needed four to six of our friends to be pallbearers for the deceased. Each would be compensated five dollars.

When our friends arrived dressed as instructed, Dad took us to a side room next to the parlor where the service was to be held. He told us what he knew about the deceased. He directed us into the chapel to sit in front of the casket or off to the side on a row of chairs or long couches. At the conclusion of the service, Dad escorted us to the room near the front door but away from the parlor where the casket was displayed. Dad wanted us, as he did with adult pallbearers, to be outside of the view of him putting things in the casket, folding the shroud over the body, and closing the lid. The lid was fastened with a latch, presumably never to be opened again. He wheeled the cart holding the coffin through the doorway and in between us six pallbearers awaiting its delivery. Dad stood at the end of the coffin. Dad began to push the coffin and let us know we should move along with the coffin, holding on to the handles. Reaching the top stair, Dad paused.

"Okay, guys, here's what you do. Stand sideways next to the casket. Take your hand closest to the casket. Put that hand on the handle. Make sure you have a good hold. You two at the front, when I start to push, I want you to take the first step down the stair, lifting the casket as you move. Those of you behind the first two, do the same. Walk down the steps. Okay, let's go."

We walked down the eight steps and stood in front of the double doors now open to the outside, no matter what the temperature.

"Good job, everybody. Now, we are going to wheel the cart to the back door of the hearse."

We proceeded on our way. The hearse driver and another undertaker waited at the open back door of the hearse. They instructed us how to guide the coffin onto the two rows of wheels located on the floor of the hearse. The coffin was placed on the first set of wheels. Once we pushed, the coffin traveled on the wheels until it reached a leather covered block to stop the casket from going further. The back end of the casket was now fully inside. One of the undertakers placed a back stopper into a hole in the floor. This stopper fit snug against the end of the casket. The undertaker closed the back door of the hearse. We pallbearers walked to the limousine. We got in and traveled behind the hearse, driven by Dad, Lawrence, or another undertaker.

When we arrived at the church or cemetery, Dad instructed us to line up behind the open back door of the hearse in the same way we stood when we loaded the casket. Working with Dad, he reminded us to take our spot at the handle of the casket as it rolled out. Once in our positions, we walked backward from the rear of the hearse. The casket came with us. Steps ascended into most churches. A casket was heavy for a sextet of adolescents.

"You got it? Are you ready to lift?" Dad said. "Okay. One, two. three."

Being a pallbearer reminds me of the scene from the musical play and movie production of *Oliver*. Mr. Sowerberry, the undertaker in the story, employed street orphans as mourners. In one scene, Oliver is carrying a feathered plume at the lead of the procession. He takes an opportunity to make an escape and get back into his street life. We pallbearers did not repeat a similar scene. We went up the stairs and stood at the entrance of the church where the minister or priest greeted us. Often there was no one in attendance. We were pallbearers *and* mourners.

We sat in the pews as the service was conducted. At the conclusion, we reloaded the casket into the hearse, walked to our limousine, and were driven to the cemetery. It was hard for me to comprehend a person had no friends or family who cared enough to say good-bye. I was left with an impression of the noble act provided by my friends and me. At the end of the cemetery service, we walked away from the coffin and were driven back to the funeral home. Dad gave us each a five-dollar bill. We came into the house for lunch, then walked or rode our bikes downtown to spend our earnings. We were part of the funeral home payroll.

Sometimes I thought the chores were a distraction to whatever I thought I'd rather be doing. Even with the welcome compensation on some occasions, I might have responded to Dad and Lawrence's request with a grimace or, "Do I have to?" I did not realize the lessons I was learning in my childhood times. Now, I distinctly appreciate how the work in the family business gave me skills in care, empathy, sensitivity to others, floral design, and conveying a sense of humor.

CHAPTER 26

It Was Not Just Funerals that Kept Us Employed

Maintaining a funeral home is more than preparing for and conducting funerals. At times, we were called upon to assist the living and those who were ill or hurt in accidents. The funeral home business also operated an ambulance service for use as needed in the community. Dad and Lawrence were the designated drivers.

I learned EMT skills as a funeral home child. In the years prior to paramedics, each of the six funeral homes in Elgin shared the responsibility of being on call once every six months with the police and fire departments for emergency situations. Dad and Lawrence kept themselves up to date with trainings. They needed to be readily available to get to the location of an accident or emergency. Time was of the essence. The oxygen tank was checked regularly. The cot was dressed with clean sheets and blankets next to a container packed to capacity with bandages. I helped Dad on some of these occasions.

My most vivid memory occurred at an accident scene involving a motorcyclist and a car. As we drove from the funeral home to the scene, Dad kept me informed. I was in my younger teen years.

"I am not sure what we are in for here," he forewarned. "The call just said a car hit a motorcycle. Follow what I tell you to do."

We quickly arrived at the scene four to five blocks from home. The motorcycle was on its side. The driver's body was sprawled on the ground near the cycle. He was on his chest with his head turned to its side. Blood was coming from his forehead, mouth, and cheek. I saw a car on the opposite side of the intersection, stopped with both the driver and passenger doors open. Two people milled confusedly near the car.

"Kevin, go to the motorcyclist on the ground, kneel close to him, and see if you can talk to him. Keep him talking if you can. I am going to go speak to the police to see about the people in the car."

The cyclist was breathing and conscious. His eyes opened and closed. He said a word or two before Dad came back. He looked directly down at the victim.

"Young man, my name is Bill. Can you hear me?"

He looked at Dad. His lips moved with a "Yes."

Dad looked at me.

"Stand up, Kevin. We need to get him into the ambulance. Two of the police are here to help. Let's get the stretcher all the way down to ground level." Moments later, all were assembled. "Okay. You two get on either side of him. I will get at his shoulders. Kevin, you stand at his feet. Put each of your hands under his ankles.

We completed our positioning.

"We need to gently lift him," Dad cautioned. "We don't know what type of injuries he has inside of him. On my count of three, let's gently lift him onto the stretcher. One. Two. Three. Lift."

The cyclist grimaced a bit. Once he was settled into position, Dad pulled a strap from each side of the stretcher and connected them across his midsection. This kept him secure from rolling.

"Now let's get the stretcher into the ambulance. I will lift the stretcher and wheel it over to the back end of the ambulance."

As we came to the door, Dad moved from the front to the side of the stretcher.

"When we lift the stretcher, push it into the ambulance. The wheels will collapse and roll the stretcher in. Kevin, get in the ambulance. When the stretcher gets all the way in, there's a belt with a hook on the floor. Put the hook into the loop at the top of the stretcher. There's another hook in the floor near the side of the stretcher. Attach the hook to the stretcher. Okay, now sit on the ledge next to where the top of the stretcher is. Keep talking to him. Watch him. When I am driving, you stay right next to him."

Dad thanked the police officers. He closed the back door of the ambulance and walked to the driver side door and jumped in. He pressed the button to start the siren sound. The lights on top of the ambulance continued to flash. He opened the sliding glass window between his seat and the back where I was sitting next to the victim.

"You okay, Kevin? How is he?" he asked.

"His eyes are open, Dad."

"Keep talking to him. Talk about anything. School. Your bike. Anything."

Dad followed the speeding squad car with lights flashing, proceeding forthrightly through intersections. The lights and sirens of the ambulance also alerted vehicles and pedestrians to the emergency. He pulled into the entrance of the emergency room of St. Joseph Hospital. From there, the hospital staff took charge. Dad conversed a bit with them and police. He came to the back entrance of the ambulance and directed me to get out and go to the front seat.

We drove back to the funeral home. When we arrived, I assisted him as we removed the sheets, pillowcase, and blanket from the stretcher. He put those in a bag to be taken to the commercial laundry. From a cabinet, he took out clean bedding and I worked with him to dress the stretcher with fresh linens. We then used rags to wipe down the surfaces of the ambulance.

"Now you can get out," Dad said. "We are ready for the next call when it happens. Thanks for all your help. I am so glad you were home when the call came in."

I don't know the cyclist's fate, but I do know this experience emphasized the skills, temperament, and care that were so much a part of Dad's character.

His character also came through when he tasked me with wallpapering. During one of my high school or college summers I worked at the funeral home, and he wanted assistance in hanging wallpaper in the bathroom located between the office and parlors. Prior to the construction of the new addition, this was *the only* restroom for the funeral home. There was no gender designation. It wasn't possible to create two bathrooms within the available space and plumbing. Patrons of the funeral home contented themselves with a unisex (an unheard-of term) restroom. I do not recall anyone ever mentioning a concern about gender orientation.

Dad provided the materials and a table on which to cut. He spread out the wallpaper, ready to apply the paste. The ceiling was about nine feet. He instructed me how to get the paper ready, stand on the ladder, and paste it to the wall. With that, Dad left me on my own. He came back when I was close to finishing. He was unaware I was intermittently draped in wet wallpaper over my head and body. He gave his approval for the work I had completed. I used this wallpapering skill in various living locations for the next thirty-five years. I felt a connection with Dad with each of these experiences.

Concurrent with wallpapering, I took on Dad's task of sealcoating the parking lot and driveway. I was twenty-nine, separated from my first wife, and had returned to residency in the back bedroom of the second floor for a month or so. I needed a place to reside and the income Dad and Lawrence provided. Filling in cracks and putting on the sealcoat is a typical do-it-yourself task for homes and places of business in Elgin. I talked to Dad about creating a crew of my two nieces and two nephews, ages ten to sixteen, to assist. I thought, *What better way to have some bonding time with them?* They would also earn some money for themselves. I bought the necessary equipment for our crew. I used the skills from my teaching profession to assign them to individual and partnered tasks. We were challenged with hot summer sun and the heat of the driveway itself. I thought our job could be finished in one day, but by the end of the first day, we had only completed about 25 percent of the project. Due to weather interruptions, a wake, and funeral, we stopped our work for a few days. On day four, no business was scheduled, and the weather was clear. The team returned. I underestimated how much sealer we needed, so I left them on their own while I made a trip to buy more. Day five followed with similar adjustments and completion of the job. A final setback left a visual reminder of our work.

While our sealing project was occurring, Dad arranged to have new indoor-outdoor carpeting installed on the front office steps and porch. When the carpet installer came to do the job, we had already completed the area near the steps. If you have ever been involved in sealing a driveway, you are aware the tar residue finds its way to shoes, pants, and gloves. As the last hour of work was winding down, I made plans with the kids for a celebratory lunch. We worked together to take the remaining empty containers, application brushes, squeegees, and gloves to the garbage area. I was feeling so accomplished in getting this job done. To my dismay, one of my directives was overlooked. Someone forgot about the condition of their shoes and walked up two to three steps of the newly carpeted stairs and quickly turned around and went back down when they realized what they had done. I am not sure if I saw it happening or shortly after. Dad came out as the tar was settling into the carpet on the stairs.

"Oh my God!" he said. (This was usually Dad's highest level of profanity.) "Who walked up the stairs? Look at the carpet!"

Dad was not easily upset. Exquisitely patient. His usual calm demeanor persisted even in this situation. He quickly retreated and came out with a scrub brush and a bucket filled with water, advising me I best take the crew with me in the car to get our lunch and ice cream treat. He was able to alleviate only some of the stain, a continual reminder of the impact of our family work on the business.

In addition to the specific tasks involving wallpaper and tar, Dad and Lawrence insisted the outside of the house was consistently presentable and maintained. When a funeral occurred, mourners first saw the yard and entrance. From the time we were six or seven, Kerry and I took turns pushing the mower to cut the lawn. We followed the mowing with raking and putting the clippings in a wheelbarrow to take to a spot in the far back yard. The lawn area was small compared to what I have encountered in my adult mowing life. In my youth, I thought the job of mowing the lawn was interminable. I looked longingly at the ending point, imagining it would be forever until I finished. In the fall, I raked and disposed of leaves. Bushes needed trimming and pruning. We planted flower beds and large pots throughout the front of the house. These had to be maintained throughout the summer.

Working in and around the funeral home was like a laboratory for the future tasks of my life. Barrett, Kerry, and I did not have aspirations to be wallpaper hangers, driveway seal coaters, landscape designers, or horticulturists. However, we did have the practical training and apprenticeship provided by Lawrence and Dad. Were they fostering a sense of filial duties or preparing us for skills we used in our future careers and residences? They were doing both.

CHAPTER 27

Pigeons, Cars, and a Broken Leg

How can there be a connection between pigeons, cars, and a broken leg? Imagine this.

Bang! Wings flapping. I woke up from sleep in my bed. Like most mornings, daylight streamed in to awaken us through our bedroom windows, set up high toward the ceiling. It was not just the daylight waking me on some days; it was the sound of Lawrence shooting his BB gun. What kid from my school or social circle awoke to this? This sound was part of life in the funeral home. The BBs were intended to frighten the pigeons who perched and roosted on the peak of the roof of our window and on the edges of the gutters. Lawrence considered the pigeons a nuisance. Their droppings landed without direction or discrimination on the evergreens and on the hoods and windshields of cars in the driveway. Those cars included our family cars and the autos of patrons who parked there to attend a wake or funeral.

Lawrence decided one way to keep the birds at bay was to fire his BB gun. On the first day I heard these shots, I got out of bed and walked down the three flights of stairs and out through the door of the office. Lawrence spotted me and spoke the first words.

"Get back in the house," he said.

"What are you doing?" I asked.

"I'm scaring the pigeons away."

"What if you hurt one of them?

"Don't worry; I don't know how to shoot this gun," he said "I'm aiming for the gutters. When a BB hits on the metal, the pigeons fly away."

"Where do they go?"

"I don't know. I don't want them around here pooping on the cars. I think if I do this shooting once a week or so, they will go someplace else. Why are *you* out here?"

"The shooting woke me up, and I wanted to see what you're doing."

"Sorry. Some days you will wake up to the sound. It's time you should be out of bed anyway. Pigeons are one of the consequences of having a house like ours. It's part of who we are as a family. Go back inside and eat some breakfast."

"Where do you keep the gun?" I asked.

"Ahh. Now that's a secret between me and me."

I turned around and did what I was told. On later mornings I ate breakfast after being awakened by gun shots. Was it marksmanship? He probably didn't want to tell me he was better at hitting the gutter than the pigeons. And in his gentle ways, I don't believe he intended to harm the birds. He was not a hunter. He simply struck a good pose in his white shirt, the master of his estate.

Scaring away the pigeons was one way he demonstrated his care for the property and its appearance. Some clients were drawn to the structure and setting of the house as the location of services for their family. Unlike an auto dealership or dentist office with a parking area of cars indicating the daily presence of clients inside, our parking lot was nearly empty in the absence of funerals. One of Lawrence's solutions was to make sure our family cars were parked in the front driveway. When Kerry and I started to drive, we parked the car we shared in the driveway. When friends or family came to visit, they knew to put their car in the driveway and parking spots. Lawrence let us know: "We need to look like we're busy with a wake or funeral. Park your cars so they can be seen." It was one of his mantras and ideas about marketing the funeral home. Visibility.

Kerry's first driving experience was not what Lawrence had in mind. Kerry's encounter with a family car at age three in the summer of 1954 involved all of us. I was in the living room, sitting on the floor beside him as we ate lunch and watched TV. Mom was in the kitchen. I was so involved in the TV program that I did not realize Kerry had departed.

I heard Sharon scream from the second floor. Mom hurried downstairs. I followed. Looking through the window to the outside, I first saw Dad and Mom's 1949 Chrysler stuck against a tree at the left side end of the driveway. Next I saw Kerry's face through the windshield. The driver's side door was open against the trunk of the tree. My family members rushed outside and pushed and moved the car away from the tree. Dad lifted Kerry out of the driver's side and up into his arms. He carried Kerry to another car and put him into the front seat. I heard Kerry's screams through the window, the volume carrying up from the open office door. He was crying but not moving. Mom joined them inside the car. Both parents were crying. I was scared and frightened. I watched as Dad backed the car down the driveway. Sharon told me they were going to the hospital. I sat frozen on the step leading to the first landing of the hall stairway, watching others scurry around the driveway. *How did Kerry get to the car?*

I wondered if I, too, should go outside. I didn't cry, but I felt alone, even with Sharon and Mildred nearby. I was tasting the bologna sandwich and chocolate milk Mom gave us for lunch just fifteen minutes earlier. Evidently, Kerry left our lunch setting and walked himself down the steps to the ground level. He ambled up to the car and opened the unlocked door. He sat in the driver's side and released the gear shift into reverse. The car rolled backward down the inclined driveway and positioned itself so the space between the passenger seat and open door was wedged against the trunk of the tree. Unfortunately, Kerry's leg was wedged as well.

When Dad and Mom arrived at the hospital, X-rays showed breaks in several areas of Kerry's leg. Dad and Mom had been planning a driving trip to southern California with Barrett as a present for his eighth-grade graduation. Kerry and I were assigned to stay with Aunt Marge and our cousins. Instead, Kerry's leg was put into traction, positioned in a sling-like position. One side of the sling near his foot was attached to a bar above the bed.

Once they got the go-ahead from the hospital staff that Kerry was okay, they proceeded with their trip. Kerry stayed in the suspended position for three to four weeks. Can you imagine? This was how a broken leg "set" during those times of medical history.

Whether it was pigeons perching on the gutters and distributing their excrement on clients' cars or Kerry finding his way into to his unfortunate first experience behind the wheel, Lawrence and Dad were continually aware of presentation. Each time a person drove by, they were perhaps viewing the mansion and its surroundings as welcoming, even alluring.

CHAPTER 28

We Were Observers, Participants, and Ambassadors

As children in a funeral home family, each of us had particular responsibilities in the operation of the business. Uncle Lawrence reminded me I was not only Kevin O'Connor, I was *Kevin O'Connor, ambassador of O'Connor Funeral Home* at school, jobs, and social interactions. He gave a similar message to Barrett and Kerry. I imagine his daughters heard the same. Our personal lives had to be intertwined with the business.

On one occasion of ambassadorship, Dad went to St. Joseph Hospital for a death call. When he arrived, he realized he needed assistance because of the weight of the deceased. No one was available at the hospital to help. He knew Barrett was at the hospital because prior to Dad's departure, Barrett had called to tell Dad and Mom that he and Pat were on their way to the hospital for the delivery of one of their children. In the 1960s, fathers waited in a waiting room, not allowed to be part of the delivery process.

Dad was in a bind. He had a person of experience in the maternity waiting room. Did he dare ask Barrett for help at this life-changing time? Of course he did. Dad opened the door to the waiting room and saw Barrett in a chair, reading the newspaper.

"Psst. Barrett."

Barrett raised his eyes and looked at Dad. Grandpas in the waiting room? Unheard of.

"Dad, what are you doing here?

"How's it going?" Dad asked.

"No news. I'm surprised to see you here."

"Hey, I need your help. I need to lift a body onto the gurney. I can't do it alone. Do you think you might be able to sneak away for a few minutes?"

"It will just take a few minutes, right?"

"Yeah. Come with me."

Barrett was no stranger to death calls but not concurrent with his child's awaited birth. Nevertheless, he knew what had to be done. He followed Dad down the hall to the room in a nearby section of the hospital. He helped Dad lift the body to the gurney, closed the zipper on the body bag, and walked into the hall with Dad. They escorted the gurney with body to the service elevator. He rode with Dad to the lower level and walked with him to the entrance where the hearse was waiting. He helped load the gurney. They said a quick goodbye.

"Thanks so much. I'm looking forward to your news," Dad said. "Get on back upstairs. Love ya."

Living in a funeral home, the connection of death and life was undeniably present. Dad drove back home and learned he was a grandfather. New life.

Our responsibilities as funeral home children extended to how we behaved in the house. When we talked loudly during games, ran up and down the stairs, or played music or TV in high volume, one of the parents reminded us: "There's people downstairs." Those three words, stated with varied intonations, sounded a signal to adapt our activity. Some people involved in grieving and visiting did not want to be disturbed with the sounds of children. On the other hand, I think our voices may have been a reminder that life does go on in the climate of death.

Have you seen the 1991 movie *My Girl* starring Jamie Lee Curtis and Macaulay Culkin? Culkin's neighborhood playmate, portrayed by Anna Chlumsky, lives in a funeral home. In one scene of the movie, the children are tiptoeing down the basement stairs looking for her undertaker father, played by Dan Ackroyd. As they reach the bottom stair, they notice that the white door leading to the preparation room is closed. Ackroyd shouts to the children not to open the door. He was preparing a body and did not want them to see what was happening. They turned around and scurried back up the stairs.

This scene deeply connected with me. On some occasions, Mom might have asked me to find Dad in the house someplace. This was in the years prior to the intercom phone system. If I arrived at the bottom of the stairs and heard the radio amid the hum of the embalming machine, I knew better than to open the door. I always knocked.

"Who is it?"

"Kevin. Mom wants to know when you will be ready to come upstairs."

"Mmm. Tell her in about forty-five minutes. I've got a few things to do, and I need to get the body put in the casket next to you by the door."

Sure enough, the casket with both parts of the cover open revealed the billowy satin of the coffin bed and the pillow where the deceased's head was to be placed. I gave this display the knowing glance of an undertaker's son. As I left my position, I heard Dad say, "Get on upstairs now."

Other times, I came upon the preparation room with the door open. My gaze was immediately on the bottom of the feet of the deceased whose body was laying on their back of the white porcelain table.

"What are you doing here?" Lawrence said. "I'm getting a body ready."

"Sorry. Mildred asked me to come down to get one of the scrub brushes on the sink in the laundry room. I'll grab it and get back upstairs."

"Okay. Close the door. Go and get the brush and then head back through the casket room and up the stairs. And stop off at the first-floor bathroom, get the rubbing alcohol from under the sink, and rub a little bit on your hands."

My brother and cousins all observed aspects of the business within our sight and reach. I spent time with Dad or Lawrence in the office when they worked. Kerry and I folded newspapers in the office to get ready to go on our paper routes. During those times, we might have needed an item stored in the cupboards behind the desk area to prepare for our route or a homework assignment. We opened the glass doors lined with sheer curtains on the inside to search for materials. In our searching we came across brown cardboard boxes about the size of a shoebox with labels printed "Remains of [name of the deceased]." The boxes had been mailed to the funeral home from the crematory, not mailed to the home of the family. Not all families responded to the calls made to them to come to take the ashes. Some boxes had been sitting on the shelves for many years prior to my birth. As I was looking for a box of rubber bands, I might have found them next to Mr. Smith's cremains. I was accustomed to moving the boxes around the shelf to find the item I sought.

This was part of the nature of our family not found in the homes of other families. As ambassadors, we needed to represent the business whenever we were in public. As residents, we knew how to monitor our behaviors according to the proceedings of the business. We couldn't help but be reminded of the beginnings of the life within our families and the remains of others left behind.

CHAPTER 29

Death of a Young Friend

I was aware of the concept of grief early in life, often reminded of the inevitableness of death. The phrase "we're busy" meant someone had died. Even closer to my sphere was the death of my elementary school friend, Francis, in August 1964, prior to the start of my high school freshman year. One day I walked into the office and found Dad sitting at his desk. He hung up the phone and motioned for me to take the seat across from him.

"The call was about Francis," he said calmly. "He died three hours ago. He was running in a field near his house and stepped on a live electric wire cut during the storm last night. It was on the ground hidden within grass. He died instantly."

I sat still. It was my first *personal* experience with the mental and physical state of shock. I had similar feelings when Kennedy died. This was different. Francis was a friend I had played with recently. With a pit in my stomach, a tear running down my cheek, and a lump in my throat, my voice cracked, "What happens now?"

"I am waiting to hear from his mom, so I will know what time she and her family can come in and talk to me about the wake and funeral."

"Where is Francis now?" I asked.

"His body is in the morgue at the hospital. I am going to call them to find out when I can go pick up his body."

"I want to call our friends," I said.

"I know you do. But I want you to wait until I know a little bit more. There may be an article in the newspaper this afternoon. Check for it when you get the papers delivered for your route."

I do not recall if the article about Francis's electrocution was in the edition of the paper I delivered that day or the one to follow. Regardless, I thought about Francis as I delivered the papers. Francis joined me on my route on some occasions. Later in the evening, Dad told me he had received Francis's body and was beginning the preparation process. Dad usually kept his own feelings in check, but his voice quivered a bit as he talked to me. He said he could not tell me much about Francis and did not want to talk about it. He gave me a hug. As a father myself now, I understand how upset Dad was. In his mind, he knew it could easily have been me instead of my friend.

The wake for Francis started in midafternoon two days later. Most of my classmates attended with their parents at various times. As their parents joined the adults in the inside parlor, some of my classmates sat with me on the side office porch. Since Dad did not tell me much, I said little to them about details. For many of us, it was the first experience of having a friend our age die suddenly and violently. We had no or limited prior experiences to show us how to act. Some of us cried; others joked and kidded around, uncomfortable in this situation. One by one, my friends and their parents went home.

The next morning there was a brief service at the funeral home and then to St. Mary Church. My classmates and I sat together in pews we had occupied for our eighth-grade graduation two months earlier. I do not recall a burial service. During the fall and the following summer, my friends and I included a stop at Francis's mother's house on our bike rides. We knocked on her door, and she would come out and talk with us. They were awkward but pleasant times.

"Don't stay away," she'd say. "Come back and see me."

We continued those intermittent visits until two years later when each of us got our driver's licenses. Our stops to see her ebbed to a close. Francis's mom went on with her life as we did with ours.

In the time following Francis's death, Dad let me know it was one of the hardest funerals he ever conducted. Without going into detail, he said Francis's body was so damaged, he was unable to make it suitable to be shown. Dad prided himself on his restoration work. Unfortunately, he had to inform Francis's family it was advisable to have a closed casket. They were upset. So was Dad.

"What funerals are the hardest for you, Dad?" I once asked.

"Funerals of young people like Francis. Whenever it's kids the same age as you, Barrett, or Kerry. When your cousin, Mary Lou, died, she was only sixteen. And your cousin Peggy's husband died at only twenty-one with a young baby and one on the way. I can't figure it out. It's hard when it's anyone I know who dies. Friends. People in my family or Mom's family."

"What gets you through?"

"I do for them what I do for the people who I only know because someone in their family has died, and they have come to us for help. I do what I can to let them know we will do all we can to help them through this time of their life."

"I don't think I can ever do what you do," I confessed.

"You will know when it is time. Don't think about it now."

I assimilated death on a daily basis. Death became a part of my life. Dad, Mom, Lawrence, and Mildred helped me understand these lessons. Through their example, I learned to live through death, day by day.

PART V

JOY OF FAMILY, FRIENDS, AND COMMUNITY

Our families were affected by the sadness and grief of the clients. Lawrence and Dad, and in turn, Mildred and Mom, related to families at a personal level. Our families respected the situations and life-changing experiences of their clients. In creating our own lives as families, it was detrimental for us to submerge ourselves into the difficulties and challenges experienced by those temporarily using the spaces on the first floor.

I perceive that Dad and Lawrence experienced their best times as brothers when they were celebrating events with our two families, our extended families, or involved together in parish activities. The function of the business did not allow for many experiences involving just the two couples. As couples and individuals, Dad and Mom participated in social circles separate from Lawrence and Mildred. Dad and Lawrence rarely participated together socially. Mom and Mildred got along especially well but did not shop, play cards, or do activities typical of friends.

Both Dad and Lawrence belonged to the Knights of Columbus, but not in meetings, committees, or social happenings occurring at the same time. Dad involved himself in fundraising activity positions. Their differences in community and social involvement were done for reasons tied to the business. In their partnership, either Dad or Lawrence had to be present at Division Street. If they both were interested or involved in the same meeting or organization, then neither one of them could be at the funeral home. Their active involvement in different organizations provided a benefit. They increased the business outreach to broader audiences.

Our parents encouraged and created times of fun with friends and family, experiences essential for our relaxation and growth away from the environment of grief. We valued the joy we experienced from family gatherings and the pets that joined us in the house. The chapters in this part of the book focus on the joy and celebrations we had as families.

CHAPTER 30

Celebrations

We celebrated small and big gatherings of friends and family in both apartments, even though it was risky to plan these festivities due to the unpredictability of the business. The families, ever ready for the possibility of a wake
or funeral downstairs, sometimes altered plans at the last moment.

It was easier to plan bigger parties on a Saturday afternoon or evening
when wakes seldom occurred. When a graduation event was scheduled on
a weekday, the *party* for the family and friends occurred on a Saturday or
Sunday. In 1954, Sharon graduated from high school and Barrett from eighth
grade. Four years later, he graduated from high school and she from college.
Sharon was one of the first in all our families to have completed college. To
celebrate the occasion, over one hundred relatives and friends attended the

party, sharing food and drink at bars and buffet tables in each apartment. People treaded up and down the steps. Three bathrooms—one on each floor of the house—provided relief services. People found places to sit at kitchen tables, on couches, side chairs, and folding chairs brought up from the funeral home. Dad and Aunt Cecil took turns playing piano in the second-floor living room for songfests. Lawrence sang and played his violin. Mildred strummed her banjo. Guests accompanied with additional instruments, as a chorus of voices harmonized to songs played and requested.

The O'Connor family is especially large, and parents have tended to give their newborns the same names: Mary, Peg, Irene, Margaret, Lillian, Tom, Lawrence, Bill, Bob, Pat, and Jim. This has the potential to be confusing to the most ardent of name and face organizers. An account of this aspect of our family fun and frivolity was written for my parents' fortieth anniversary celebration book by Dad and Lawrence's cousin, Jim O'Connor:

"The O'Connors are a fairly large clan who sincerely love each other, and they manage to get together occasionally. There is a strong resemblance among the members of the clan, and as a result, individual members sometimes are not quite sure who is who in the early stages of a large family gathering. For this reason, the greeting 'Hi, Cuz' is very common during the initial hours. Some reunions are more memorable than others—some more amusing.

One such occasion I recall was the day of Maureen's wedding. Following the reception in the school hall, the clan retreated to the O'Connor brothers' home. I had drifted about and had just sat down in Marion and Bill's kitchen for a cup of coffee with Bill and a couple of other men when my brother, Bill, and his friend, Jack, arrived (late) from Chicago and were directed upstairs to the bar.

My brother, Bill, spotting me in the kitchen, figured that I had had time to sort out the names of all the relatives present and so could readily introduce Jack to the clan. I had just introduced Jack to the group in the kitchen (with brother, Bill, carefully noting the names) when Marion came into the kitchen door and then said, 'Hi Bill, good to see you' to my brother, whose mouth dropped open over the fact that she had recognized him so quickly (not realizing that all of the of Chicago members of the clan had been there for hours). He in turn could only reply, 'Hi, Cuz.' Marion started another pot of coffee as brother, Bill, continued to stare at her. As she finished, she said, 'You seem to be having some trouble,' to which Bill replied, 'Yes, I know that you're a relative ... but where do you fit in around here?' Marion ran her fingers through her hair, as though trying to figure that one out, and then responded, 'Would it help any if I said that you are sitting in my kitchen?' Brother Bill said, 'Yeah,' and then turning to Bill (Elgin) added, 'She's your wife?' to which Bill (Elgin) only replied, 'God, I hope so. My kids are calling her Mama.'"

As the size of the business and family grew, Dad and Lawrence came together to create a way to mix the business with their desire to entertain by establishing a space for social gatherings. They knew the perfect spot.

Lawrence's purchase of the property included a barn built behind the house. In its earlier days, perhaps prior to the 1887 construction of the house, the barn had accommodated the business of raising cows whose milk was shipped to dairies in Elgin and the Chicago area. The slope of the hill on the property allowed the barn to have two stories. The lower story was accessed via a gravel driveway. This level had a ceramic tile floor and contained stables for horses and livestock. The upper floor of the barn was at the same level as the driveway extending from the house. At the structure's front, two side-by-side barn doors covered an opening about the size of a three-car garage. The upper level's floor was made of sheets of plywood, supported by wooden beams attached to sixteen posts. An open cupola pirouetted itself in the middle of the roof. With no windows on the walls, air was exchanged between the open door and the slatted shutters of the cupola. Pigeons roosted between the slats of wood. This level originally housed the horse-led carriages. But from 1939 to the mid-'50s, Dad and Lawrence used it to store the hearse and ambulance. Barrett and the girls stored their bikes next to the hearse.

When I was five or six, Kerry and I adventured one day to climb up to the cupola. We succeeded but had to yell for help, as we were unable to get down. Sharon and Mom brought us down to safety. That was my first and last view from the top of the cupola.

Lawrence and Dad had a vision to convert the barn to be functional for social occasions and storage of funeral home vehicles and supplies. The entire structure of the main level floor was raised with a hoist and a crane. This resulted in an increased height of ten feet for the lower level, which eventually became a three-vehicle garage area. After the structure was lifted, a cinder block foundation was constructed to strengthen the foundation of the building. As the cinder blocks were being put into place, additional new beams reached from side to side to support the upper floor of the barn.

At the front of the barn, contractors removed the existing barn doors and reinforced the four walls. They added green siding over the outside walls and a new shingled roof with gutters and downspouts. In place of the garage door, they installed a single door in the middle of the wall with a porch of three steps extending to ground level. These steps accommodated the new level of the raised barn. The construction crew used the blacktop area, formerly the entrance to the ground-level barn entrance, as a patio area surrounding the porch on three sides. Landscapers created a lawn and vegetable garden beyond the patio surrounded by a redwood fence separating the space from the parking lot.

Electricity for the barn had been installed in the early 1900s. Prior to installing Sheetrock during the renovation, electricians threaded wiring and sockets between the studs and across the ceiling beams to provide outlets for lighting, appliances, hi-fi players, and fans.

No plumbing was provided in the original design of the barn, except for a faucet and hose on the outside wall. Plumbers used that water connection to install plumbing for a kitchen and bathroom. Carpenters cut two small window areas on the east side and one on the north side. The window openings included a screen and a plywood piece with bottom hinges. When a window was opened, the plywood rolled on the hinge and found a resting spot against the wall. The barn was never described as fancy.

The ceiling of the barn remained with the original open beams, adding to the visual character of the structure. Little to no insulation was placed between the beams prior to the installation of the Sheetrock walls. As such, the barn heated up like an oven during summer months and was as cold as an igloo in the winter. Technicians installed a furnace but no air conditioning. In the cooler and cold months, heat to the barn was essential. In the coldest of winter months, it took two to three hours for the barn to heat up enough for entertaining. When the barn wasn't being used, the furnace was set at 40 degrees to keep the water in the plumbing from freezing. Sometimes, we forgot to keep the furnace set or a power outage occurred. The pipes froze and burst. We mopped water on occasion.

From the time of its completed refurbishing in the late '50s, the barn became a refuge for entertainment and a place to get away from the funeral home. Mom's brother-in-law built a two-section bar placed between the kitchen area and bathroom. The kitchen was designed with an oven, range, refrigerator, and sink. Long tables framed the kitchen area, providing preparation and serving areas for buffets. We now met in the barn for celebrations formerly held in the two apartments of the house.

Our families appreciated the scheduling options provided by the availability of the barn. If a wake or funeral occurred concurrent with a party or meeting already planned in the barn, Lawrence or Dad excused themselves and spent time in the funeral home. When their job was done, they came back to the barn. No longer did a need occur to postpone or cancel a celebration, as was the case when a funeral or wake occurred at the same time during in-house events.

A spinet piano, positioned where a floor opening to the stables below used to be, marked a keystone area of the barn. Most events with family or friends showcased Dad and other piano players. When he played the first chord people began to gather. I became further familiar with the melodies and lyrics of songs from the '20s through '60s. Dad kept adding to his repertoire each time he heard a new song or we played one for him. If it was an engagement or wedding party, he played "Sadie, Sadie" from 1963's *Funny Girl*. When *A Chorus Line* became popular in the mid '70s, singers readily engaged in songs he played from the score, including "What I Did for Love," "Tits and Ass," and "One." With "One," performers raided kitchen cupboards for pots, pans, lids, and plates to simulate the top hat and tails closing number from the play. Dad continued to play when Lawrence added his voice to "You'll Never Walk Alone," "Some Enchanted Evening," and other songs from his repertoire.

In addition to friends and family, Dad and Mom both brought people together through involvement in philanthropic and volunteer organizations. They enjoyed "having company" to their apartment or in our back yard area. Dad made references to entertaining in the barn in letters he wrote. Here's mention from one letter written in mid-August 1977:

"We had thirty-two. We had a bar and tables set up in the yard at the barn. It was such a gorgeous night, so all we had to do was set up seating chairs and table service, and it was a great menu. At 12:30 a.m., there were about eight of us having 'one for the road' when these cars drove in the driveway. Six more couples came over from the Elks Club after it closed. They all came over to tell us we were missed. With all the confusion, we ended up in bed at 3:30 a.m. If nothing else than the good time, this party really got us going."

Another letter dated September 10, 1977, provides a further glimpse of their celebrations:

"Last Saturday we put an 18 lb. ham in the oven and went to play golf with our cronies at Burr Hill. We all came back to the barn. There were twenty-two in all. It was a party to end all parties. Somewhere along the we way we lost control. We were playing old Mitch Miller records. Everyone danced. I really think we drank too much, but we had a ball...."

The barn wasn't only a fun spot for the grown-ups. Barrett, Kerry, and I also made the barn a welcome place for small and large parties of our friends. These started during Barrett's high school years and Kerry's and my elementary years and continued through college and into our thirties. We entertained ourselves with card games, Ping-Pong, and stacks of 45 RPM records and albums on the record player, singing and dancing with abandon. On hot summer nights, we sweated profusely in the heat and escaped to the sometimes-cooler air to sit on the steps of the porch and outdoor furniture in the yard. In our late teens and twenties, we added beer and alcohol to these activities.

We hosted sleepovers with friends during our school years. I felt independent being "far" away from the house. Mom and/or Dad greeted our young guests and made sure we settled in. With the installed business phone in the barn, we called to the second- or third-floor apartment phones to make requests or report a problem. We used the kitchen in the barn to prepare pizzas, popcorn, and other snacks all on our own. For breakfast, we ate cereal and milk, juice and toast, or made pancakes.

After Dad and Mom visited, my friends and I knew to expect a knock on the door from Uncle Lawrence sometime between eleven and midnight. To prepare for the inevitable knock, we knew to put away anything we did not want him to see or be aware of (e.g., alcohol, feathers from a pillow fight, or female friends). We opened the door and there stood Uncle Lawrence.

"Everything in here okay, boys?" he'd ask, surveying the barn with a glance.

"Yes, Lawrence," I'd say.

"Yes, Mr. O'Connor," the guests would echo.

"You be careful. Be careful with matches. Be sure the burners are turned off on the stove."

Lawrence might walk through on the pretense of introducing himself while at the same time checking behind the bar and the kitchen. Within three to five minutes, he made his exit.

"Good night. Get some sleep. You know who to call or where to come if you need anything."

Who knows what he knew or what he may have suspected? As wary as I was of his visits, I do appreciate his ongoing attention and the way he wanted to know our friends. He was happy we did our own entertaining.

Barrett, Kerry, and I each celebrated our graduation parties in the barn. The family hosted showers prior to the arrival of Barrett's and my kids. We surprised Mom and Dad with a fortieth anniversary party at the barn. When I married the first time in 1975, the rehearsal dinner was in the barn, decorated with low lighting, the colors of the holiday season, and tables set with white tablecloths and matching dishes and glassware. When our cousin and husband asked to use the barn for their twenty-fifth wedding anniversary in 1981, Dad made sure contractors came to assess if the floor was strong enough to support the number of people planning to come. The contractors added steel beams under the floor.

In our elementary years, we played with friends in the lower-level garage area, next to the hearse and ambulance and the traveling caskets. These caskets were made from plywood and used to transport bodies via air or truck from places beyond the Elgin area. Dad and Lawrence kept some traveling coffins available for times when they might need to ship a body. Dad helped us to move these caskets to an area on the garage floor. We created imaginary houses and forts within them. Our neighborhood friends took this all in stride. It was not unusual to us. The garage provided items for imaginary play. Four pails contained black and white ceramic tiles of octagon, rectangle, and square shapes, remnants of the removal of tile floors from this area formerly used as a milking stable for dairy cattle. We laid the tiles from the buckets side by side to create the walls of rooms within the casket. We placed dolls, toy soldiers, and plastic farm animals in the casket's imaginary rooms. We ventured into the ambulance. We pretended to be carried on the cot. In the hearse, we acted as the deceased and laid out our body.

The funeral home property was sold in June 1984. Three months prior, we planned a final party for the family to celebrate St. Patrick's Day. Unfortunately, the worst snowstorm of the season started in the afternoon. Many guests cancelled. The others celebrated together and harbored themselves for sleep on the floor or came into the house to take over any available bed, couch, or floor space.

The barn became well-known among our friends, family, and community. For some invitations we just indicated to meet at "the barn." We provided no address. People knew where to go.

CHAPTER 31

Feathered Friends, Canines, and Hares Bestow Expressions of Life

O ur families on Division Street fostered a bevy of pets in the apartments above the funeral home. The first memory I have of a pet on the second floor is Shakespeare, a parakeet with dominant green coloring. He resided in a cage hanging from a metal floor stand in the dining section of the kitchen. Mildred took particular pride in the way she taught him to repeat phrases:

"What's cookin' Mildred?"
"Goooooood morning."
"How's about it?"

When he wasn't talking, he was busy jumping from perch to perch, swaying in his swing and feasting on the food and water from the beak-size containers attached to his cage. Shakespeare usually stayed confined. When he got out, he flew to rooms in the apartment and back to the kitchen. One day, Shakespeare flew out of his cage, found his way to an open unscreened window, and took off on his runway to the outdoors. Mildred, Lawrence, Dad, Mom, and others began quickly to canvas the neighborhood, shouting, "Shakespeare! Shakespeare! Shakespeare!"

We echoed his name throughout the yard and up and down the streets. He did not return. I discovered his name on TV, theater productions, and literature classes in middle and high school. You may think of *Hamlet* when you hear a reference to Shakespeare. I think of Mildred's parakeet.

The third floor was in fact a bird sanctuary. During the time of Shakespeare, we too had a parakeet. Dad mounted a curved hook on the chimney wall centered between the two small square windows of our kitchen. This hook supported the cage. Mom and Dad steadfastly kept the cage clean. Feathers rarely found their way to the kitchen table or floor.

In addition, Dad's pursuit of canaries continued our family fascination with birds. One of Elgin's department stores included caged canaries in their springtime store displays. Upon entering the store, the birds greeted customers with chirping sounds and songs. The displays finished in early June, and the birds and cages were sold to customers. Dad and his sisters put their names on the list to be notified when the birds became available. They traveled together to pick up the birds and take them to each of their houses. Dad called his sisters on the phone, comparing their bird experiences.

Mom wrote about Dad's birds in a letter written to me on June 4, 1973:

"Forgot to tell you the story about your Dad's bird. Anyway, Cease and I were eating dinner one night, and Cease said how bad she felt about Dad's bird dying, and I looked at her kinda stupid and said,

'When did that happen?' Seems the bird had left this world about a week before. Given I just wasn't that close to it, I didn't know it was gone. So much for me. Then your last letter, the one before Saturday, Kerry was home, and I said something to him about your letter, and he said he was sure glad he read it because that was the first he knew about the bird dying! We really cracked up. Dad is thinking about getting another one!"

A visiting family parakeet met its mortal fate at Division Street. In the early '70s, Barrett and his family took a trip. Dad and Mom took care of their pets: a dog, a parakeet, and a goldfish. During the time of this caregiving, they awoke to find the bird at the bottom of the cage, dead as a corpse in the preparation room. Dad and Mom considered two options. Do they let Barrett's kids know? And what do they do with the bird? They decided to wait until the family returned from vacation. They also decided to wrap the bird in cellophane, insert it in a plastic bag, and inter (using a funeral word) it into the freezer in the basement we used for food storage. This freezer was in the newer area of the basement, not near the preparation or casket room (in case you're thinking, *Did they really have a family food freezer in the basement by the embalming room?*)

The announcement of the death was taken well. Dad explained that the bird was in the freezer and a proper burial was in the future. Nothing happened. The poor bird was missed no more than Dad's canary was missed by Mom or Kerry. Years later when one of us went to the freezer to retrieve frozen strawberries and ice cream, the cryogenically preserved parakeet was rediscovered behind a bag of berries. We closed the door, and the bird stayed. I am not sure if the bird was ever buried or deposited in a garbage can.

Dad was also fascinated with wild birds. The late '60s and '70s was the dawn of the bird feeder hobby. No tree branches or greenery extended to the third-story windows. This made it difficult to attract birds. Dad made it his business to install bird feeders on the ledges of the kitchen windows, filling the feeders with different types of seed. The bird feeders had, as Dad said, "no action" for weeks. Mom added a PS to a typed letter she wrote on April 17, 1974:

> "Most important news. Last night a blue jay was feeding at the bird feeder Dad got as a Christmas present. First bird that ventured near it. Now, if he just tells his friends."

In Dad's eyes, the appearance of the jay was akin to Apollo's landing on the moon. Mom reported Dad shouted as loud as the broadcasters did on that night. Once the jay came, he acted as a sentry, leading other birds to feast from the feeders. When the first cardinal appeared, it was worth at least three or four phone calls from Dad to aspiring ornithologists. Soon squirrels followed. When the first one appeared, Dad experienced a bit of frenzied disappointment about their invasion. Taken from the squirrels' points of view, I envy the canny effort it took for them to navigate the structure of the house to arrive at the bird feeders. Amazing. For the next ten years prior to Dad and Mom's departure from their apartment, Dad engaged in a battle to keep the squirrels away. Eventually, he surrendered. He bought squirrel food for a larger feeder by one window. He placed feeders at the neighboring window for small birds. He was in his own aviary with bird activity on the windowsills three stories above the ground.

Birds were one element of pet menagerie. The dogs of the second floor came before I was born. I did not know them. Checkers, a Boston terrier, entered our home when Barrett was in his teens. Checkers was then a popular name for dogs. In September 1952, the GOP candidate for Vice President, Senator Richard Nixon from California, was accused of improprieties regarding a fund established by his backers to reimburse him for his political expenses. To protect his position as the VP candidate, he delivered a thirty-minute televised speech. It was viewed by 60 million people, the largest television audience at that time. He defended himself and attacked his opponents. He asked the audience to contact the Republican National Committee to tell them he should remain on the ticket. During the speech, he affirmed he intended to keep a gift from one of his donors, a cocker spaniel named Checkers. In political history, Nixon's speech was called "The Checkers Speech." The speech worked. Nixon received a surge of support, remained on the ticket with Eisenhower, and became Vice President.

Our Checkers nearly died during a summer hot spell. Sometimes, we put him on a chain in the backyard by the barn. One day Mom was getting us in the car to take us to the swimming pool at Wing Park. We noticed Checkers lying on the ground. The water bowl was upside down. Checkers had been outside for six hours or so. We walked toward him. He laid extremely still, except for his open mouth and white drool running to the ground. Mom told us to get the garden hose and bring it close to the dog. We put water in his bowl. He did not go to the bowl. Mom poured water from the hose on his body. She gently placed the hose on his tongue and into his mouth. The water kept coming back out. Mom took off his chain, picked him up and brought him to the car. She laid him in the backseat between Kerry and me, and we drove to the vet. Being funeral home kids, we knew the look of near death.

At the vet, Mom carried Checkers inside and laid him on the stainless steel examining table. I heard the word "dehydration." The vet hooked Checkers up to an IV. As the fluid ran through the tubes into his body, he started to revive. The vet instructed us to leave Checkers with him overnight. We went for the ultimate hydration at the swimming pool. Checkers returned home in excellent condition the next morning.

Another time, Checkers acquired celebrity-type fame when he journeyed on a freight train. I can hear you asking, "Freight train? *How?*" We noticed his absence from the house. We looked through the neighborhood and other areas of town. We called friends and the police. Checkers wore a medal identification tag attached to his collar. After two to three days of searching and phoning, we concluded Checkers was either dead, had found a new home, or took off to live in the wild. Then the phone rang. The voice on the phone introduced himself as a railroad worker in a Wisconsin town freight yard three to four hours north of Elgin. He found Checkers when he opened the sliding door on a freight box car. The freight man read Checkers' dog tag and telephoned.

We went on a road trip with Dad to pick him up. The *Elgin Courier-News* printed a story about his journey. In journalistic vernacular, the story indicated it was "a slow news day," or perhaps it was a worthwhile human and canine interest story. If we had only used Checkers' story and written a children's book, later becoming a movie leading to a Broadway musical, the family's production company could have supported the publication of this book you are reading. I will let you make up a title for Checkers' story. In these current times, I picture the movie similar to Spielberg's remake of *West Side Story*. Without the death scenes.

When Barrett left for college in 1958, Kerry and I took over the caretaking of Checkers. We unenthusiastically set up turns to take him for walks. Dad and Mom reached exasperation and took it upon themselves to walk Checkers, as they did not take well to his stains on the carpet. One morning as Kerry and I were taking our first step down the stairs to walk to school, Dad spoke to us from the living room couch.

"Boys, Checkers will not be here when you get home from school."

"What?" we said.

"Your Mom and I decided Checkers will be better off at a farm out in the country."

"You mean the farm where we took him last summer to mate with a girl dog?" Kerry said.

"A different farm," Dad replied.

"Can we see him at the farm?" I asked.

"I don't know. We will see what the new owners think. You get going. I don't want you to be late for school. We will talk when you get home."

Kerry and I talked about Checkers on our four-block walk to school. We came home to our apartment with no sign of Checkers. We never took the trip to the farm to visit Checkers. Did he go to a farm or a kennel for pet abandonment? It remains a mystery.

In Checker's absence, other dogs came for visits. When Barrett and Pat traveled with their family, Mom and Dad cared for their dogs. One of their dogs was an Old English sheepdog named Carrie. Not Kerry. *Carrie*. Carrie left the property on one occasion. Dad's letter of October 21, 1974, to Barrett and Pat and carbon copied to me explains what happened:

"I went downstairs (Mother went to bed) to give Carrie a night airing before I took her upstairs. We were out in the front and back yard playing around. She had her leash on, but I never keep hold of it when I have her out. It gives her a little more freedom and room to do her job. We chased around the front yard funeral home sign; she was barking at me, and I was clapping my hands at her. She apparently got mad at me or thought I was an enemy cause she took off like a bolt down Division Street toward the corner. The more I chased her, the faster she ran. So, I ran all the way back home and picked up the car and started to go looking for her.

I went to the police station first and reported it, so they could have the squads looking for her. I drove over to your house and turned on the outside lights in case she went home. I couldn't leave the garage door open because of all the kids' bikes, etc. From there I called Valley Security Patrol and told their patrol cars to be on the lookout. I drove all over sections of town, but I'd always end up back at your house thinking she'd be there.

In between time, the police had seen her on State Street near the railroad tracks, so I was sure she found her way across the bridge and would go home. By 2 a.m. I was tired and discouraged and stopped at the police station. I came home and laid down. I couldn't sleep but could picture Carrie being caught or tangled in some bushes because she had her leash on or someone picking her up. (Some Saturday nite, drive through town at those hours and see the characters around!) I also thought someone might see her in a back yard and shoot thinking she was a bear!

I dozed off and was mad when I woke up at 3:45 a.m., and the cops hadn't called and no dog. I tried to go back to sleep until daylight came, so I could get out and start searching and call the radio station, etc. But I couldn't sleep, so I washed my face and started out again. I drove around and looked downtown and drove over to your house and searched all around again. I drove around your church, looked there, and told and asked God to help me find that dog. Decided to go get a cup of coffee and a roll and wait until it got bright outside, but decided I wasn't hungry.

I decided to check in at the police station again. When I crossed the bridge on Kimball Street and came near the library parking lot, my heart pounded like crazy 'cause I thought it was a mirage. Dumb me. I tooted the horn, but she just jumped and started walking along east on the sidewalk. So, I drove until I got quite a bit close to Carrie and pulled to the curb and stopped. Thank God, I was driving your station wagon. I opened the back door and I just kept saying softly, 'Carrie.' But she went past the car.

I opened the window and called 'Carrie' again. She came back, smelled the car, and put her paw in the back seat, and I grabbed her collar and pulled her in! Thank God no car or person came along during all this, or it may have scared her off. I held on to her while I closed the door and windows, and I just couldn't believe I had her. We came right home, and she really was a mess. Don't know where she was. We'll never know. I keep wondering if she went to your house and was on her way back to our house? I brushed and brushed and gave her water. And finally fell asleep on the couch.

Mother got up and was relieved, too, naturally. Kept thinking that the last time the bird died and this time you're gone and there's a missing dog. Whatever made me get up at 4 a.m. again, I'll never know. Thanks to God I did. She's been fine ever since, and we had decided if she wasn't back by 4 p.m. Sunday, we wouldn't have the heart to tell you when you called and spoil your trip. I thought *I've been thru these things so much before, why am I going thru them again?* Lost dogs, lost kids, etc., etc. I wouldn't let mother tell this tale before or during the party we had yesterday. We had Carrie out there with us all day and night, either in the yard or in the barn. All of you have fun. Was so glad when you called to say you had arrived. Love, Dad"

We did not experience a continual canine presence in the households. When Checkers departed, Mom and Dad did not seek a new dog. I imagine that had as much to do with the inconsistent care Kerry and I were providing as well as Checkers' decreasing ability to hold in his bodily waste. The rugs and furniture were too vulnerable. Dad and Mom led active personal and professional lives. Other than visits from Carrie and other canines, there was no interest from them to continue.

We also had rabbits in our family pet chronicles. It was Easter Sunday in 1963. Barrett and Pat awaited their first child in less than a month. They arrived in the early afternoon for dinner. I was thirteen; Kerry almost twelve. They carried a shoebox tied with ribbon. They handed the box to us and insisted we open it. We gazed at a small white baby rabbit who twitched and extended its nose out the top of the box. Irresistible. We took it out of the box and held the fluffy creature with resolute oohs and ahhs.

The gift was a surprise to Dad and Mom as well. I am not sure when the rabbit deposited its first dropping on the carpet. Dad carried a rag and spray with the directions for us to "find a place to put the rabbit, so it doesn't further mess up the carpet." We carried the rabbit down the three flights of stairs and outside where we let it scamper in various parts of the yard. The rabbit kept us intrigued and entertained throughout the day.

Barrett and Pat departed after dinner. We fed the rabbit bits of lettuce and used an eye dropper to provide water. We let it move about on the floor in the back room. We watched TV shows with Dad and Mom, intermittingly each of us holding and playing with the rabbit. At some point, we realized the rabbit had escaped our view. We scanned the room and noticed the open door from the back room to the rest of the apartment. As we exited into the dining room, one of us peered over the side of the railing dividing the floor area and down stairway.

"It's at the bottom of the stairway."

"It isn't moving."

We realized the bunny had found its way under the railing and fallen over the edge of the stairwell. Mom, Kerry, and I ran down the stairs.

Once again, our experiences as funeral home kids gave us the knowledge this rabbit reached the end of an all too short life. No resurrection, in spite of Easter. Death is unexpected. One never knows when a death call will come in. Even on Easter Sunday.

"Who's going to tell Barrett and Pat? They will be so mad," I stated.

"Do you mean sad?" added Kerry.

"Both," Mom concluded.

Nobody called. We did not have school the next morning. It was customary in Catholic schools to have a holiday on the Monday after Easter. It was the nuns' way of avoiding children filled with sugar and chocolate. We buried the rabbit in a spot next to the driveway at the bottom of the back stairs. The shoebox in which the rabbit arrived became a casket. Kerry, Mom, and I took turns with a small garden shovel to dig a hole deep enough to place the stiff body. We covered him with the soil we just dug. In line with our Catholic upbringings, we made a cross using two sticks from nearby bushes. After the funeral and a bit of grieving, we did what we probably should not have done. We went to a pet store and bought another rabbit. This cottontail was welcomed in similar fashion.

We convinced Barrett and Pat this replacement was the same bunny they gave us. This rabbit grew rapidly. Dad purchased a cage and set it on metal sawhorses. We kept the rabbit in the yard in front of the barn. Kerry and I made sure this second-chance rabbit was fed and given water regularly. He grew accordingly. In the weeks to follow, the burial area of the first rabbit next to the yellow blooming forsythia bush near the back stairs was full of the greenest grass and plantings in the yard. The decomposing hare was a powerhouse of nutrients. Six months later, winter arrived. Dad suggested we bring the cage into the barn. We laid newspapers on top of plastic sheeting placed under the cage. Kerry and I were less than regular in our duties. On the days we checked, the rabbit seemed content in his cage, though the aroma of his droppings and urine permeated the barn. One rabbit produces excrement proportional to a baby of similar size. Problems occur when these remains are not cleared regularly. This rabbit lived a good life with no predators in a converted barn with gas heat set at a temperature to keep pipes from freezing. I honestly don't recall what happened to him. Did we set him on his way in the yards to fend for himself?

Dad and Mom, Lawrence and Mildred buoyed the ongoing interest of pets in the house with canine experiences, caged birds, outdoor feeding aviaries, and quickly replaced rabbits. They were amused with experiences of life in the midst of the death readily apparent with the business. I felt togetherness with the family through our shared animal experiences.

PART VI

LETTING GO: CELEBRATING TRANSITIONS IN OUR FAMILY

Did we become accustomed to the grief of our clients and immune to the possibilities of losing members of our own family? I observed or heard about our client families' reactions and coping with their loss. Their experiences mirrored our own. We were not ready for the inevitability and unexpectedness of death in our own family or any more prepared to live through the lingering illness and death of a family member than those who came to us for help. For all we experienced in our own business, we too navigated grieving for those who left us.

I've viewed all episodes of the 2001–05 HBO series *Six Feet Under* written by Alan Ball. Set in a funeral home and family apartment of similar interior design to ours, I connected with the family portrayed. Each episode focused on the story of a client—how they died and their arrangements, wake, and funeral. This story was interlaced with stories about the lives of the funeral home owners. The final episode was a flash-forward to tell the stories of how each of the surviving family characters met their end. In similar fashion, this final part of the book highlights the end-of-life occurrences, wakes, and funerals of the four owners of O'Connor Funeral Home and our three cousins.

Deaths do not happen in sequence. This was affirmed to me in a letter I received from my father's sister, Lillian, when their brother, Dan passed away in July 1973:

> "Dan's death was a shock from which it will take us a bit of time to recover. The law of averages says we should die as we were born. Oldest to youngest. But . . . he, the third born, broke the law of averages. Needless to say, the rest of us are looking at each other furtively."

Barrett, Kerry, and I are the remaining survivors of the original Division Street residents. A sobering and contemplative thought. We remain furtive.

CHAPTER 32

Mildred Kruzan O'Connor

MARCH 6, 1971

Mildred was my aunt and godmother, a vital conduit of the connections between our second- and third- floor families. One treasured memory for me is when Mildred came to my rescue as I prepared for my junior prom. This was my first experience wearing a tuxedo. A white one. Dad and Mom left for the evening. With some direction from them, I prepared for the event on my own. I was in the third-floor bathroom doing my final prep work, attired in the white jacket. Posing in front of the mirror, I saw a pubescent whisker, maybe two, on the area above my lip. I was as new to shaving as I was at wearing a tuxedo. As gentle as I tried to be, I managed to nick a piece of skin. Blood found its way to my finger as I tried to undo the damage. One drop went from my finger to the collar of my coat, leaving a red spot. I ran from the bathroom and down the stairs, crying out, "Mildred!"

She was in the kitchen.

"Look. Blood on my collar."

"Stay right there," she said. "Do not move."

Rather than scold or ask why I was shaving a lone whisker with my tuxedo coat on, she went to the sink, took a rag, and rinsed it in cold water. She then gently dabbed the blood on my collar until the redness of the blood was absorbed.

"Looks like you're ready," she said, judging her handiwork. "Are you sure you don't want to look for another whisker? Let's get over to the living room and take a picture. Your Dad and Mom asked me to get one." She took a picture of me posed next to the living room mantle on the second floor. I have the picture to this day. A close-up of the photo reveals a slight pink smudge on the collar of my white tuxedo.

When I said goodbye to her three years later at my departure for Rome in August 1970, I had no idea it was to be our last time together. Her passing reminded me sternly of the unpredictability of death. As much as the years living in the funeral home inculcated this understanding into me, her departure from life was still incomprehensible.

I received the news via a phone call. Phone calls were a rare occurrence when I lived in Rome. In the apartment building where male students resided, a phone was located near the stairway vestibule of each floor. It was connected to the switchboard on the main campus and not used for outgoing calls. Few incoming calls came in. On Sunday evening, March 7, 1971, I heard the phone ring. Someone came to my room and let me know the call was for me. Picking up the receiver, I heard my cousin's voice. She was calling from Germany where she lived.

"Kevin, it's Lani," she said. Mildred died yesterday."

I gave no response. Sniffles and sobbing were heard from both of us.

"Your parents will call you. They told me to tell you they don't want you to come home. Stay. They are still planning to visit in a few weeks."

"What happened to her?" I asked, still numb to the news while images of Mildred and our times together sprinted through my memories.

"She had a heart attack when she was in the car with Uncle Lawrence. They were coming home from Sharon's house in Menomonee Falls. She and Lawrence had gone to Sharon's for Scott's second birthday. Lawrence tried to get to the hospital in time. She died shortly after."

"But I got a letter from her yesterday," I said. "She sounded fine."

"I know. My mom told me she has had some spells lately but hadn't been complaining."

"I want to go home," I insisted. "I can't miss her funeral."

"I know. I feel the same way. I want to go, too. But everyone in Elgin wants both you and me to stay where we are."

"How am I going to get through this?"

This was the second time during my year in Rome I experienced the death of a close relative. My grandmother had died three months earlier. Her death was not a surprise, yet I had difficulty in only reading about her wake, funeral, and celebration gathering. I really wanted to be with the family. I got through that occasion. Now I was grieving from a distance for a second time.

"I am right here; you know you can call me," Lani said kindly. "For now, get with some friends. Tell them what is happening. Don't call home. They will let us know when we can call."

"When is her funeral?"

"I think it is Tuesday. Do you want to stay on the phone with me?"

"I've got some friends standing right here next to me. I will stay with them."

My friends, Jim and Jance, both knew and had spent time on Division Street with Mildred. They asked me what I wanted to do. I told them I wanted to walk, so we walked across campus. Along the way, I asked my girlfriend, Sue, to join us. The four of us continued to meander the paths and roads of the campus. I needed and treasured their support.

Dad and Mom called me the next day. They explained about Mildred's passing, how happy she was, and how much she enjoyed my letters. I listened more than I talked as different voices came to the phone. Dad and Mom further convinced me not to come home for the funeral.

Mildred's wake and funeral were held a few days later. Her daughters, sons-in-laws, and fifteen grandchildren arranged themselves in bedrooms on the second and third floors. In their grief, Dad and Lawrence were supported by colleagues from other funeral homes to help in making the arrangements. In the morning preceding Mildred's afternoon and evening wake, Lawrence and others in the family noticed Dad's extended absence from the second and third floors. They thought he found his own private place to grieve his sister-in-law's death. Later, he came up the stairs and entered the second-floor kitchen filled with relatives.

"Bill! Where have you been?" Lawrence asked.

"I've been with Mildred," he replied to all. "Working on her hair. I got her ready in the casket. She looks so good in a beautiful dress and jewelry she liked. I was determined she was not going to be shown in a wig. She hated those wigs. I worked and worked to fix her hair. Her own hair. She looks beautiful. She's going out of this world with her own hair. I also decided to keep her glasses on. She doesn't look like herself without her glasses. Nobody knew her without her glasses. She looks like herself now."

"Thanks, Uncle Bill. She's smiling right now. And she will have 20/20 vision."

Humor and light talk was customary at our family wakes. Living two floors above grief, we had the capacity to not conceal moments of laughter and cheer. Dad positioned Mildred's coffin in the parlor closest to the bottom of the stairs. As family and friends came down the front stairs, they walked directly into the viewing area. The funeral home and living area became as one, similar to funerals conducted in people's homes, before the practice of funeral homes separate from family residences. Mildred was an owner and resident on

Division Street for more than thirty years. The blending of her personal and final environments provided a comfortable atmosphere.

After an evening wake, funeral the next morning, and burial at the recently purchased plot at Mt. Hope, the family gathered back home for food, libation, and music. Aunt Lillian carried a cassette recorder with her, inviting relatives to speak in the microphone and taking time on her own to add commentary. She mailed the tape to me within a day of the funeral. Hearing the voices, music, and Aunt Lillian's commentary helped me to feel I was at the celebrations with them.

In the months prior, Mildred was making plans to bake and ship me her raisin cake, one of my favorite desserts, to celebrate my birthday. In her letter dated December 3, 1970, she began to unveil her plans:

"Oh yes—I really thot [sic] of you when I baked a raisin cake recently, so I weighed the cake on my bathroom scale, and it registered five pounds—and I mentally added two pounds for packaging and called the PO to see how much it would cost to send a seven-pound package to Italy, and when he said $14.90, I decided you will have to eat Italian pastries until you get home. Kathy had a good suggestion when I told her about this when she said, "SEND HIM THE RECIPE!" So now it will be up to you to find a cook!—or a kitchen in which you can try baking! I know the cake is good—BUT I DON'T BELIEVE THAT GOOD, to cost $15.00!"

Her last letter to me was dated March 1, 1971. I received it after she died. In the upper left corner, she sketched an impression of herself with a poof of hair and closed eyes with distinctive eye lashes. She sketched tears coming from her eyes flowing into a beer stein with "Hamm's" imprinted on the side. She typed these words next to the sketch:

"ME—cryin' in my beer because I just heard—that my gorgeous curly red hair lover boy is leaving me for that female upstairs—and he has such sexy lips! Oh well—(I can't think of any foreign words that mean "SO BE IT"), so in my own Chinese—SO BE IT!"

Her lover boy was a wooden sculpture bust of an African man I purchased during the trip I took the prior December to Kenya. I purchased artifacts in addition to this one and mailed them home with directions about who was to receive each item. There was confusion about the designations, and she thought she was going to get the bust. Evidently, the bust went to Mom on the third floor. The bust eventually came back to me. It is sitting on the shelf behind me right now as I write this story. It serves as a reminder of not only my trip, but the letters about the gifts I sent, and Mildred's humor in conveying the confusion. Her letter continued:

"Haven't heard your latest tape that arrived today, but your Pop was saying you are off to Spain in a few weeks. Maybe you could find a Latin Lover for me. You see, I never gave up hoping. The 1971 22nd annual Mardi Gras Ball has come and gone . . . the costumes were quite plentiful . . . of course members of our Catholic Charities board looked charming in baseball uniforms. I couldn't have looked more ridiculous, so I jazzed it up by wearing large loop earrings, gold necklaces—high heels and nylons—and a child's baseball cap on top of my head. Should have had my picture taken for my grandchildren who could say, 'This was my grandmother—before she was captured.' Oh well, it was fun and just about twelve months before the next dance. Good night for now—I NEED lots of beauty sleep—"

Her signature was handwritten. *Love, Mildred.*

As a surprise for my birthday, Mildred went ahead and made the cake, packaged it, and mailed it to me in Rome. She sent it from Elgin on March 1, five days before she died. Dad's letter dated March 10, 1971, made reference to me receiving the raisin cake in Rome:

"Eat the cake and pass it around in the spirit in which she planned, investigated, baked, and mailed it—full of anticipation and joy. Hope it's good; so, whoever goes first can tell her when they get there. Dad"

When the cake arrived, it was wrapped beautifully in layers of paper recommended by Mildred's local baker to preserve it in the mail. I shared the cake as Dad suggested. I gathered friends in the kitchen of the apartment residence of one of our administrators. I cut the cake and passed it around. Raisin cake is an acquired taste. It's not for everyone. Yet, each friend to whom I gave a piece, took a bite. Eating my piece was one of the most difficult experiences in my twenty-one years. I felt a lump in my throat and stomach. I held back tears pushing to be revealed. It was a hard moment knowing Mildred's hands were the last to touch the cake before my unwrapping and cutting. I felt the joy of her preparing, baking, and doing all necessary to make sure it was packaged correctly and shipped in time. Of course, I wished she was alive and imagined writing to her about my friends and I sharing in her baking skills. It's been a long time since I've eaten a piece of raisin cake. Now I'm a diabetic, which has lessened my desire for cake. Nonetheless, I have the recipe. As Kathy told her grandma years ago, "Send him the recipe. Let him make it."

Raisin Cake Recipe from Mildred's mother, written by
Maureen O'Connor Osborne. Date unknown.

Mildred's death resulted in changes. In the weeks and months that followed, Lawrence decided to sell the funeral home to our Uncle Bob Allanson and my Aunt Lillian. They owned Wait Ross-Allanson Funeral Service two blocks from our house. Our families did not consider ourselves as competitors. Barrett, Kerry, and I were included in a 1971 Christmas holiday gathering typical for all of us with Lawrence, his daughters, my aunt and uncle, and their children. I thought it was a social gathering. Unknown to me, it was also a business gathering with an announcement of the sale to Uncle Bob. They advised us to not share the information with our friends. Even in the prior years, we knew not to share that Lillian was a sister to Dad and Lawrence. Some people did know because our families had common friends. Conversely, others who did not know may have considered it unusual that the sister of the O'Connors was married to one of their competitors.

To the best of my knowledge, Dad was not included in the decision to sell the funeral home. He was never a co-owner. Lawrence was the owner. Dad was his employee. My first thoughts were, *Why wasn't Dad given an opportunity to buy the business and make the funeral home his own?* I do not remember if I asked questions about it. Bob's purchase offered benefits for Dad and Mom. They became co-owners. He was no longer an employee. Over the next thirteen years, Lillian, Bob, Dad, and Mom were partners, meeting regularly to review their business plans, maintaining and strengthening their relationship. They had no secrets in their business relationship or surprises like Lawrence leaving suddenly for three-to-four-day trips. When Dad and Mom wanted to take a short or long trip, Lillian and Bob easily accommodated them. The two couples made time together at dinners, social situations, and community events. In 1974, the four of them arranged to take a trip together to Hawaii. These events were in contrast to the separateness of the relationship as couples Dad and Mom experienced with Lawrence and Mildred.

I am a believer in unearthly, celestial interventions. Changes and adjustments in life sometimes result after a death. When I hear the phrase, "at death's door," when someone is terminally ill or in the midst of passing, I do not think of the door as closed. The door is open, not only for the deceased but for survivors they are leaving as well. In her transition, I imagine Mildred orchestrated the new character of O'Connor Funeral Home. She longed for Lawrence and Dad to have a social as well as business relationship. She enjoyed the relatively few times that she, Lawrence, Dad, and Mom spent social times together. I'd like to think that perhaps she wanted Lawrence to sell the business to Dad. Yet, she loved Lillian and Uncle Bob and knew the business would be in good hands. Perhaps, she guided Lawrence's decision about the sale. She figured out a way to intercede and have the four of them create the ultimate family and business she had perhaps envisioned in 1930.

I believe death can unfold new possibilities and opportunities in the lives of survivors. That was the case in the business and family years that followed. Mildred lived on.

CHAPTER 33

William Virgil O'Connor

SEPTEMBER 9, 1984

Some members of the extended O'Connor family do not readily disclose ailments and physical conditions. Dad followed a similar practice. In summer of 1982, Dad was diagnosed with a cancerous prostrate tumor. His diagnosis came within the same timeframe of Lawrence's artery burst in his leg. Lawrence was in Kansas visiting Maureen and her family. His leg was amputated below the knee. Rather than come back to Elgin, he stayed in Kansas for the three- month recuperation. Although Lawrence was no longer the owner of the funeral home, he had continued to occupy the second-floor apartment. While he was recuperating, he and his daughters made the decision to move him out of the apartment and into a building in which he could use an elevator to access his living space.

Lawrence's time at Maureen's changed the dynamics of the shared living space on Division Street and Lawrence's capacity to assist with the business. Due to these changes, Dad kept his cancer diagnosis to himself, Mom, and Uncle Bob. They collectively made a decision not to tell Barrett, Kerry, and me, hoping the medical help Dad was getting would provide a promising outcome. They wanted to maintain the business without letting others in the family or community know. For a time, this arrangement worked well. The employees at Wait-Ross-Allanson were accustomed to helping Dad. He went to his appointments and treatments. In spite of his changing medical diagnoses and proposals for treatment, Dad and Mom wanted us to maintain our own lives with our families and friends.

Dad did not adhere to all the medical advice given to him. He felt the more he worked on his own condition, the more he put increased burden on Lawrence and his condition. Without following all the recommended components of his regimen, his cancer advanced. Throughout the remaining months of summer, fall, and the winter holidays, I was unaware of Dad's illness. His concern for the rest of us interfered with his self-care.

In January 1983, Mom made individual calls to Barrett, Kerry, and me to let us know about Dad's condition. The next eighteen months sent us all on a trajectory of treatments, hospital stays in Elgin and Quebec, and research into the cancer as it spread from his prostrate to other areas of his body. Remarkably, he kept up with business and social activities. He traveled with Mom to Naples, Florida, from February to April, returning every two to three weeks for treatments in Elgin. When Dad and Mom returned to Elgin in April, they became readily involved in their social and golf games throughout summer and fall. During the Christmas holidays in 1983, Dad maintained his eager, hardy pace as he tended to decorations on all floors of 364 Division Street. He never indicated any pain.

In March 1984, Gina, our toddler age son, Nick, and I, six weeks away from the birth of Mark, visited Dad and Mom for the second consecutive spring break trip at their rented condo in Naples. Dad and Mom extended an invitation to Gina's parents to join us. Dad found a rental down the street to accommodate them. Dad and Mom guided us all on trips to pick oranges, shop at markets, eat dinners at restaurants, make family meals at home, and relax at the beach. Everything seemed normal. Mom told us later that Dad did not let on about his pain. "He wanted you all to be there and for things to go well."

Over the next six months, Dad, Mom, and Uncle Bob made the decision to look for a buyer for the funeral home. By this time, it was clear that neither Barrett, Kerry, nor I were interested in pursuing the family business. Bob was also sick with cancer. When they first consolidated the businesses, they envisioned the creation of three to five funeral businesses in Kane and McHenry counties. The dream was radically impaired due to the effects of Lillian's passing in 1978 and the health conditions of Bob and Dad. They consulted with attorneys and funeral director associations to find a buyer. They did not want a potential buyer to know O'Connor's was owned by Allanson. They did not want the buyer to know Dad was sick.

The business plan stated Dad and Mom's intentions to continue working while the new owner became established. The sale was completed in June 1984. Dad and Mom moved out of their apartment. Lawrence's furnishings and memorabilia went to his daughters. Closing the doors marked the end of the fifty-four-year history of the business with an O'Connor as owner.

On moving day, Dad moved slowly and deliberately but with a renewed sense of energy for home ownership. This was the first time they lived in a house owned by them. Dad was readily involved with contractors to add a bathroom. Depending on Dad's health, he and Mom helped the new owner of the funeral home. They provided a presence at the funeral home during wakes and funerals, especially for families and friends familiar with Dad, Mom, and Lawrence.

In August, as the medications lost their effectiveness, Dad spent periods in the hospital ranging from two to five days. Other times he rested at home. My brothers and I took turns staying with him. We visited with him in a chair beside the couch or in his bed. I was talking to him one night about how I felt good about how I was adjusting to fatherhood of a two-year-old and three-month-old infant. I asked him how he and Mom adjusted in their lives when they went from parents of a single child to three children. He responded: "Kevin, you will not regret the times you could have had with friends while you stayed home to be with your kids. You kids were what was most important in our lives. There will always be parties and dinners to go to. You can only be a parent and an influence in your children's lives for a short time." Even then, Dad was nurturing—he at 71, laying on the couch in all his pain and me at age 34, listening. He was nurturing me as a father speaking to a son-father. I incorporated his words into my fathering.

In the first week of September, Dad and Mom made the decision to acquire hospice services at their house. On the evening of September 7, Gina and I took Nick and Mark to visit Dad and Mom. Dad faded in and out. I laid the boys on either side of him in the bed. Dad and I talked.

He advised in his always practical but now strained, whispered voice, "Your condo has been on the market for almost a year. You need to get something bigger. What is happening?"

"We changed realtors," I said. "We are now with Cindy. She has done real estate work with friends who have been happy with her. She listed the place today. We will see what happens. Something has to change. Not one person has looked at the place in a year."

"Yes, we have to do something, so these boys have a yard to play in, and you and Gina have more room," he replied.

Those were the last words I heard from him that night before he drifted away. He died thirty-six hours later at 7 a.m. on Sunday, September 9. My brothers and I assigned each other responsibilities. I went to Lawrence's apartment to let him know. He had already become adept at maneuvering his wheelchair from room to room. He was dressed in his white short-sleeve shirt, to which I had been accustomed all of my life. I stayed with him for an hour.

We conversed, consoled, and comforted each other.

Dad's passing put the new owner of the funeral home in the unexpected position of making arrangements for the funeral of the man with whom he was planning a business relationship. The wake started on Tuesday afternoon. Mom, Barrett, Kerry, and I took our positions near the casket. A line formed, extending from inside to the parking lot and sidewalks in front of the funeral home. Each time I looked up at the line, no end was in sight. A friend of mine has remarked that Dad's wake and funeral were the largest she ever experienced.

At the funeral service the next day, the pastor of St. Mary's offered a eulogy:

"Bill's service as a funeral director was much more than a business enterprise. It was a ministry of service to the grieved and bereaved. How many families in more than fifty years did he comfort at a time in their lives of greatest stress? How supportive he was to the clergy and all those involved in a funeral event. Many of us here can testify to this. But I use the word 'ministry' very deliberately. Ministry means service. The one clear indicator of a follower and believer in Jesus Christ is that he/she is a servant. Bill O'Connor was one who served and served with dignity.

No one who really loved him would want his suffering to continue. It was a difficult period these last months with cancer taking over his poor body. But his spirit and optimism and good cheer never flagged. He didn't want attention or sympathy. With Marion at his side and his children there in full support, these last months were opportunities given to him to let other people, especially his family and friends, serve him for a change. And they did, so unselfishly.

In one of my best and last visits with him a few weeks ago, we talked about how important it was to let those around you know you love them. For Bill this was no problem. He did let people know he loved and appreciated them.

Bill was an optimist, a pleasure to be around. He knew deep down that there must be a cross if there is to be a crown. His professional life taught him that lesson countless of times over, too.

Each one of us enjoyed this man's great gift of personality, his sense of humor, and the strong confidence that seemed to always emanate from him.

And today there is a group of men here that should be acknowledged. In fact, a special fraternity: the many funeral directors who knew and worked with Bill. All of you have lost a vital member, and he appreciated you. He relied on your support and understanding, your willingness to help, and your friendship. I know you leaned on him often, too. It is my fervent prayer that all of you will rededicate yourselves this morning in Bill's honor and memory, to see your important professions as a ministry of service to God's people in some of their loneliest moments. I hope you will exert that extra patience and compassion that marks the best of your profession. Bill O'Connor and his dear brother, Larry, have been examples to emulate. Never underestimate your important role in people's lives as they struggle to face grief and loss.

Human life is a passage from one finite life to eternal life. The white vestments, the funeral pall on the casket, and the candle burning are all baptismal symbols, and they remind us of the promise of Christ that 'Where I am, you also will be.'

So, 'well done good and faithful servant. Enter now into the joys of the kingdom.'

You know, I believe Bill is here with us, and I can almost hear him say as he sees the large number of people here, 'Gee, isn't that great.'

And it is great. A large outpouring of love and affection, a tribute that is beautiful and prayerful. A memory to cherish. Bill is a man none of us will forget, and we are all richer for having known him. We join Bill in his living spirit as he approaches Christ in whose arms and heart he now rests secure."

Sitting in the pew, I started applauding. The pastor gave me a disapproving look. No applause in church allowed. The congregation joined me in applause. Dad, the performer, was receiving the adulation he got when people sang along with him as he entertained at whatever piano he was playing.

Dad's Celebration of Life was typical of the family. Food and libations were served at the local Elks Club, one of Dad's favorite places to play cards and have meals with friends. One of our family photographers took pictures of the Division Street offspring. Maureen, Kathleen, Sharon, Barrett, Kerry, and I posed together in a brother/sister/cousin picture.

Picture taken at Bill O'Connor's funeral, September 12, 1984. Front row seated: Kathleen and Sharon. Back row standing: BarreH, Maureen, Kevin, Kerry.

After lunch, many among our extended offspring came back to Division Street for a picture on the front lawn. We went from there to Mom's house. Food and drink flowed. And there was music. Definitely music.

While at the wake, our realtor, Cindy, came to me.

"I found a young man who wants to look at your condo. I haven't had a chance to list it yet. I was asking around the office, and somebody said they thought he might be interested. He is coming to look at the place tomorrow. I know you will be at the funeral. I will show him your condo."

"Cindy, this is incredible," I said. "In the year the place was listed, not one person has shown any interest. I was telling my Dad about you last Friday night. The last time I was with him."

"It looks like your Dad heard you. He went to work and found this guy. I'll let you know what happens."

The day after the funeral, Cindy called Gina and me to tell us this prospective buyer made an offer for purchase. She recommended we take it. We did. As Dad was making his transition, he was helping. I am convinced he found the buyer.

Dad lived on immediately when we were searching through his wallet in the days after the funeral. Inserted into one of the pockets was a folded piece of small stationery with a note written presumably in his terminal days. In his exquisitely stylized handwriting, he scripted: "Marion, I've loved all of you so—but especially, you! Please enjoy life. Good luck. Me."

Under a glass top on my desk, I keep the birthday card I sent to dad on his sixtieth birthday in 1973. I was twenty-three. My sentiments written inside the card convey: "Happy 60th. You're not older, Dad, just better! I think of you and hope that when I am 60—or even 30, 40, 50!—I will be as much an open thinker, open tryer, and open doer as you. You're always willing to expose yourself to new ideas, new people, new places—always growing and growing and growing . . . and always having that spirit of adventure. So many people tell me: 'Kevin, you're so much like your father.' I consider that a real compliment. I hope I can always live up to it."

I received a gift of a music box in the shape of a grand piano from a friend. She often stood by Dad and sang with him at gatherings. On the music box, right in the spot where the name of a piano brand was usually shown, I was caught by two words engraved on a brass plate. "Play On." Dad plays on in my thinking, my fathering, and my relationships.

CHAPTER 34

Lawrence Stephen O'Connor

SEPTEMBER 13, 1993

Lawrence died in Babylon, NY. He was living in the coach house apartment behind the house where Kathleen and Frank raised their children. After his leg was amputated in 1982, he moved to an apartment on Chicago Street and later to another apartment on State Street in Elgin. He learned how to drive his car with his prosthetic leg. He traveled via air or car to visit his daughters' homes. In the late 1980s, he moved to Babylon. He was able to visit with his grandchildren as they finished college and started their professional and married lives. He became acquainted through church and choral groups. His coach house was a visiting place for the family.

When he died, the Martinos arranged a wake for him in Babylon and shipped his body to Elgin. His wake in Elgin was held at our house. David

Osborne remembers arriving to the sound of the family singing around the organ while Lawrence's body was laid out in the casket. After his funeral at St. Mary's, we gathered at a reception hall. This was followed by a stop at the Division Street house, where we positioned ourselves in front of the funeral home sign for our offspring picture. Most people stopped at their hotels or homes to change clothes and headed to Kerry and Linda's for further festivities full of food, drink, music, and singing. For hours. We did our best to emulate his baritone tones in renditions of "Irish Eyes are Smiling," "Wild Irish Rose," and "Danny Boy." We relied on Linda's piano playing to lead us in the songs, vamps, and intonations characteristic of Dad's style. We cleared some furniture and did Irish jigs. When some sought further entertainment, we proceeded to a country and western bar in Elgin. What a contrast to our usual musical repertoires! We went because some of the grandchildren were fans of that genre of music. We stayed till the closing hour after circle dancing and Texas two-stepping in a variety of partnerships. Together we were making the transitions from Lawrence's melodic beginnings to the musical tastes of his offspring. A joyous time, in spite of our loss.

I was blessed to be a part of Lawrence's life. Living in the same house, I knew him in everyday, routine ways. Lawrence considered me and my brothers as his sons. He wanted us to be a part of shared experiences. Kerry and I— or sometimes me alone—accompanied Lawrence and Mildred for trips to Clinton, Iowa, to spend the day with Maureen and family. Lawrence knew his way through the back roads and towns west of Elgin to Iowa. He made stops to visit priests who were formerly stationed in Elgin and currently residing at a parish rectory along our route. He may have called ahead of his departure to alert them of his arrival or stopped at a phone booth on the way to make the call. Sometimes, he walked to the rectory door and knocked without prior announcement. When we headed back home after visiting in Clinton, Lawrence insisted we recite the rosary with him. We knew not to offer resistance. If I didn't fall asleep during the recitation, I was asleep soon afterward.

I slept until about halfway through the trip when he stopped at a coffee shop or diner he knew was open. Lawrence knew those places were open until late hours. I assume he made visits to some of these towns during his getaways from the funeral home. We walked into these establishments and sometimes were the only customers at the late hour. He ordered a cup of coffee and urged Kerry and I to have a sandwich, piece of pie, or a sundae. We got back in the car and continued to Elgin.

Our longest driving trip with Lawrence was in April 1959 a few weeks after the birth of Kathleen and Frank's firstborn child, Stephen. Mildred had flown or taken the train to help them at their Farmingdale, New York home. Lawrence made plans to visit and bring Mildred back to Elgin in the car. He invited Kerry and I to go with him. Dad and Mom took us to school to meet with our teachers to get our schoolwork. Kerry and I took turns riding in the front seat with Lawrence as we headed east. On the first night, we slept in Youngstown.

Lawrence taught Kerry and I to determine how many miles the car was getting per gallon. Before we pulled out of the driveway in Elgin, we recorded the mileage on the car's speedometer. At our first stop, he showed us how to find the current mileage on the car and subtract it from the previous recorded mileage to determine the number of miles driven. He instructed us how to divide the mileage amount by the number of gallons of gas put into the gas tank. The resulting quotient provided the number of miles we got for each gallon of gas. We repeated this process at each fueling stop. Now of course, all those numbers are recorded automatically in car computers. We computed with pencil and paper, without calculators. Lawrence was a teacher. To this day, I can estimate these figures in my head, thanks to what he taught us.

Lawrence showed me how to be the type of uncle I have strived to be for my nieces and nephews. He was interested in my schooling, activities, friends, and children. Not just interested. He wanted to be a part of my life. He was. Still is.

CHAPTER 35

Eileen Sharon O'Connor Safar

MARCH 1, 2004

Sharon was the first of us Division Street children to die. We suspect she knew she was sick and kept the information mostly to herself. This secrecy about health is not unusual in our family. At a party to celebrate my son Mark's graduation from high school in June 2003, some of us noticed changes in Sharon's appearance. By Thanksgiving, we knew cancer was weakening her body. By early January 2004, she was in a hospital care unit. During those months of January and February, many of us made trips to see and visit with her. The visits I made coincided with visits from Maureen and Bill, Kathleen and Frank, and other cousins. We spent time with Sharon's husband, John, and children-Shannon, Lynn, Scott, and their families. We savored a few moments of hope while coping with the inevitable finality of her condition.

Sharon's wake was similar to others in the family. Music played as we meandered in each other's presence. Some of us offered verbal tributes and remembrances. At the conclusion of the evening wake, we engaged in the customary frivolity of food and drink at a local restaurant. We stayed overnight at an area hotel. We awoke the following morning and positioned ourselves at numerous tables for breakfast. Pallbearers Barrett, Kerry, Mike and David Osborne, Jim and Vincent Martino, and me wore white gloves embroidered with Sharon's name and a shamrock. After the funeral at her parish church, we gathered in the community room for lunch and posed for a group picture of all the family in attendance. We then headed back to our homes to move forward with our own lives.

A few weeks later, some of us gathered in Milwaukee at Alverno College where a tribute was held for Sharon in honor of all the work she had done as a counselor for students and staff. We made plans for a family reunion to be held at Maureen and Bill's house the following summer in Lawrence, Kansas. It was a record-breaking day of heat. We sweated in unison, each taking a momentary break in the air conditioning of the house. We joined in keyboards and instruments, playing as our voices regaled in song outside under the canvas tents. More than one hundred of us posed on a sloping area of their yard for a group picture, testimony not only to Sharon but to the continuity of our family.

CHAPTER 36

Kathleen Margaret O'Connor Martino

JUNE 26, 2010

In the months prior to her passing, Kathleen's health challenges resulted in surgeries and amputations. Leon and I made trips to Long Island to visit her. On one visit, she asked me to go to physical therapy with her. She was a stubborn patient, sharing her humored resistance at each exercise station. I hope my encouragement helped in some way to provide sustenance. My visits provided time for conversation. Talking was not a problem for her. Ever. Throughout my life, I knew there was an undetermined end to our conversations when we talked on the phone. I thrived on those calls. We talked about her kids, her grandkids, and my kids. We talked without boundaries and secrets about marriages, divorces, and family situations. As I felt with her sisters, I was a close brother.

Family spent the wake and funeral days at a Babylon area hotel. We joined with family at restaurants or the homes of the Martino children. When we gathered at the wake, we shared stories during one-to-one conversations. During the service, we shared our own personal tributes and memories. Kerry, Barrett, and I were once again pallbearers. Cousin Michelle was the officiant at the funeral home, at the church, and cemetery. She rode in the car with us. We insisted she was not allowed to pass on until she conducted each of our own funerals. We said collectively we wanted to make sure she was to be our officiant. As of this writing, Michelle is holding on, enhancing the prospect she will officiate at our funerals.

We concluded the funeral day with a luncheon for all in the family in attendance. We took the pictures standard for our funeral gatherings. We lingered with goodbyes at the restaurant and hotel as each of us departed. We gathered later at Kathleen's son Jim and Kim's house for togetherness. Emblematic of funerals in our family, there was no rush into goodbyes.

CHAPTER 37

Marion Helen Ciraulo O'Connor

OCTOBER 1, 2010

The prologue of this book opened with the story of Mom's last hours. There is more to the story of her final years and her funeral and services in Elgin.

I was with Mom at her Huntley home during the spring of 2007. Her arm was in a cast from a fall. She wanted to take a shower. I moved with her as she maneuvered her walker into the bathroom. Although the shower area was handicap equipped, she told me she was not steady on her feet enough to get into the shower.

"Darn, I really want to take a shower. What can I do?"

"How about if I use a warm washcloth and give you a sponge bath?"

"I want to get my hair wet and get a shampoo."

"Okay, Mom. Here's an idea. I will get you undressed, but in order to keep you steady, I will get in the shower with you."

"Oh, oh, oh, I am not sure about that," she said.

"Would you feel more comfortable if I kept my briefs on?"

"Yeah. Are you sure you're okay with that?"

"Do you mean you'd be okay with my briefs off?"

She smiled. "That's not what I meant."

She laughed.

"Let's do it."

I positioned her on a stool in the shower. I assisted her in taking off her clothes. I helped her to hold on to the handicap bar on the wall of the shower area.

"Mom, I don't want you to peek, but I am going to take off my clothes, except for my briefs. I am going to stand right beside you."

"Okay. This is something we've never done before."

"Yeah, a new adventure," I joked.

I turned on the faucet and adjusted the temperature while the water flowed through Mom's hands.

"Tell me when the temperature is right."

"Okay, that's good."

I wet her hair, massaged her scalp with the shampoo, then rinsed.

"Oh, that feels good. I am so glad."

I continued with washing and rinsing her body.

"Time to get out. I will turn off the water now."

I wrapped towels around her shoulders and across her lap. I dabbed at the towels until her skin dried. I helped her stand briefly while I removed the stool from underneath her and repositioned it on the floor in front of the counter and mirror. I helped her to move from the shower area to the stool. I replaced the towels.

"Time to dry your hair. I've got the dryer in one hand and a brush in the other."

I stood behind her to keep her from falling.

"How do you want me to comb your hair?" I asked.

"I can do that myself. I don't need you for that. You hold the dryer. I will brush my hair."

By the time her hair was dried and brushed, her body was dry too.

"Mom, hold on to the stool. I'll get clothes for you."

I expeditiously went to her drawer and closets. I returned with clean undergarments, pants, and a blouse. I helped her get dressed. We went back to the living room.

"I feel so much better," she said gratefully.

"I am glad you are comfortable with this. I will be glad to do it again."

"That would be nice."

The scene was replicated in the months that followed.

After retiring as principal from Maplewood School in Cary, Illinois, in June 2007, I moved to Hollywood, Florida. Mom was living in Naples each year from October through May and in Elgin from May through October. Hollywood is a ninety-minute drive from Naples. I welcomed the privilege and opportunity to be with her two to three times a week to provide respite for her caretakers. In the summer of 2009, we hired Amy as Mom's caregiver in Elgin. Amy moved with Mom to Naples after the 2009 Christmas holidays. In the summer of 2010, Barrett, Kerry, and I agreed to move Mom and Amy to Hallandale Beach near Hollywood, so I could be readily available. Leon's daughter-in-law, Orli, a real estate agent, found an apartment on the eighteenth floor of a building overlooking the Atlantic. Mom was so happy to be living with a view of water.

"I've always wanted to live on the water. Now, here I am," she'd say proudly.

I spent my times with Mom in conversation, reading aloud to her from letters and newspapers, playing cards and Rummikub. I spoke to either Kerry or Barrett on a near daily basis.

Mom was a voracious reader. In her last few years, she lost the ability to comfortably read and pay attention. It was difficult for her to hold a book or newspaper. I suggested I read the letters referenced and shared in this book. She agreed. The letters provided a sense of history for me and Mom. Sitting on her terrace overlooking the Atlantic the month before she died, I read aloud one of my letters written to Dad and her in September 1970:

"Dad and Mom, thank you so much for writing to tell me you will save my letters. Someday we will be able to read these letters and remember what we were doing and the adventures we had."

A revelatory and predictive comment. I felt a chill when I read those sentences aloud to Mom on her terrace. I looked at her as she smiled. I caught a tear in her eye.

"Isn't that amazing?" she said. "Here we are forty years later. What you said would happen is happening."

Fifty years later, I use the content of these saved letters to share stories about grandparents, parents, and relatives. The personalities of our family come to life through the stories in their letters.

She liked to read herself to sleep. One time when I was putting her to bed, she lamented, "I wish I could still read in bed."

"How about if I read from one of your novels?"

"That would be nice. It's been a long time since someone has read out loud to me from a book."

I picked up the romance novel that appeared to be the most current from her bedside. I opened to a bookmark. "He stroked her along the top of her shoulder," I began to read aloud. "He gently touched between her breasts."

Mom said nothing.

"He reached one finger to her protruding nipple as he gazed into her eyes."

"I don't recall this part."

"Keep going?" I asked, gauging her comfort level.

"Sure. We've come this far in our lives together. What's a few words like these between us at this point?"

I continued. She fell asleep. She did not ask me again to read from a romance novel.

Barrett visited her in Hallandale the week before she died. Barrett and I talked about Facebook as we looked at laptop screens. Mom inquired.

"What are you doing?"

Barrett explained about Facebook.

"How do I do it?"

Barrett and I set up a Facebook account for her.

A few days later I sat with her on the couch with my computer opened to her Facebook page. By now, she had a number of followers making comments to her.

"I am so confused about this Facebook thing. How does it happen? Why is my picture on there?"

"Facebook is like writing a letter or making a phone call to someone," I replied. "You can write to someone on Facebook. You can see what they have been doing by looking at pictures and comments they write. People write comments back to them. It's like a conversation."

On Tuesday, September 28, Amy called me at 1:45 in the afternoon to tell me she had called 911. I arrived at the driveway of the condo building as paramedics lifted Mom aboard the ambulance. I followed the ambulance to Aventura Hospital. Mom was taken to the emergency room, examined, and moved to the cardiac care unit. I experienced a series of serendipitous events in the following days. The first thing I noticed upon entering Mom's room was an Elgin clock hanging on the wall. It was not common to see Elgin wall clocks. When Mom was sleeping, I looked at the clocks in each of the thirty rooms in the unit. I counted three Elgin clocks. What were the chances Mom was randomly placed in one of the rooms with an Elgin clock? Serendipity.

She napped intermittingly. She awoke wide-eyed from sleep and blurted out, "Facebook, Facebook." Somehow in her oxygen induced sleeping, she was coming to an understanding of social networking. She was updating her contact list or putting a post on her wall. Not knowing or ready to accept what was happening during her hospital stay, I perceive Mom, in her sleep, was re-initializing direct connections with Dad and others who were reaching out to her. She was in the ultimate social network.

Mom exhibited an accepting outlook on death. She remarked to me she was ready. She said this in a matter-of-fact, not sad way. She kept her sense of humor. Always. She woke the next morning, opened her eyes, looked at me, and smiled. "Oh, I'm still here."

"Yeah, Mom. Where did you think you'd be?"

"Well, I thought it might be MY time."

"Not now. Let's have some breakfast."

The following morning the doctors informed me of Mom's deteriorating condition. I met with the nurse in charge of the hospice wing of the hospital. She introduced herself as Catherine, but her name tag was printed "Margaret C." I asked her why.

"Margaret is my given, legal name, but I go by Catherine."

Mom's deceased sister's name was Margaret. Another sign of serendipity.

Thursday morning, Kerry made plans to fly to Miami. The doctor recommended Mom stay on oxygen prior to moving to hospice. He wanted to be sure Kerry arrived to spend time with her. It was serendipity this empathetic doctor was assigned to her case.

Barrett called to remind me, "Did you contact a priest?" I met with the front desk nurse. She contacted a priest from nearby St. Lawrence Church. St. Lawrence does not rank among the top names assigned to Catholic parishes. Another St. Lawrence Parish was located in Elgin. [Also, her brother-in-law, Lawrence, was a significant person in her life.] What were the chances the priest be from St. Lawrence Parish? Serendipity.

I told Mom the priest was coming from St. Lawrence Parish to give her the last rites. She grinned and said, "Lawrence?"

An hour later, the priest arrived. Mom and I looked at his name tag. My eyes filled with a tear or two. The name on the name tag? William.

"Mom, look at this name tag. His name is Bill."

She whispered one of her commonly used conversational phrases, "Heavenly days," through her oxygen mask. At that moment, I think there was connection attached to "heavenly." Mom smiled at the coincidence of the priest's name. Serendipity.

Kerry arrived at the hospital at 8 p.m., after Father Bill departed. Kerry took some time alone with her, followed by conversation with Mom, Kerry, Leon, Amy, and me. Mom was fading. Two hours later, the nurse came in.

"Are you ready, Mrs. O'Connor?"

"Yes, I am."

We stayed with Mom as the nurse disconnected the devices attached to her. She stayed alert and talked a bit. We all accompanied the nurse and attendants as they wheeled her bed through the halls of the hospital to the hospice area where the attendant, Millicent, introduced herself. We all looked at her and each other. You can't get much closer to the name Mildred than the name Millicent. Again, serendipity.

Millicent took her into an available room, gave her a sponge bath, and placed her into bed. We came into her room and sat on the sides of her bed. It took just a few minutes for her to make her transition. Mom died a few minutes past midnight on October 1. This date was significant to her bookkeeper skills because that date is the beginning of the fourth quarter and the start of a new month. Mom earned her full Social Security check for October by living to the first half hour of the first day of that month. To her last breath, she attained the balanced checkbook and up-to-date financial records she regularly accomplished. To the penny. Serendipity.

Mom died far from Elgin. She *was* assigned to a room with an Elgin clock representing her parents and Elgin upbringing, a hospice intake person with the name of her sister, Margaret, a priest named Bill from St. Lawrence Parish, and a hospice greeter with a name closely akin to Mildred's. This was ultimate serendipity, a strong connection to the key players in our lives from Division Street. Kerry and I knew Mom was home.

In designing the program cover for the funeral, my niece, Keli found a picture of Mom she thought to be the right one. This particular picture of Mom was taken fifteen years earlier when she exited St. Mary's Church arm in arm with her sister Margaret. Was it uncanny for Keli to choose a picture of Mom taken in St. Mary's, the church where she was baptized, married, and attended Mass regularly? Not uncanny. It was serendipity.

Kerry stayed in Hollywood for three days. We continued as sons of undertakers. Kerry made arrangements for us to be on the same flight to Chicago as Mom's coffin. We boarded the plane and watched through the window as she was loaded into the baggage area. When we landed in Chicago, we exited the plane and watched from the terminal window as her transport coffin exited the plane and was placed on a cart pulled by a golf cart. So appropriate for Mom's coffin to be pulled by a golf cart. The cart drove to meet the hearse. We met the hearse in a cargo area and rode with Mom from O'Hare back to O'Connor-Leetz Funeral Home in Elgin. We met with the rest of the family later in the day to make arrangements with Lucy, the employee assigned to Mom's case.

Mom's body was placed in one of the original funeral parlors. The wooden sliding doors dividing the parlor from the front vestibule and stairway were left open. Many of those who came to the wake took up positions on couches and chairs at the bottom of the stairs leading up to the apartments. Some sat on the stairs for their conversations. This was home to all of us. At the conclusion of the wake, we went out to eat like we had done for earlier family wakes.

We arrived for the service at the funeral home the following morning. We decided to bury Mom with her gold bracelet with charms attached representing various milestones in her life. I wish we had not buried her with it. The charms might have been shared with individuals in the family as remembrances of her. Too late now. Barring an exhuming of her body, Mom is keeping the bracelet.

Mom's nieces and nephews and Leon served as pallbearers. As they exited the front door of the funeral home and placed Mom's closed coffin in the hearse, Kerry, Barrett, and I traded quick, knowing glances. We stepped quickly to the front seat of the hearse, placed ourselves behind the wheel and drove in the procession to escort Mom's body four blocks to St. Mary's. After the service, we continued the drive to Mt. Hope Cemetery for the graveside services. Mom, Mildred, Lawrence, and Dad were now together in a shared cemetery plot under a tombstone purchased almost forty years prior when Mildred passed away. The four of them together. As they were on Division Street. At the conclusion of the graveside prayers, a vibrant, interactive atmosphere occurred at her graveside. There was no rush to get into cars. It felt like a cocktail party without the alcohol. People milled about from one conversation to the next. Suddenly, a family friend who owned a funeral home in Elgin mentioned to Kerry, "Your mom's coffin is in the wrong direction. As it is now, her feet will be next to your dad's head."

Thank goodness for the trained eye of an undertaker. We summoned the pallbearers to let them know their job was being continued. Amidst laughter of all those learning what was happening, the pallbearers turned Mom's coffin and repositioned the head of her coffin to be level with Dad's. All in a day's work for undertakers. It makes me wonder how many coffins do go into the ground in a reverse position. Mom was in the care of so many, right up to the very end. And now she and Dad are reclined side by side, head-to-head.

CHAPTER 38

Maureen Frances O'Connor Osborne

MARCH 20, 2014

Maureen was the seventh of our original Division Street family to make the transition from her earthly position.

Throughout our lives, I spoke to Maureen frequently on the phone. My last call to her was on March 8. We talked about her prognosis and debilitating condition. A few days later she lapsed into a period of difficulty speaking on the phone.

Her Celebration of Life was held in Lawrence, Kansas. I traveled to join her immediate family. We repeated the rituals in which our family had been involved in prior years. We gathered at hotels and restaurants to tell stories and treasure our time together. We met at the funeral home for the memorial service attended by her friends and family. We arrived at church the following morning for Mass and then to a luncheon. We came together for the family picture. When I returned to my hotel room, I received an email from a publisher accepting my proposal for this book. Maureen was at work already. She wanted the stories to be written.

After a respite in our hotel rooms, we met back at Maureen and Bill's house for more food, libation, and to look at Maureen's superbly organized picture albums. This was all done amidst a music fest with instruments and voices singing songs with lyrics from Maureen's teen years up through the contemporary songs of her grandchildren. We shared smiles and harmonies to moderate our grief and move us forward. We closed the evening at the community room of the hotel.

I stayed for a few more days and helped with whatever assignments came my way from Bill and the Osborne cousins. I helped to organize the cards from family, floral gifts, and charity donations, and I addressed the envelopes for acknowledgment. Per my training on Division Street from Dad and Lawrence, I was in my element. Always an undertaker's son and a Division Street offspring.

The family met together in Elgin a year later to inter Maureen's ashes in an area next to the marked graves of her daughter, Marie, her parents, Mom, Dad, and her in-laws.

PART VII

STORIES AND CELEBRATIONS CONTINUE

Each time I used my fingers to retype the thoughts and letters of other family members, I felt myself relocating into their hands and minds. This physical act of reading and typing connected me to them in ways I think of as spiritual.

I was blessed to live in the richness of nurturing family experiences. My two sets of parents provided me with a secure life with their successful business. If the business was so good, what prompted me or my brothers and cousins not to continue in our family's professional line of work? It was not customary in the 1940s and 1950s to encourage females to be funeral directors. Dad and Lawrence respected my brothers, cousins, and me for the lives we were creating. They did not pressure us to continue in the business. They wanted us to build on the experiences from the funeral home as well as the relationships we had with friends and the other jobs we had outside the home to guide us to our own choices for careers and livelihoods. I learned from the jobs I had as newspaper carrier, fast-food provider, grocery and liquor store clerk, hospital kitchen dishwasher, and manufacturing line worker. I knew I would be welcome to be readily involved in the funeral business. I liked the aspects of the business that focused on people in need. Watching Dad and Lawrence's care in dealing with people, I knew I had a personality that accommodated to the work. Yet, experiencing the business firsthand, I had difficulty with the irregularity and absence of schedule, the aspect of being on call at all times, and the emotional challenges and unpredictability of outcomes involved with an ambulance call or violent death. The perceptions I had about the business, coupled with my parents' and Lawrence's and Mildred's encouragement to explore what life had to offer, influenced my decision to pursue a career in education.

I don't think Dad wanted us to follow in the profession. Lawrence found himself in the funeral industry in part due to economics of the late '20s and his desire to have a business with his name attached. He influenced Dad to join him. Dad worked hard but felt more tethered to his work and responsibilities than he liked. He wanted his sons to have the freedom he felt he did not have as a funeral home director. I don't recall having a single conversation with Dad or Lawrence about the possibility of me following in the business. I knew if I was interested, I could talk to them.

Lawrence, Mildred, Dad, and Mom provided a life for us connected to the backgrounds they brought with them from their own experiences of family and living together with brothers, sisters, parents, and grandparents. For many years I have thought about the importance of conveying our history. There are few families engaged in the comparatively small funeral home business. According to data from the U.S. Bureau of Labor Statistics, there are just under 25,000 licensed funeral directors in the United States. [4] Undertaking is a necessary, small profession compared to the many other careers in which Division Street offspring and spouses/partners are engaged.

I offer this book as a gift to readers and an opportunity to reap the benefits of our storied history. I encourage individuals to take our stories and use them as an inspiration to research and tell your own stories.

Letters are an essential part of our stories. This book includes Mom's letter to her parents the day after her wedding, the letters I wrote as a child to my cousins, and the letters, aerogrammes, and writings sent between my father, mother, uncle, aunt, and me. I am indebted to my parents for saving the letters I wrote to them. I am pleased for saving the letters I received. Some in my family say they don't know about Mildred's humor and laughter without reading her saved letters. I have also conveyed the political thinking of my mother and the care and concern of my father in the letters they wrote. The content of these letters has provided me with the assistance to support the purpose stated at the beginning of this book of inviting and engaging readers to learn about and be involved in the lives of two sets of parents who created a loving environment for their six children.

The letter writers sometimes composed their correspondences simultaneously without each other's awareness. The news in these letters may have been duplicated. However, the voices in these letters taught me to interpret their different viewpoints. I am reminded about their differences and how they thrived in their relationships, in spite of their various ways of thinking and doing. In reading the letters and sharing them in this book, I have the benefit of discovering aspects of my life about which I was not aware when my past was the present. These letters have been jumping off points for me to make connections I was unable to make in earlier years.

Today we have the immediacy of text and email. We have the ability to make an international phone call at a moment's notice. This was not the case prior to the mid-1980s when email and cell phones first came on the scene. During the first thirty years of my life, letter writing was considered the way to communicate. Letters written, sent, and received were essential to the development and continuity of families like ours. I embrace history through the written words of others.

CHAPTER 39

Record Your Own Family History

You have read this far—or maybe you skipped to this section because the title enticed you to consider delving further into your own family history. Genealogical records provide the information of dates in our ancestors' lives. This information is limiting. The listing of dates and tracing of locations of our ancestors do not provide the stories of why or how they moved from one place to another, decisions made about jobs, or the creating of their families. A friend from college commented to me recently that she appreciated the autobiography her grandfather wrote. She now knows about decisions he made leading to her own history. Let the stories in this book provide a base to relate to your own lives and share with your generations and those to come. Keep looking for your roots. Let yourself be inspired.

For my continued inspiration, I am writing parts of this chapter from my son Mark's house in St. Paul. The structure of his house is built in a similar, but smaller, Victorian style as the Division Street house. Coincidentally, both the funeral home and Mark's house were built in 1887. I marvel at the architectural similarity of both houses. Mark's house was built as a one-family home. It was converted into a first-floor apartment and two second-floor apartments.

Mark's house built in 1837.

Kerry and Linda made a trip to St. Paul to join Leon and me with Mark in the initial refurbishing of the house. Kerry worked alongside Mark to swing the mallet to remove a wall and reroute electrical wires. We are continuing our legacies of uncle and father working together with son. I am enjoying additional assumptions about how our Elgin home may have looked. In the physical sense of the two houses' similarities, Mark's venture provides testimony of the longevity and legacy of our family. Each of the Division Street offspring are creating lives as single people, or with partners, spouses, and children. Each are building relationships. The offspring have the potential to establish continued links to the family.

I marvel at the coincidence of Mark's purchase and renovation of this house during the same months I have been writing this book. While painting the stairway leading to a second-floor apartment, I have been reminded of the front stairway on Division Street. When I am on the second floor, I notice the three-windowed curved bay area resembling the second-floor living room of Lawrence and Mildred's apartment. When I enter the kitchen and adjoining bathroom of this apartment, I assume these rooms had formerly been a single bedroom area, similar to Division Street.

While working at Mark's house, I have a perception of scenes in which Lawrence and Dad first started doing the work on 364 Division. As I learn about plaster and lathe walls in Mark's house, I realize the work he and I are doing is similar to the changes made in converting a single-family house to a funeral home and apartments. Working in Mark's kitchen, I imagine the butler's pantry and kitchen on the first floor converted into the office area for the funeral home. Working alongside Mark and hearing his stories, I find myself in the minds, hands, and feet of Lawrence and Dad when the house was first occupied by them in 1939 and the years that followed. There was always a repair or a remodel needing to be done. Even though built in same year, I consider Mark's house as the "grandhouse" of "grandfather" 364 Division Street.

Mark asked me to will him the framed painted rendition of the Division Street house. It was painted in the mid-1950s by Janice Sokody, an art student at Elgin High School, the alma mater of both Dad and Mom. Students painted their renditions of houses and sites in the neighborhood. She gave her finished artwork to Lawrence and Dad. They framed and displayed it in the funeral home. I have been the caretaker of the painting. My niece, Keli, a muralist and fashion retailer, refurbished the painting in a way similar to art historians who touch up a Rembrandt or Van Gogh. Mark's future possession of the framed painting will continue our family history.

Painting of 364 Division Street done by Elgin High School art student Janice Sokody Asp mid-1950s.

The adventure Mark is having with his house is an extension of what Dad and Mom, Lawrence and Mildred created with their unique business and family history embodied by their characteristic optimism and happiness. Mirth and fun were natural to them. They knew the importance of joyful experiences to contrast with a business built on grief, sadness, and stress. The experiences of elation have continued with their children, grandchildren, and the generations beyond. Our family history reaffirms that we are continuing traditions started over one hundred years ago. Offspring will continue to grow and have families. Reading through our history of nearly a century of stories provides the launchpad to continue telling and writing stories of family legacy.

One of the mottos and advertising logos of the funeral home was "It is better to know us and not need us than to need us and not know us." The slogan was printed on combs, pens, fingernail files, and other materials they distributed to advocate their business. During the Christmas holidays each year, the business provided copies of a month-to-month calendar to the parishioners at all the Catholic parishes in Elgin. Each time a family referred to the calendar in their homes, they saw a picture of the funeral home with Dad and Lawrence's name, address, and phone number plus the slogan printed in italics.

Recalling the motto of the funeral home, each of us knows and needs each other. This needing and knowing invests us with the continuity of our history and our family culture.

There is no "THE END" to this book.

Continue. Let your stories flourish and be shared.

ENDNOTES

1   "5 O'Clock Edition: A Million Dollars," *Elgin Daily Courier,*
    Vol 7, No.78, 1, http://www.idaillinois.org/digital/iiif/
    newgailbord01/11736/full/full/0/default.jpg.

2   "364 Division Romanesque Revival Built 1887," *Gifford Park
    Association 28th Annual Historic Elgin House Tour*, September 12,
    2009, 6-7, https://gpaelgin.org/wp-content/uploads/2022/08/364
    Division_2009.pdf.

3   E.C. Alft, "Days Gone By: The Division St. Mansion," *Northwest
    Herald*, March, 24, 2007.

4   "Occupational Employment and Wage Statistics," Bureau of Labor
    Statistics, U.S. Department of Labor, accessed August 18, 2022,
    https://www.bls.gov/oes/current/oes394031.htm#nat.

Invite Kevin to
Your Book Club!

As a special gift to readers of *Two Floors Above Grief,* Kevin would love
to visit your book club either via video conferencing or in person.

Please contact Kevin directly at
kevinoconnorauthor@gmail.com to schedule his
appearance at your next book club meeting.

ACKNOWLEDGMENTS

My development through childhood to my current senior citizen status is rooted in the Division Street family: Bill and Marion O'Connor, Lawrence and Mildred O'Connor, Maureen O'Connor Osborne, Kathleen O'Connor Martino, Sharon O'Connor Safar, Barrett O'Connor, and Kerry O'Connor.

I offer gratitude to family and friends who inspired me with their encouragement to keep writing and put stories in print. Thanks particularly to those who provided feedback to drafts of the writing: Mark O'Connor, Bill Osborne, Barrett O'Connor, Kerry O'Connor, Ron O'Connor, Sister Michelle Dermody, Kathy Colson, Eileen Rohwer, Stephen and AnneMarie Martino, Scott Safar, Martina Nicholson, and Susan Howell Pagnucci. Their interest provided the tenacity I needed to look beyond the conception of my ideas toward the finished product you have in your hands. They engaged me in conversations to ensure I was staying true to the events and dates conveyed in each story and the imagined written conversations of the characters.

I am indebted to Stacy Ennis of Nonfiction Book School. Her leadership and instructional skill provided the process for me to congeal the years of stories and perceptions stored in my memory. The organized online schooling of her staff, guest speakers and colleagues in my class guided me in an inspiring and rewarding process.

I recognize Patrick Price of Ask a Book Editor. I have learned from his astute observations and steadfastness in assisting me to winnow and define the stories of my immediate and extended families.

Recognition goes to the staff of the Elgin History Museum and the publications of The Gifford Park Association. They have been a valuable resource to define the locations, names, and information of the businesses and neighborhoods essential in the stories of our family history. I am obliged to artist Laura Marie Sanchez for her rendition of the original structure of the house used on the cover. Thanks to Jack Hubbard and Amber Hubbard for facilitating the interview with my brothers and me on "Jack Rants," his broadcast on LinkedIn. Steven Shires of Fort Lauderdale is known for his photography in the Fort Lauderdale area. He assisted with pictures included in the book and on the cover and photos used on my website. I extend appreciation to Catherine Fishman, Polly Letofsky, Laura Dent, and Victoria Wolf of My Word Publishing. June Noel has guided me in the creation of my author website. These people and organizations provided the support to convert my final drafts into the finished product.

Ultimate thanks are extended to my husband, Leon Rudolph. He sustains a caring and supportive atmosphere to keep me on schedule, insisting that I take the needed breaks from my sometimes-intense zealousness. Through his reading of the drafts, he helped me define my close and broader audiences. He shared in the vision of my stories.

ABOUT THE AUTHOR

Kevin O'Connor enjoys chronicling the stories of families and friends through tracing genealogical histories and writing. His prior writing includes a dissertation, personal letters, articles, anthologies, and presentations delivered at conferences, seminars, and webinars. He brings people together personally and professionally. Collaborating with friends and relatives, he plans family and class reunions.

He sings and performs in theaters and is active with SMART Ride, a bicycling group that rides annually from Miami to Key West, raising funds for HIV awareness, treatment, and education. Kevin was an elementary teacher, principal, professor, and curriculum coordinator in California, Illinois, and Florida from 1973 to 2020. He authored content and provided training in areas including support for substitute teachers, LGBTQ advocacy, and Sexual Health/Family Life.

Kevin resides in Ft. Lauderdale with his husband, Leon. Their family includes five sons and seven granddaughters.

To have Kevin speak to your group or visit your book club, contact him through www.kevinoconnorauthor.com.

Made in the USA
Monee, IL
30 June 2023

37968995R00199